THE GRANITE STATE

THE GRANITE STATE

NEW HAMPSHIRE

An Illustrated History

Ronald Jager and Grace Jager

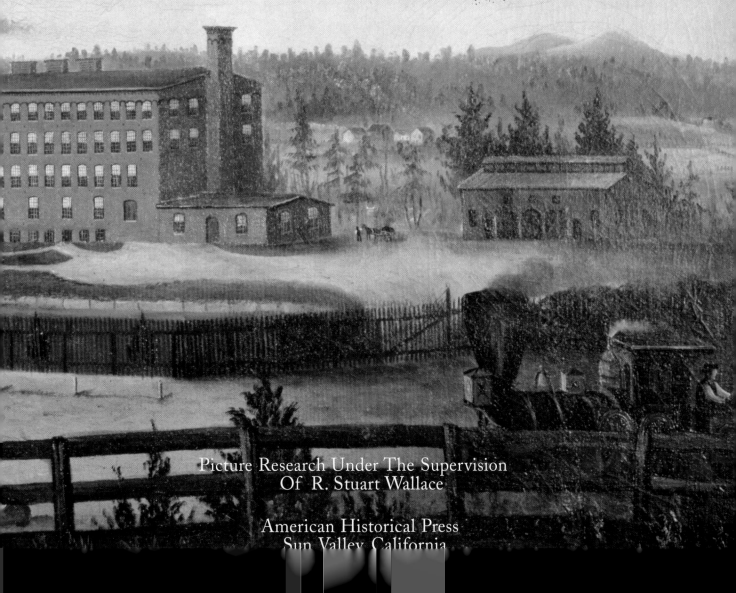

Picture Research Under The Supervision
Of R. Stuart Wallace

American Historical Press
Sun Valley California

Frontispiece: Upon its completion in 1870, the China Mill was a major addition to the tiny mill village of Suncook. George McConnells idyllic painting China Mill *captured the grandeur of the mill in 1871 without reference to the mill's unsightly tenements (built for its workers and known collectively as "China Village"). New York State Historical Association, Cooperstown.*

Excerpt from "The Gift Outright" from *The Poetry of Robert Frost* edited by Edward Connery Latham. Copyright 1942 by Robert Frost
Copyright ©1969 by Holt, Rinehart and Winston.
Copyright ©1970 by Leslie Frost Ballantine.
Reprinted by permission of Holt, Rinehart and Winston, Publishers

Map. Courtesy, The Collection of Vince Feeney

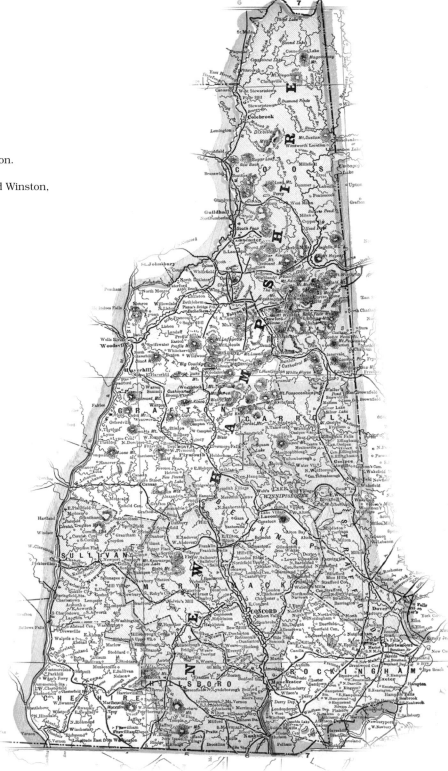

© American Historical Press
All Rights Reserved
Published 2000
Printed in the United States of America

Library of Congress Catalogue Card Number: 00-108799
ISBN: 1-892724-15-4

Bibliography: p. 228
Includes Index

CONTENTS

FOREWORD

It is no small task to summarize New Hampshire. Although a small state, New Hampshire seems to have a little bit of everything—mountains, lakes, seacoast, rivers of varying sizes, and weather conditions to match. When Dartmouth historian Edwin Sanborn published his *History of New Hampshire* in 1875, he concluded that the landscape and harsh weather shaped the character of the state. "Liberty lives where the snow falls," he wrote. "Man is enfranchised only in the temperate zones." While that may seem a bit extreme, the fact remains that New Hampshire has many faces—and many characters. It is perhaps the most representative of the New England states.

It is also no small task to summarize the history of New Hampshire. Jeremy Belknap, New Hampshire's first state historian, took three volumes to accomplish the task. Several multi-volume histories have followed. These histories have been long on text—testing the patience of the most avid history buff—but short on illustrations. Readers have long needed a readable text of reasonable length, accompanied by illustrations that let them sense New Hampshire. Ronald and Grace Jager have remedied the problem with the publication of *The Granite State: New Hampshire, An Illustrated History.*

This volume is both a revision of an earlier work and an entirely new book. In 1983, the Jagers wrote the text to *New Hampshire: An Illustrated History of the Granite State.* The book met with immediate success, but it was soon out of print. American Historical Press acquired the rights to the volume and asked the Jagers to revise and update their text. Not only have they added another chapter, but a timeline, dozens of new illustrations, and a separate section on the state symbols or "icons" through which we define ourselves as a state.

As before, Ronald and Grace Jager have taken a great deal of New Hampshire history and condensed it into one

Gosport Village on Star Island is depicted circa 1977—in the white light of the Shoals—by John Hatch of Durham. Courtesy, Amoskeag National Bank & Trust Company

volume. This is by necessity a selective process. And as before, *The Granite State: New Hampshire, An Illustrated History* is wonderfully readable. It is hoped that between the text and pictures, readers will be "hooked" on New Hampshire and its history.

Like the earlier book, *The Granite State is* an example of "subscription history," in that is has been funded in part by subscribers or sponsors. The organizations that have helped to sponsor the publication of *The Granite State* have had their stories told in the last section of the book entitled "Chronicles of Leadership." Subscription history has been with us for a long time. Jeremy Belknap relied upon subscribers to help him publish the first *History of New Hampshire* better than two centuries ago. Most New Hampshire state histories published since that time have relied upon subscribers as well. One benefit of subscription history is that it gives future readers a chance to look at businesses and organizations at a particular moment in time. This section of the book might be thought of as a form of time capsule.

Anyone reading *The Granite State: An Illustrated History of New Hampshire* may reach the conclusion that elements of New Hampshire's land and its history are not unique. That is partially true. New Hampshire's land has characteristics common to other New England states; its people have experienced episodes similar to people elsewhere in America. Yet Ronald and Grace Jager give us a large picture of New Hampshire. It is in the particular blend of human experience and environment that we discover and define New Hampshire. Wallace Nutting once wrote that "to live in New Hampshire and not to breath[e] deeply, think strongly, love truly, is a crime against the landscape." Hence, for the sake of honesty, a thorough reading of *The Granite State is* recommended.

R. Stuart Wallace

INTRODUCTION

New Hampshire is a small state, heavy with history. It began life as we know it in the 1620s, that decade of New England beginnings, and grew up to become a vigorous seacoast province and one of the 13 original states. Livelihood for the early settlers lay in lumbering and fishing, and only later in husbandry. In the 19th century the rivers of New Hampshire worked harder than any rivers of record, turning manufacturing wheels and propelling massive textile industries. Late in the 20th century came the high technology businesses.

New Hampshire has an 18-mile coastline, a bright edge of sand between Maine and Massachusetts, with a superb harbor at the outlet of the Piscataqua River, long the center of a maritime culture. Inland the terrain quickly becomes uneven, then rugged, and is eventually crowned in the north by the bold beauty of the White Mountains. In 1850 half the land in the state was cleared for farming, but today nearly 90 percent of it is wooded. However, pastoral landscapes abound, and there is considerable farming still, especially in the southern half, tucked into the spaces between the peremptory suburbs and the equally peremptory woods. In the shades at the edge of live farms are scenic ruins of dead farms: old roads pockmarked with cellar holes and former pastures embraced by stone walls of green and gray, a pain in the back for those who built them then but balm to the eyes of those who view them now. Though some of the memories of the state are maritime and some are industrial, the fondest memories of New Hampshire are rural memories.

The state is somewhat culturally self-conscious, in the manner of New England states generally. Residents suspect that elsewhere in the nation old New England is thought to be something of a national antique—to be kept dusted off and displayed for its authenticity, but a bit too fragile or fussy for the daily grind. Against this is blunt New Hampshire assertiveness: high in electronics, first in mountains, last in taxes, the Presidential primary state, Live Free or Die... uneasy sloganeering. No poise there. Abetting the self-consciousness is a long, long ambivalence toward Massachusetts, dating as far back as 1640, when New Hampshire towns first joined their governments to the Bay Colony, and continuing through the centuries as Boston capital intermittently funded and drained New Hampshire enterprise. Persistent voices say that New Hampshire is part Vermont, part Maine, part Massachusetts—no center. Such voices are from elsewhere and invite retort in New Hampshire accents that the state has the assets of its neighbors—bucolics, wilderness, coastline-without the liabilities.

The strength of the state, the source of its surprising coherence, may be simply its history—long, complicated, densely packed, and very much present. It is a past unavoidably present in every stone wall and meetinghouse green and in every native disposition to believe that, for almost anything from town meetings to old roads. durability automatically confers distinction. Appropriately, the New Hampshire State Constitution is older even than the U.S. Constitution. A long unity of historical experience, much of it governmental if not political, binds the state top to bottom, just as it had earlier bound the old seacoast towns with the young Connecticut River towns through the political stress of the Revolutionary War, which nearly uncoupled them. The experience has overcome the burdens of major economic shifts and the accidents of location, size, topography, and the arbitrary cut of state boundaries. New Hampshire is a small state, a large community. Any resident can drive to Concord, the capital city, there to look in upon a legislature that has accumulated over 300 years of bent but unbroken legislative history, and still get home in time for dinner.

From the first, the town in New Hampshire was chartered as the locus of government and society: it created schools, hired pastors, elected selectmen, passed ordinances, sent representatives to the General Court, imposed its own taxes, marked its own bounds, thought its own thoughts. It was New Hampshire towns that recreated the state government when English authority faltered at the outset of the Revolutionary War. In New Hampshire the town possesses a memory; and one of the things it remembers is that it was there before there was a state. Cities came much later: Manchester was first in 1846. Counties are only collections of towns. No wonder it is still widely supposed that the town is the natural instrument of social cohesion and the town meeting the automatic standard of political democracy.

The state itself is the other unit possessing a memory, and one thing it remembers is that its origins and career amount to far more than the sum of town parts. Over time towns and townspeople have come to see, sometimes eagerly, often wearily, that in many areas the state is the unit of significance. This book is a state history. Readers may or may not find here that favorite vignette from a favorite town. We hope they do; but there are too many favorites.

History books are keepers of the public memory and also imaginative creations. Only the inert matters of fact are absolutely given: the rest is endless choice and decision and revision for authors. What data, what context, what meaning? Seen in what light and pattern? Like any book of history this book, too, is full of facts, but it is not meant to be the largest possible pile of information about New Hampshire. History is also color and yarn and connection and drama and nuance—a way of repossessing the past. Sometimes a few big, rough ideas are helpful in nudging the pesky little facts gently into place.

We try to lay out the New Hampshire drama in terms of the four large themes that we think best accommodate the historical experience of the state. These four are: natural history, political-social history, economic history, cultural history. Each dominates one of the first four parts of the book. Once the big themes presented themselves, the historical order in which they demanded attention was automatic, for they build upon each other.

The theme of the first part, "Land and Water," is the natural environment, primary encounters with primary things: the terrain the New Hampshire pioneers found, the shords they fished, the boundaries they drew, and the transformation wrought in the land as it evolved from wilderness to farrnland to abandonment to a sometimes fragile ecology. That part looks at New Hampshire as possession, commodity; the second part, "Government and People," looks at the state as place, community. What political and social institutions arose upon this land? How did they work and who worked them? What was/is it like to live here? The third part, "Economy and Industry," looks at the Granite State as it became part of an industrial world, through its transportation, manufacturing, textile, granite mining, and lumber enterprises. Though that story pervades the whole life of the state, it focuses on the 19th century and thereafter. We regard the independent contemporary Part VI, "Chronicles of Leadership," though not written by us, as a continuation of a this same theme.

The theme of the fourth part, "Mind and Spirit," reaches across the whole spectrum of the state's history to reflect the way religion, learning, and art colored other things, supplied meaning and restated historical experience. Artists of the 19th century made New Hampshire's mountains the symbol of the early American wilderness; likewise, in our own century the poet Robert Frost enlarged New England again and made it, almost, a symbol of America. There have been mythic contours to the New Hampshire landscape ever since the White Mountains were first admired from the sea, and ever since the land was first deplored—and relished—as "this remote and howling wilderness."

Switching the emphasis, the fifth part, "Into the 21st Century" endeavors to look carefully and selectively at the very recent New Hampshire past. Of course, the last years of the 20th century are much too near to offer a reliable historical prospective, but the four themes of the earlier parts provide a working framework. So this reviews some of the main elements of New Hampshire's recent natural, social, economic, and cultural history as of the beginning of the new century. There follows "400 Years: High Points of New Hampshire History, " a timeline which means to highlight the major events—the splendid, the embarrassing, the heroic, the memorable—in the long story of the Granite State.

Ronald Jager
Grace Jager
August 2000

I

L A N D
A N D   W A T E R

Perhaps more than any other painting, Maxfield Parrish's New Hampshire, also entitled Thy Templed Hills, has been used to extol the state's rural splendor. Parrish, one of America's most popular painters, lived and kept a studio in Plainfield, New Hampshire, from 1898 until his death 68 years later. Painting from the collection of the Vermont National Bank, Windsor Office. Photograph courtesy, The Magazine Antiques

CHAPTER
ONE

NATURAL
BOUNDARIES

Under the forests of New Hampshire, under the earthy mantle, the texture of the rocky substratum has a certain grain, a grain weathered and worn down by the ages, but yet visible, just as the grain is visible on the old pine boards of a country barn. The grain in the rock of New Hampshire, unimaginably old and going back to the ancient convulsions that broke the crust of this part of the Earth, runs essentially north-south and, like any weathered grain, it is brought out by the wearing away of the softer rock that exposes the harder lines. The Connecticut Valley is a worn-away part, as is the Merrimack Valley and, farther north, the Androscoggin Valley and the great notches, Pinkham, Crawford, and Franconia. Between the notches, accenting the grain, are ranges of mountains and, farther south, there is the long range of hills and highland from Kearsarge to Monadnock. The grain is conspicuous farther west in Vermont, in the wrinkles of the Green Mountains and the worn-away Champlain Valley. In lots of New Hampshire ledges and outcroppings of rock the fine grain appears.

Before man came, before the Ice Age, before the Old Man of the Mountains settled here, before the dinosaurs, millions of years back into the mists of time, there were already hills and high mountains in these parts. The Earth's surface, a layer of ancient rock, surged under the hills. Molten granite was cooking in the bowels of the earth, boiling up, heaving the crust, buckling it, making long tears in it, squeezing granite toward the surface to cool, creating the infrastructure of a future Granite State. That was two or three hundred million years ago. The pressure from below, bending and tearing the surface, also tilted the entire New England landscape southeast toward the Atlantic and poured out the ancestors of the Connecticut and Merrimack rivers toward the sea. The rivers cut down along the grain through northern Massachusetts to the Atlantic. The Connecticut River, too, such was the tilt, might have spilled out eastward but for the heave of the Monadnock and Berkshire ranges. Perhaps already then the ancestral Contoocook River, also spilling eastward because of the tilt, got caught in the lines of the grain and was sent northward—

odd for a New Hampshire river then, and unique now—eventually breaking out and dashing across the grain again to join the Merrimack.

Thereafter, very slowly, through eons and eons of time, New Hampshire settled down in bedrock, gathered vegetation, gathered topsoil, gathered composure. The mountains wore down to stumps during millions of years of calm. Erosion exposed granite that had cooled under the rocky crust. Lakes drained or died. The rivers of the land ran smoothly without waterfalls through long and shallow valleys. Dinosaurs roamed. New Hampshire lay as if it were in the summertime of some grand and transcendent rhythm of the seasons.

Then came the Ice Age. Earth's temperature dropped just enough to affect the snow level in Canada. Each summer as usual the snow melted northward from Pennsylvania to northern Canada; but each fall, when the new snow started, the point of melt-back was a bit farther south. The glacier that, then as now, caps the North Pole was creeping south two steps each winter and retreating one step each summer. No matter if the steps were but a few hundred feet a year. There were thousands and thousands of years for the glacier to grow down out of Canada—thin and benign at the edge in summer, rigid and deep farther back, packed by its own weight into ice. Creeping through the St. Lawrence Valley, up over the ridge, down over the Connecticut Lakes, toward the White Mountains it came, a long white slither, winter by winter, deeper and deeper. Winds scooped up water from the ocean and poured it out on the glacier as snow. As it grew the glacier folded the forests of New Hampshire along its advancing edge into its soft, mushy embrace at first; but inevitably the summer came when it didn't release the trees but froze them rigid in its grip and sheared them off or ground them up.

Maybe a thousand years, maybe two, it took the ice sheet to grow and shove its way from the White Mountains in the north to Mt. Monadnock in the south, then to plow on for ages more. Miles deep it piled up, a frozen flood of Biblical proportions covering the White Mountains, range after range. The sheet

weight of the ice turned the bottom of the heap to mush—an ever-shifting, melting, freezing, rocky mass endeavoring to ooze southward from the greater pressure to the north. Walls of rock were torn from the lee side of cliffs—the south or southeast side—or jammed into the ancient channels where they broke up the floors of the old rivers and formed, for future waterpower, the Amoskeag Falls, Bellows Falls, and all the others. As the glacier plowed on like a bulldozer, its force and pressure ground up 10 to 12 feet of bedrock and scooped out lake and river valleys, while rocks, frozen in the slush, sandpapered the surface of the mountains, leaving scours still visible today on top of Mt. Kearsarge and many other places. Altogether it was a mighty drama in white and in slow motion, ghastly, gorgeous, and irresistible—sweeping everything in its path.

Geologists agree that in the Eastern states the glacier reached approximately to Long Island, paused, and then from a slight shift in climate, began slowly to recede, melting back north as deliberately as it had crept south, dropping cargo in its tracks. Then the whole thing, start to finish, happened again. And again. Probably four times. In New Hampshire the Ice Age with its four separate glaciers extended from about a million years ago to what is, in geological terms, only yesterday. As the last glacier melted back, only 12,000 to 15,000 years ago, films of debris accumulated at the edges of temporary lakes, settling down into future farmland. Streams of melt water ran through tunnels in the lower glacier, piling up long veins of sand and gravel, called "eskers." Left in place were large boulders ("erratics") miles from their now-known place of origin. Smaller rocks on the tops of mountains, including Mt. Washington, show by their mineral composition that they came from other mountains. During the sum-

mers of the melting, temporary lakes dropped the sand that washed into them, and when the lakes froze in winter, dropped the clay suspended in the water, dropped sand again the next summer, clay the next winter—thus creating the "varves," the sand/clay layers familiar to every New Hampshire bulldozer operator.

When the last glacier peeled back northward the region lay as if at springtime. And, indeed, behind the retreating ice the New Hampshire landscape would have been as attractive as an abused and muddy driveway on a sullen March day. Moreover, the last glacier that had passed its rough edges against the face of the state and had chiseled away at the rock where its predecessors had chiseled, had finally completed and left there a glacial trademark as if to herald a wholly new era. In that springtime, 15,000 years ago, there peered out from under the masses of rotting ice and rock and mud the Old Man of the Mountains—an eerie human profile glowering upon a scene devoid of vegetation and still intolerable for human life.

All that then remained was to clothe the bony nakedness of Earth with the soft green of virgin forests, the work of just a few centuries. That is when the New Hampshire whose lush and rugged contours we now know and love really began.

The White Mountains

At the basis of history itself is the story of encounters with the land, bringing it into the service of human need; this is especially true of New Hampshire's history, where so much of the terrain, fiercely inhospitable when first found, was developed with such hardihood and patience.

The White Mountains are the centerpiece of the New Hamp-

Pascatway River in New England by I:S: *is the best map of its time of the coast of New Hampshire and the area around the Piscataqua River. Drawn in London and now owned by the British Museum, the map is remarkable in its overall accuracy, its rich historical detail, its decorative figures, and even its doggerel verse dedication to the Duke of York, later James II. Internal evidence dates this masterpiece about 1660. Courtesy, the British Museum*

To artists the light on the Saco River has often seemed golden, and the river "sweetly sinuous." In 1899 Benjamin Champney wrote, "if one was a poet, no more charming scenes (than the valley of the Saco) could be found to inspire a pastoral." Photograph by Bill Finney

Colonel George Boyd's country seat at Portsmouth, built in the 1740s, served as the country seat of several other owners before Boyd purchased it in 1771. Located on a tidal creek with a wharf and available timber, the estate also included two warehouses, a garden, turning mills, and gristmills. This "South-West Prospect" was painted in 1774, the year Boyd left Portsmouth for England to wait out the Revolution. Returning in 1787, Boyd died on board ship two days before reaching his estate. Courtesy, Lamont Gallery, Phillips Exeter Academy

This William H. Bartlett colored print entitled Mount Washington and the White Hills *was published by S.T. Davies circa 1836. Courtesy, New Hampshire Historical Society (NHHS)*

From earliest times cormorants have been a common sight on the rocky ledges of the New Hampshire coast. Photograph by Timothy Savard. Courtesy, New Hampshire Times

A telephoto lens brings out the Paleozoic wrinkles in the face of the Old Man of the Mountains. Photograph by Dick Smith. Courtesy, State of New Hampshire

shire landscape, and the Reverend Jeremy Belknap of Dover is the dean of New Hampshire historians. These two met just 200 years ago, when Belknap was writing a history of New Hampshire going back to the English settlements of the 1620s. Like any educated man of his age, he regarded history as having two major themes: "natural history," and what was then called "civil history." On both he was eager to examine all the evidence at hand. For the natural history part of his book it was appropriate, therefore, for him to go and study directly the White Mountains. Nobody had ever studied them; few had climbed them, and fewer had written anything about them.

It is likely that Jeremy Belknap had read the first known account of the ascent of Mt. Washington in John Winthrop's famous *History of New England.* Winthrop's journal for the year 1642—which was before white men had even climbed the Berkshires—records that someone named Darby Field of Exeter, New Hampshire, first "went to the top of the white hill." Indian companions accompanied him "within eight miles of the top, but durst go no further, telling him that no Indian ever dared go higher, and that he would die if he went." Perhaps the Indian fear had been originally based upon the solid fact that the weather on Mt. Washington is notoriously treacherous and severe. Sudden storms break, mists and clouds often shroud the top, a world-record wind of 231 miles per hour has been recorded there, and avalanches are common in the winter. It is said that more people have died on its slopes in the last hundred years than on any other American mountain. But Winthrop says that "two Indians took courage by his example and went with him." Field climbed Mt. Washington a second time that same summer and seven years later he died, still a young man. The Indians would not have been surprised.

In Belknap's library there were other tidbits about these mountains. One might have been the Englishman John Josselyn's book *New-England's Rarities,* which describes the outlook from the top of the highest mountain: "the Country beyond the Hills Northward is daunting terrible, being full of rocky Hills, as thick as Mole-hills in a Meadow, and cloathed with infinite thick Woods." The thick woods reach up to about 4,000 to 4,500 feet on the average, leaving nearly two dozen peaks above treeline, like molehills in a meadow.

Fragmentary statements such as these were the main written accounts available to supplement the hearsay and Indian lore of the White Mountains in Belknap's time, more than 150 years

New Hampshire's White Mountains are crowned with the snow-covered peaks of the Presidential Range. Mt. Hancock is in the right foreground, while Webster Cliffs, marking the southern entrance to Crawford Notch, is right of center. Photograph by Dick Smith. Courtesy, Society for the Protection of New Hampshire Forests (SPNHF)

after New Hampshire had been first settled at the coast less than 100 miles away. But if Belknap was to write about New Hampshire, he would have to write about the white hills—"white" because sailors frequently reported seeing the frosted peaks against the blue horizon on clear autumn days. So he organized a scientific expedition to the mountains.

Belknap and six or seven others set out from Dover in July 1784 for the top of the mountain that was later named (by Belknap, most likely) Mt. Washington. They took with them all kinds of clumsy gear: telescopes, compasses, a surveyor's chain, a barometer with a bag of mercury, three muskets, and pistols. It was quite an ordeal for a collection of overloaded scientists, strangers to mountains: a steep and pathless climb led by the rotund and enthusiastic preacher with his notebook. They would have struggled up through the hardwoods and then into the white and black spruces, through stunted evergreens beaten shapeless by the wind and seven months' snow. Finally, breaking into the open they would find themselves climbing up around and over great slabs of rock, seemingly thrown up in heaps. The loose rocks strewn over the peaks are more the result of frost breaks than of glaciers. At the top they could look out upon two dozen neighboring rocky peaks, all kept bare by the cold and incessant wind. Belknap's main party made it all the way, but the leader himself gave out and returned to camp before treeline. "In great enterprises," he said afterward, "to have attempted is enough." The barometer broke on the ascent and the main crew gave a reading at the mountaintop that they knew was inaccurate—9,000 feet. Belknap wrote that an accurate instrument would show that Mt. Washington was more than 10,000 feet high. It is actually 6,288 feet above sea level.

Beneath that summit New Hampshire was spread out before them, an irregular triangle, today comprising 9,282 square miles, 90 miles wide at the base and 120 miles long. From the mountaintop the encircling view, but for the bare peaks, was one of rocky slides and "infinite thick woods." "Nature has, indeed, in that region," wrote Belknap, "formed her works on a large scale."

Why, more than a century earlier, had anyone come at all to this inhospitable terrain? Part of the answer is that the English settlers had not really known what they were getting into.

Jeremy Belknap, Congregational pastor in Dover from 1766 to 1786, was the first historian of New Hampshire, and it is commonly said that he remains the best. He knew firsthand the last years of the colonial era, and he saw the Revolution come and go. Loyal to the American cause, he also retained friendly relations with Royal Governor John Wentworth. Belknap's History of New-Hampshire *was published in three volumes between 1784 and 1792. Its thorough scholarship and literary merit place it among the best historical writing in 18th-century America. Courtesy, Massachusetts Historical Society*

CHAPTER
TWO
POLITICAL
BOUNDARIES

At the beginning of the 17th century, with the Spanish Armada defeated, the English mind, dreaming of lordship of the seas, turned with fascination toward the strange new continent beyond the ocean to the west. Helping to bend English thoughts toward America was the work of international promoters such as Sir Walter Raleigh and Captain John Smith. There was also Sir Ferdinando Gorges, who by 1615 had three native New Hampshire Indians living on display in his household in England. What stories they told of the riches in the valley of the Piscataqua we do not know. We do know that a few probing voyages and quite a few glowing reports pictured a store of natural resources in New England that could never be used up: fish, furs, timber, perhaps even farmland. Maybe there was gold, too, and possibly still a passage northwest to Asia. By 1620 the King had been persuaded to create a Council for New England, with Gorges as president and with authority to grant land and create trade and settlements in North America between the 40th and 48th parallels—roughly between the present Hudson and St. Lawrence rivers. The wealth of the New World was to be tapped.

The Council for New England
Retrospectively, the Council for New England seems to be the spiritual ancestor of that legendary Yankee who inherited a hundred measured acres and later sold them as three lots, each of "40 acres more or less." One thing to be said for the council is that under its aegis New Hampshire got started. On the other hand, the council didn't always know what it was doing. Within little more than a decade (1622-1635) the council's grants created boundary and ownership confusion that 150 years of litigation, and the fattening of teams of lawyers, politicians, and developers, could never sort out. Bounds of council grants were vague and sometimes overlapped; some lands were granted several times. True, they had only very poor maps and scant knowledge of the land; but this seems to have enforced no discretion. Their grantees, who included members of the council, fully expected to make money off developments, and that didn't work out either. New Hampshire was born struggling for life: a collection of rather poorly conceived settlement efforts that cen-

tered around the Piscataqua River and didn't do very well.

It started out directly enough with David Thomson of Plymouth, England, a clerk for the Council for New England, who was paid for his services with 6,000 acres and an island in the New World—somewhere in the council's territory. Accordingly, his ship *Jonathan,* having followed the *Mayflower* out of Plymouth by a bit over two years, eventually arrived at what the Indians called Pannaway—now Odiorne's Point in Rye—on April 16, 1623. Claiming this land as his own, he and his wife and their small company built a house and set about planning a trading post and a fishing operation. Though still without its name, New Hampshire was on its way. Within three years, however, Thomson moved away to Boston and took up life on an island in the harbor; and his little settlement, the first in the state, is presumed to have passed to the brothers Hilton who were supervising the activities.

Meanwhile, back in England the Council for New England had been giving away this very land to others: once to John Mason and Sir Ferdinando Gorges in 1622, next to John Mason alone in 1629. Also in 1629 the council granted several other "patents" (land grants) of uncertain location; and in 1631 John Mason and eight others were granted yet another, called the Piscataqua patent. It included, sure enough, much of the same territory. Then the council collapsed, a disaster; no one at the time realized the extent of the mischief.

John Mason, who probably never set foot on New Hampshire shores, named "his" land, wherever it was exactly, New Hampshire, after his native county in England. He at least had the broadest and most complicated claims to the largest grants. An adventurer by nature, he was also a man who ardently wanted to see this part of the world settled—preferably by Anglicans, not Puritans. It was to be for him both a business and an extension of the Church of England, and he hoped to achieve the development of colonies as an absentee landlord by maneuvers from London.

Under the grants by the council before 1635 there were, besides Thomson's beginnings, a number of other meager efforts directly under John Mason's supervison: a fur trade on the Piscataqua (the natives, however, couldn't supply enough furs), a fishing base, a saltworks (it didn't pay), a lumber mill, and some farms. The records of the time, thin and fragmentary as they are, make it clear that before 1640 most of these scattered efforts struggled more than thrived. Fishing near the Isles of Shoals was immediately successful, but the station there was more a base of commercial operations than a settled colony. By the mid-1630s the community in the Piscataqua Harbor at Strawbery Banke seems to have made some progress at farming—it was recorded in 1632 that 16 hogsheads of corn were being sent from there to Charlestown for grinding. Cattle, horses, and hogs arrived from England, and a few ships returned to England with lumber that found a ready market there.

The harsh truth of the first two decades was that the New World resources were much harder to tap than the early entrepreneurs had expected. A visitor to the Thomson settlement in 1624, Christopher Levett, had summed the matter up in a letter that the next decades could only confirm. "There is fowl, deer, and fish enough for the taking if men be diligent," he wrote of early New Hampshire; but he added, "I will not tell you that you may smell the corn fields before you see the land, neither must men think that corn doth grow naturally (or on trees), nor will the deer come when they are called . . . nor the fish leap into the kettle."

Partly because the settlement was such a struggle to maintain, the question of the ultimate ownership of these large tracts of land could often be ignored by most of the settlers. The uncertain boundaries of the council grants were like time bombs shallowly buried when John Mason died conveniently just as the council itself was killed by internal English politics in 1635. Mason's grandson dug up the claims a generation later and triggered a century of litigation. Considered as real estate, the province of New Hampshire had a curious parentage in John Mason and the Council for New England—fathered by adventure and mothered by indiscretion. Politically, the infant province was an orphan from birth. Granting land was one thing; granting governmental authority was another.

Masons and the Masonian Proprietors

One of the council grants to John Mason put a western limit of 60 miles on the grant. To this day, two-thirds of the residents of New Hampshire live within that 60-mile arc from Portsmouth, and every piece of land owned there has in its legal ancestry the weirdly tangled tale of Masonian claims.

Captain John Mason, who had a strong though questionable claim to New Hampshire up to the 60-mile limit, died in 1635, leaving his New Hampshire claim to a grandson, Robert Tufton Mason. Robert started litigation to recover the land, protesting the "unjust encroachments" of Massachusetts upon his property and trying to collect rent from the residents. His efforts got confused in the political shuffle whereby New Hampshire was established as a Crown Colony in 1680. When Robert Tufton Mason died in 1685, he left his claim to his sons John and Robert, who, as Londoners, found the New Hampshire problem tedious and in 1691 sold the claim—through a London court transaction—to Samuel Allen. Allen got himself appointed lieutenant-governor

Captain John Smith helped to popularize the New England coast with the publication of his book A Description of New England in 1616. Unfortunately, while helpful with most of the area, Smith's account had little to say about the portion of New England that was to become New Hampshire. He visited the Isles of Shoals, immodestly naming them after himself, and virtually ignored New Hampshire's Great Bay area. In preparing an otherwise excellent map of New England, Smith compensated for ignorance of the region by placing this engraving of himself over present-day New Hampshire. NHHS

If Captain John Mason and Sir Ferdinando Gorges had had access to accurate maps of the New England coast, perhaps some of the overlapping and otherwise conflicting land grants for "New Hampshire" would have been avoided. Unfortunately, they did not. Pictured is a rather fanciful illustration of "Gorges and Mason naming their provinces." NHHS

of New Hampshire and made a number of moves to take possession of the lands that he now governed. This made him few friends in New Hampshire. Eventually a bargain was struck that would give him all "the waste and unimproved lands" up to 60 miles west in return for his not pushing claim to settled towns in the east. The document was drawn up, and on the day before it was to be signed, Allen died. His son inherited the claim, discovered that there was a mortgage on it, sold half of what remained to a Boston man in August 1706, and then he died. *His* son, then an infant, having inherited the claim or problem, whatever it was, ignored it for 40 years.

Enter another Mason. In the 1740s a great-great-grandson of the original Mason appeared in court claiming that since his grandfather's sale to Allen had been transacted in London and not in New Hampshire, it was invalid, and that therefore *he* had inherited New Hampshire. There was some slim legal basis for this and a lot of smoke in it too; and before the claim was vindicated or the smoke had fully cleared, Mr. Mason shrewdly sold his alleged inheritance to a new corporation of 12 prominent Portsmouth businessmen—friends and relatives of New Hampshire Governor Benning Wentworth.

Calling themselves the "Masonian Proprietors," the new "owners" quickly offered quitclaim deeds to their somewhat nonplussed neighbors in the settled towns and started speedily surveying, mapping, and granting dozens of townships in the "waste and unimproved lands" to the west—Hopkinton, Hillsborough, New London—the boondocks of the day. It was a smooth professional and profitable operation by the Portsmouth aristocracy. Who was to say them nay?

In these transactions—first to last, 1620s to 1740s—it is impossible to sort out exactly what was legal from what was bluff, what was merely complex from what was entirely confused. Obscure inheritance laws and blatant politics colored nearly every move in a game wherein many a reputation and career was made, and many lost. For intricacy and duration as well as for the extent of the stakes, the Masonian controversy set the colonial record in North America. Eventually it was just easier to let the Masonian Proprietors boldly pretend that their title was clear right back to the Indian chiefs and the English kings. The controversy was never resolved; it was dropped.

Land ownership disputes may be dropped for good, but land boundary disputes are often only shelved—to be dusted off again in troublous times. Moreover, boundaries of states are often arbitrary, unnatural, indifferent to ownership of the land and to the grain of the landscape itself. Politics, not nature, determines state boundaries. Or so it seems. Yet there is a complex reciprocity between the claims of the land and the claims of the politicians in the three major boundary controversies that determined the main outline of New Hampshire. In the controversies with Massachusetts and with Vermont, both land and the future of the state itself were very much at issue.

The Massachusetts Boundary Controversy

The northern reach of the Massachusetts Bay Colony had originally been set as "all those lands . . . which lie and be within the space of three English miles to the northward of the . . . Merrimack River *or to the northward of any and every part thereof*" (italics added). The Englishmen who penned those words in the 1620s thought that the entire Merrimack flowed easterly as it does at its outlet. By the time it was common knowledge that it flows south and then cuts sharply east 30 miles to the ocean, there was no one to care, for the settled New Hampshire towns along the coast were part of Massachusetts anyway. Even when the New Hampshire colony was separated off in 1680, the boundary, yonder in the wilderness, didn't much matter. Indeed, when the 10 italicized words were left off the newly chartered description of Massachusetts in 1691, it also concerned few people. Though they had separate assemblies, Massachusetts and New Hampshire shared a governor, and they had common worries about very practical problems such as Indians and Masons. The conveniently vague assumption grew that for some distance, the Merrimack was three miles inside Massachusetts; west of the Merrimack was only wilderness anyway.

About 1720, between Indian wars, Massachusetts opened the dispute with a trivial question—three miles from the *center*, or from the *bank* of the river? A much bigger issue promptly took over and dominated politics for two decades: (a) three miles north of the Merrimack outlet and then on a line straight west? (New Hampshire's claim); or (b) three miles north of "any and every part" of the river? (Massachusetts' claim). Moreover the north-south line that now divides New Hampshire and Maine was also in dispute. Massachusetts, which then "owned" Maine, drew that line so as to put much of upper New Hampshire into Massachusetts (Maine) as well. In Massachusetts' eyes, New Hampshire was just a little coastal enclave like Rhode Island. At issue was more than three-quarters of what is now New Hampshire.

Lieutenant-Governor John Wentworth led the maneuvering for New Hampshire. Local commissions having failed, he managed to present the case in London as the latest version of the Crown's problems with Massachusetts—with New Hampshire loyal to royal interests. Back on the frontiers the legislative assemblies of Massachusetts and New Hampshire were poised like boys drawing a line in the gravel between them, daring the other to cross. Both dared.

First, in the 1720s, there was only pushing: Massachusetts reached up and granted the township of Pennycook (today's Concord); New Hampshire reached over and granted the township of Bow on much the same land; Massachusetts retaliated by granting Suncook on top of parts of Bow and dividing the township into lots; New Hampshire responded by superimposing Bow lots on top of Massachusetts' Suncook lots.

This was confusing, so they started shoving: Massachusetts chartered the whole line of towns straight across the southern edge of present-day New Hampshire. New Hampshire sent distress signals to the King about Massachusetts imposing taxes on New Hampshire citizens and bullying "this poor little province." New Hampshire then boldly raised the ante by entering pleas for a separate governor. The common governor of the two provinces, Jonathan Belcher, wrote to London that the unfortunate inhabitants within these disputed and shifting boundaries had to "live like toads under a barrow," yanked now into the jurisdic-

When the New Hampshire/Massachusetts boundary controversy was settled in 1740, authorities in victorious New Hampshire were quick to prepare an accurate map of their enlarged province. As George Mitchell's 1745 map indicates, however, a number of smaller boundary disputes remained to be settled, particularly Kingston's and Londonderry's. The map-making convention that top is north was not yet firmly established when this map was made. Here top is west. The double line of square towns running west was conceived as a defense line, primarily against Native Americans. For this purpose a major fort was completed (1746) at No. 4, and was authentically rebuilt late in 1961. Courtesy, Public Record Office, London

Provincial New Hampshire's commerce passed through the busy mouth of the Piscataqua River. James Grant mapped the island-studded harbor in 1774 shortly before the outbreak of hostilities with Britain. His watercolor "plan" was later used in making Samuel Holland's map of the "state" of New Hampshire. NHHS

tion of one state, now into another. To complicate matters further, at this time, after nearly a century's lapse, Anglicanism was being carefully revived in Portsmouth. Dr. Arthur Browne, a distinguished Rhode Island cleric, arrived in 1732 to head the new Queen's Chapel in the capital. John Thomlinson had arranged this as the London agent for the New Hampshire colony—explaining carefully, no doubt, the attractive prospects of a compliant "Anglican" New Hampshire colony next to the perpetually troublesome Puritan Massachusetts. Thus the plot thickened.

In London the Privy Council investigated the boundary dispute and made a recommendation to King George II, which he then decreed on March 5, 1740. His decree settled 20 years of contention with a victory for New Hampshire that outreached anyone's wildest dreams. The north-south line with Maine on the east was set where New Hampshire had claimed it and essentially where it is now, securing the North Country for New Hampshire. The south line cut deeply into the traditional claims of Massachusetts: three miles north of the "Course of Merrimack River" to a point north of "Pawtucket Falls and a strait line drawn from there due West cross the said River *till it meets with his Majesty's other Governments*" (italics added).

That fixed the boundary officially, though a satisfactory survey of it was not achieved until 1901. The King's decree clearly put 28 former "Massachusetts towns," hundreds of square miles, into New Hampshire. Many of these towns immediately petitioned Boston and London pleading for readmission to Massa-

chusetts. They got no hearing. The petitioners, wrote New Hampshire's London agent, were "full of false facts, false geography, false reasoning—a most weak but wicked attempt of the unruly province of the Massachusetts Bay." For good measure, Governor Belcher of Massachusetts was fired and replaced by a new governor for that state; and a separate governor, Benning Wentworth, an ardent Anglican, was appointed to the now vastly enlarged province of New Hampshire.

Enlarged to the west, "till it meets with his Majesty's other Governments." Where was that? Of course His Majesty had no idea at all. Presumably, it was wherever New York was bounded on its east—which was very unclear. Thus the explicit solution of the boundary dispute with Massachusetts on the south just as explicitly created—with those eight inexact words—a boundary dispute with New York on the west. Out of the resulting affair between New Hampshire and New York, Vermont was born.

The Vermont Boundary Dispute

Governor Benning Wentworth made the opening move, casually telling Governor Clinton of New York in 1749 that he was about to start making grants "in the unimproved lands within my government" to the west. He then reached far across the Connecticut River and granted a new township to a group of friends who promptly named it Bennington (now Bennington, Vermont; *then* Bennington, New Hampshire). New York's Governor Clinton complained, cited some century-old docu-

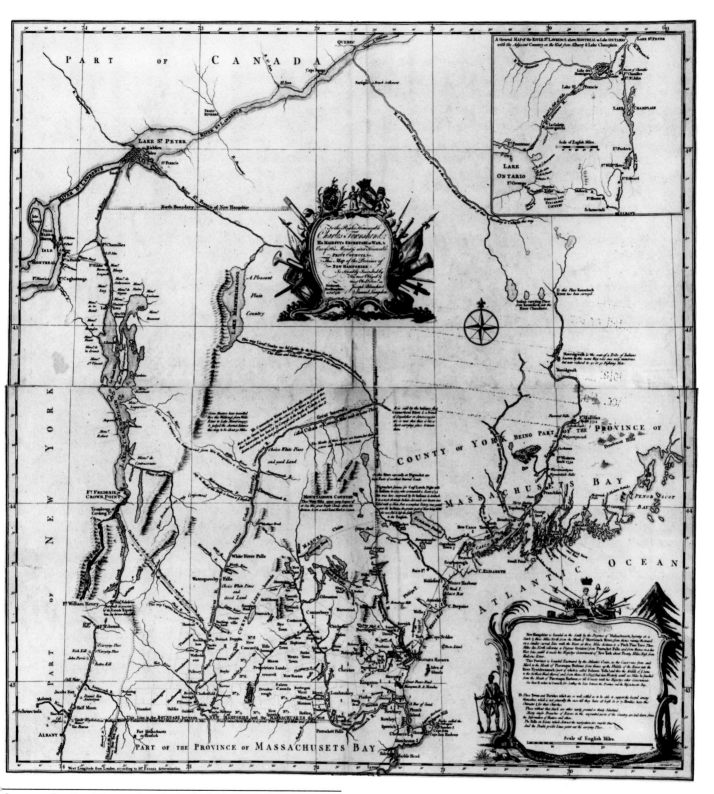

Governor Benning Wentworth undoubtedly had nothing but the greatest admiration for the cartographic skills of Colonel Joseph Blanchard and the Reverend Samuel Langdon when they completed this map of New Hampshire in 1761. The boundaries were somewhat generous. Not only does "New Hampshire" seem to extend well beyond the Connecticut River, but the province's northern boundary lies well north of Lake Memphremagog. NHHS

ments, and let the matter be referred to the Crown. Governor Wentworth simply went on chartering towns, dozens of them, all across the southern part of present-day Vermont. These territories beyond the river came to be called the "New Hampshire grants;" "iniquitous grants" was what the New York governor called them. Well before the Revolutionary War they were populated with a class of stalwart pioneers who, having carved their homes out of the remote wilderness, were serenely defiant of *all* distant governments, whether in Portsmouth or Albany, let alone London.

The problem as it developed was not only that the boundaries were uncertain, but also that the residents of the towns along both sides of the Connecticut increasingly felt an economic and social cohesion among themselves which they shared with neither New York nor the New Hampshire coastal towns.

Though King George tried to clarify matters in 1764 by decreeing the western shore of the Connecticut River as the eastern boundary of New York, this turned out to be just one round in a complicated skirmish that echoed the "line in the dirt" game New Hampshire had played earlier with Massachusetts on the Merrimack. Now the line was the Connecticut River and the adversary was New York. Now the "toads under a barrow" were the New Hampshire grants in "Vermont" as well as a row of New Hampshire towns on the eastern bank who felt akin to them. An association of river towns, first called New Connecticut and then Vermont, appeared and thumbed its nose east and west. By the time the Revolutionary War was well under way Vermonters had a government of sorts, authorized by themselves. Eventually two rows of Connecticut River towns in New Hampshire, long dissatisfied with that state's government, were leaning toward affiliation with Vermont. Dartmouth pamphleteering, arguing that there is "no legal power subsisting in the [NH] colony," and that the future lay with Vermont, encouraged the rebellion against the wartime New Hampshire government. All kinds of jurisdictional claims flared on both sides of the river. Who owed taxes to whom? Which courts had what jurisdictions? The old boundary dispute showed signs of becoming a full-scale civil war. In 1781 Vermont boldly asserted jurisdiction over not only the New Hampshire grants but also over all the dissident towns in New Hampshire and began dropping broad hints of direct negotiations with England. "Unless Congress interferes," wrote President Meshech Weare of the New Hampshire Council, "very probably the sword will decide it." But Vermont was not listening to Congress.

Forty years earlier the King had simply settled matters concerning the Massachusetts border. One longed for a King George again; but this was 1781 and the country was at war with the King. A novel tactic suggested itself, and it turned out to be a masterstroke, namely, to appeal to George Washington. The Commander in Chief of the American army was in Philadelphia with a war on his hands, and he needed to be brought into a turf fight in New England about as much as he needed another Benedict Arnold. But Washington was deeply wise, knowing full well the force of his authority and how to use it with casual grace. The letter he struck off to Governor Chittenton of Vermont pulled everybody up short, and changed the course of New England history.

Chittenton had written to enlist Washington's sympathy for Vermont's ambition, which was essentially this: admission to the Union for Vermont with territories extending into New York on the west and across the Connecticut to the east, including the string of 16 rebellious New Hampshire river towns. Washington replied on January 1, 1782, saying that he could not of course respond in any official capacity, but the request "gives me an opportunity of offering you my sentiments, as an individual," suggesting that this was also "the prevailing opinion of congress." The message was: let Vermont be content, as Congress had earlier proposed, with a western boundary on a line southerly from Lake Champlain to the corner of Massachusetts, and an eastern boundary at the western bank of the Connecticut River, and on that basis apply for admission to the Union as the first new state. The letter went on about how Washington dreaded the thought of restraining territorial claims by "coercion on the part of congress," which in Vermont's case would lead to the "ruin of that state"; how talk of Vermont joining Great Britain had sown "seeds of distrust" and must have been intended only as a clever ploy to deceive the enemy. The letter was shrewd, respectful, conciliatory—and very threatening.

No king could have acted so effectively, for this voice spoke with accents of native authority, earned and conferred in the course of a democratic revolution. The Vermont Assembly, with the New Hampshire delegation temporarily absent, accepted the proposal in principle; and the New Hampshire towns, cast adrift at the river's edge, eventually came back to New Hampshire. The borders of Vermont were essentially set as proposed by Washington and from that time the general territorial and political integrity of both New Hampshire and Vermont were assured. (The definitive resolution of the New Hampshire-Vermont boundary came only with a 1934 U.S. Supreme Court decision that set the boundary at the low-water mark on the western bank of the Connecticut River.)

The natural social and political unity among the Connecticut River towns on both sides of the river was self-evident to everyone: the lines of nature itself provided on the west the Green Mountains and on the east the Kearsarge-Sunapee-Monadnock range, with the river between. As a political idea, centering the new state of Vermont athwart the river reflected the patterns of development and historic experience of the people and it was true to the run of the ancient grain of the rocky substratum. However, Washington's proposal, though it did not originate with him, turned out to be decisive for subsequent history, and it involved for New England an explicit political self-assertion against the shape of the land. Politics conquered the landscape.

The Indian Stream Republic

The Treaty of Paris of 1783, which concluded the Revolutionary War and, incidentally, paved the way for New Hampshire to unite under a new constitution and for Vermont to be admitted to the Union as the 14th state, also planted the seeds of a new boundary dispute to the north. This dispute was with Great Britain, and the entire U.S./Canada line from New Brunswick to New York was at issue. Once more the language that had fixed

the New Hampshire part of the boundary was ill-chosen. The Treaty of Paris described a part of the new line as running from the source of the St. Croix River to "the northwesternmost head of the Connecticut River." A few words had done it again. Three tributaries might claim the honor of being the "northwesternmost": Halls Stream on the west, Indian Stream in the center, and Perry Stream to the east. Depending upon the choice, about 100,000 acres of excellent, reasonably accessible timberland belonged either to one country or to the other. Many a fine tree went from seedling to sawmill during the 60-year boundary dispute. Indeed, commissions and committees formed to solve the problem came and went, resolutions multiplied and gathered dust, and a whole series of United States Secretaries of State, preeminently John Quincy Adams, wasted their diplomatic skills on non-solutions. While diplomats dithered and quibbled over big issues, a little independent republic grew up in the New Hampshire part of the disputed territory.

The saga of the Indian Stream Republic is a droll bit of history, charming to distant viewers, but far more earnest than charming to the participants. The contest over political authority within the region that is now the town of Pittsburg was more than a generation old when in June 1832, a committee of five Indian Stream residents was appointed by their fellow citizens to draft a constitution for an independent republic. Their document had a preamble and a bill of rights, and laid out the several branches of government, including an assembly composed of all men over 21. In July the constitution was ratified by a 56-3 vote and the new country, the United Inhabitants of Indian Stream Republic,

was in business. They created a militia of 41 men, and one supposes—without direct evidence—that they may even have planned a birchbark navy. However, there quickly developed two political factions in this remote nation; one faction inclined toward annexing Canada, and the other leaned toward an international merger with the United States. In 1835 unrest was so severe among the Republic's inhabitants that civil war seemed likely, and 50 New Hampshire militiamen were sent abroad to restore order. Rocks were thrown. The next year the New Hampshire legislature sent up another commission—which duly recommended, to no one's surprise, that the nation become a part of New Hampshire. The Assembly of the Indian Stream Republic contemplated this for a few years and then agreed. In 1840 the area was incorporated as the town of Pittsburg.

None of these goings on, however, helped anyone to locate the northwesternmost head of the Connecticut River, or to solve the initial boundary question. Eventually the true head of the Connecticut River was located by Lord Ashburton of Great Britain and Daniel Webster, native of New Hampshire and U.S. Secretary of State. Over dinner in Washington, D.C., and no doubt over a map and port that Webster supplied for the occasion, they easily agreed that Halls Stream on the west was indeed the "northwesternmost head" of the river; this "discovery" was incorporated into the larger border resolution. Accordingly, on August 20, 1842, the United States Senate formally ratified a major document, the Webster-Ashburton Treaty, which established the entire northern New England boundary and incidentally defined the boundary of New Hampshire and of Pittsburg.

CHAPTER THREE

THE USE AND ROMANCE OF THE LAND

In the London of the 1620s they told tall tales of New Hampshire lakes bubbling with beavers. Captain John Mason would have heard the tales and he hoped to develop a major fur trade in his colony. Three years of effort by his agents in the early 1630s produced just 500 pounds of furs, mostly beaver traded from the Indians. The frail project collapsed when Mason died in 1635. Others continued the trade in increasing competition with the more aggressive traders and trappers who came north from Massachusetts. In 1640 Dover tried to regulate activity by encouraging trade with the Indians but forbidding sale of "arms" and "strong water." After 1641 the Massachusetts General Court asserted a monopoly on the New Hampshire fur trade and enforced it by licensing fur traders and forbidding unlicensed trading. Nevertheless, fur trading remained a small-time business in New Hampshire, profitable for only a few. The custom records for 1692 show 54 pounds of beaver and 130 small "furskins" sent from New Hampshire to London that year. After that, fur exports from New Hampshire virtually stopped, though local furriers and hatmakers continued using local furs for the next 200 years.

Fishing was another story. Throughout New Hampshire's first century, it was a major enterprise, though it suffered several ups and downs. The 1660s were a high point, the 1690s and the 30 years thereafter were a low point, and the 1720s were another high point.

Already in the 1640s, when the young colony was barely established on the mainland, the Isles of Shoals—some eight miles out from the Piscataqua Harbor—had become a well-known spot for processing fish, and by the 1660s there were as many as 1,500 men working there. Mackerel were salted and cod were dried and both were sent all over Europe, especially Portugal and Spain, as well as to England, the West Indies, and the wine

islands off the African coast. The palate of Catholic Europe became addicted to Isles of Shoals "dun fish," dried cod.

The fishing business broke down drastically in the 1690s. Along the coast severe Indian troubles, including several massacres, demoralized the communities, often bringing enterprise to a standstill. A tax imposed by Massachusetts on its section of the Isles of Shoals so annoyed the fishermen that hundreds of them left Appledore (then called Hog Island), many moving across the bay to Star Island in tax-free New Hampshire. At sea, vessels were being harassed by the French around Nova Scotia. The Shoals population had dropped to about 100 by the end of the decade.

But by the 1720s fishing was back in high gear. The Shoals were booming, New Castle was almost completely a fisherman's town, and fish were used as currency in Portsmouth. One hundred fishing vessels were based in Piscataqua River in 1720, and many of them were owned by merchants who systematically fished off Newfoundland as well as the Shoals regions.

However, after the first dramatic spurt in the 1660s, New Hampshire was always far overshadowed in its fisheries by Massachusetts Bay. Ultimately, fishing was to be Massachusetts' speciality as lumbering was to be New Hampshire's. Indeed, in April 1770 Governor Bellomont of Massachusetts complained to the London Board of Trade that New Hampshire fishing had fallen off because the people there were too preoccupied with lumbering.

Lumber and the Broad Arrow
"Lumber" is an American word, invented in colonial New England. For years the English avoided it in official documents, preferring "timber." New Hampshire was clear on this from the beginning: timber goes into a mill, lumber comes out. There

were 20 sawmills in New Hampshire in 1665, 50 by 1700. Most of the lumber that came out of the earliest ones and was not used locally went to Boston. Already by 1680 more than 50 vessels carried New Hampshire lumber to Boston, and in the year 1695 alone more than 100 vessels carried nearly two million board feet of lumber from Portsmouth to Massachusetts.

The building of Boston provided one market, the rebuilding of London after the Great Fire of 1666 provided another. Then there was the barrel-stave business for trading rum and molasses with the West Indies and wine with the islands off the coasts of Africa and Spain. But something bigger still was in the air: England's wars with Spain, then with the Dutch, then with France, decimated the Royal naval stores. Trade problems with Sweden threatened to close off the Baltic Sea area, which for centuries had supplied the British navy with planking, masts, and naval stores. New England pine, oak, and pitch were discovered just in time to keep Europe supplied for its traditional pursuits of mercantilism and warfare.

Since the 1630s entrepreneurs looking for return cargo had bought and taken to England shiploads of lumber, including pine masts, but it was in 1652 that the British Admiralty itself began annual purchases at Portsmouth. Soon thereafter the mast trade came to be the dominant area of the New World timber industry, and for more than 100 years—long enough for a second generation of masts to grow—it continued with little interruption. Portsmouth was the New England center of the trade. Initially, the Admiralty purchased at the dock the lumber, masts, and spars that had been cut, hauled, sawed, and finished to specifications by the New Hampshire loggers. Very soon everybody involved was making money at the business, and the pine and oak forests along the New Hampshire coast were being harvested with a cheerful abandon from the common lands of the four towns and from the no-man's-land up the river. One reason that farming developed so slowly in New Hampshire was that timbering developed so rapidly. So efficient was the Piscataqua River in

draining the pine from its slopes that the British Parliament began to take steps.

A broad arrow was the longstanding insignia of the Royal Navy. A kind of three-toed turkey track, it had for years been branded on cannon, ships, and slaves; and in America after 1685 it was regularly cut into the bark of a pine tree by six blows with a hatchet. That was the year the office of Surveyor of the King's Woods was created for New England and was charged with identifying and branding the trees to be reserved for masts.

The vital question was "Who owned these trees?" Was it those who owned the land on which they grew? By 1699 the Crown, going as far as it dared, officially laid claim (first only in Massachusetts and then, through the legislative Assembly, in New Hampshire as well) to all trees of 24 inches in diameter and upward on land not previously granted to a private person. Inevitably, this opened a blast of disputes about land ownership, to say nothing about the precise meaning of the laws. But the Royal intent was clear and increasingly effective: the Crown was bent on claiming all the large trees in all the future land grants in townships of New Hampshire. (Royal ownership of large trees on private estates had been standard policy in Old England, abolished by the Civil War in 1647, to be reasserted 50 years later in New England.)

Top: Stone walls give definition to the Charles French farm in Washington, New Hampshire, circa 1880. Courtesy, Ronald and Grace Jager

Left: Exactly what use these women will make of their day's catch of kelp is impossible to determine. The year is roughly 1905, and the place is Little Boar's Head. NHHS

Rural New Hampshire is portrayed in this circa 1836 lithograph, View of Meredith, *by William Bartlett. NHHS*

The policy was enforced by stiff penalties for unauthorized cutting, and by the high price offered for finished masts: usually it paid to be legal. Although the government controlled the business through the appointed surveyor, his licensed mast agents, and the network of subcontracting tied to it, such was the demand for lumber in general and masts in particular, and such was the extent of the resources, that it was still a profitable business to be in. It was profitable also for those who ignored the law or who continued to sell masts and lumber to Spain and France after it was made illegal in 1740.

Exact shipping records before 1695 are scarce, but in that year 56 masts of record went to England and an unknown number elsewhere. In 1718, two hundred went to England. In 1742 more than 500 masts of record were exported from the Piscataqua, nearly a fourth of them to the Caribbean and other North American colonies. In 1752 alone, the record year, 554 masts were sent to England.

Too soon, however, the profits were being siphoned off from the choppers and sawyers to the merchants and politicians. Understandably, enormous numbers of the King's mast trees simply disappeared at night and there was, coincidentally, everywhere in the lumberyards an endless supply of boards 23 inches wide. By the middle of the 18th century, New Hampshire Governor Benning Wentworth, who was also Surveyor General of the King's Woods, and whose brother, Hunking, was mast agent for

New Hampshire, was well aware that there was far more profit in controlling the market for himself than in enforcing the law for the King. He kept to appearances, though: every charter the governor authorized for a hill town, no matter how remote from the sea or from any plausible masting route, dutifully carried a clause that reserved all the white pines for His Majesty. When "His Majesty" was George III and the New Hampshire yeoman felt aggrieved against His Majesty's government, he could vent his feelings by going out and chopping down a big pine tree on his own land—if there were any left.

Nearer the coast, the woodcutters in the sawmills and logging crews developed into a class by themselves, hardworking, hard drinking, hard up. Belknap wrote, "The too free indulgence of spiritous liquor, to which this class of people are much addicted, hurts their health, their morals and their interest. They are always in debt, and frequently at law." Casting an eye back from the 1780s over the long New Hampshire experience at thinning its thick woods, Belknap opted for "husbandry; which, after all, is much preferable to the lumber business, both in point of gain, contentment and morals."

Husbandry

Contrasting the life and character of the lumberman with that of the farmer, a contrast still common today, was already a cliché 200 years ago. Farming always gets a better press than lumbering, and it is the "family farm" that has long been a staple in the nation's mythology. "Those who labor in the earth are the chosen people of God," wrote Thomas Jefferson, and many a contemporary who followed a plow wrote in the same vein. The romance of lumbering lies not in the humdrum of labor with the ax but in the great dramas of the business: the spring river runs of the logs, the mast trees, the logging railroads. No one ever wrote, "Those who chop down trees are the chosen people of God."

The New Hampshire "yeoman" settled into "husbandry" (standard colonial terms for "worker" and "farming") with an industry and optimism that compels admiration even at a distance. Incredible natural obstacles were simply taken for granted: they would yield to labor and patience. Hardly any reports come down to us suggesting that New Hampshire was thought inhospitable to farming. An exception occurred in 1738 when the grantees of what is now Bradford lost heart and sought a refund. To the Massachusetts General Court they sent a petition:

. . . shewing that the lands in said township are so rocky and mountainous on a View thereof that renders the settlement impracticable; praying they may be allowed to take up a Tract of Land in lieu of the aforesaid Township, lying West . . .

Shortly thereafter the King took all this territory from Massachusetts and put it in New Hampshire, and the Masonian Proprietors regranted the township to settlers undeterred by things "rocky and mountainous." Bradford thrived as did all its neighbors. So it went throughout the 18th century and into the 19th.

Moving inland, the pioneers shaved the hills to make way for cornfields, hewed the logs, and built sturdy post-and-beam buildings. Land too steep or rocky to cultivate was grazed. Buildings and fences they constructed as if to last forever, as if every farm established would be a farm forever, as if they had no inkling at all that the land was perverse and resilient enough to retrieve these fields from their grandchildren and restore them to forests again. From one end of the state to the other the development of New Hampshire farming shows a remarkably similar, repetitious pattern for 200 years—starting in 1650, when development was very slow, and ending in 1850, when it had virtually stopped. The pattern had certain stages.

First a group of perhaps two dozen adventurers would secure a grant of a township, lying 20 or 50 or more miles away, beyond roads, perhaps six miles square, roughly surveyed and laid out on a very imperfect map of the state. Little or no money was involved, but choice lands in the township were reserved by the grantor and conditions were attached to the grants depending on local circumstances and grantor's aims and shrewdness. If the date was 1750, the grantor was likely to be either Governor Benning Wentworth, acting ostensibly for the King of England, but pretty much for himself and his friends; or the Masonian Proprietors, acting for themselves. The governor and the Masonians "owned" New Hampshire, so to speak, and both were ambitious. Conditions normally attached by the Masonian Proprietors included: development to a certain point within a specified time (for example, 20 families settled and 200 acres cleared within eight years); 200 acres reserved for a minister; 200 free acres for whoever put up the first mill; 200 to be sold to finance a school; and things of that kind. When conditions were not met, the grant was forfeited, and in some cases the township was then regranted to others. Nevertheless, between 1750 and 1775 more than 100 successful townships were planted in New Hampshire.

Having secured the township, the grantees engaged a surveyor to measure and divide the land into lots of several hundred acres, which they then divided among themselves. Each got 1,000 acres or more, which he then further divided and offered for sale. Many surveyors' maps are still extant: they look more impressive than they are, for they were often made up in a Portsmouth office and show little knowledge of the actual terrain. Broadsides, word of mouth, and, after 1756, advertisement in the *New-Hampshire Gazette* publicized the availabilty of land. Here was opportunity undreamed of in Europe: hard work virtually guaranteed security on land of one's own. Settlers poured in from Massachusetts, Connecticut, and England. In the 40-year period 1790-1830, New Hampshire's population nearly doubled, going from 141,885 to 269,328.

Every lot partially cleared and built upon enhanced the value of the remaining ones: land development, whether by the Council for New England in 1625 or by Benning Wentworth in 1755 or by Samuel Tamposi in 1975, is a very stereotyped operation. In the colonial period many grantees never saw their land, but stayed at home in Dover or Portsmouth to speculate on land in other towns. Others went to their lots, cleared the land, settled down, and sold other lots to new neighbors. Many cleared and developed a lot, built on it and cultivated it, then sold out at a profit after a few years and took a wagonload of goods over the hills to the next town. Then they did the same thing over again, sometimes a third and fourth time, restlessly preferring the ax to the plow. Pioneers.

A township had reached the next stage in its life when sawmills and grist mills were running, a few dozen farms were cleared, and permanent houses had been built to replace the log houses that were often erected as temporary quarters for the first few years, when a meetinghouse was planned or being built and when starting schools and getting a pastor were being actively discussed. A township might then reasonably petition the legislature for incorporation as a town. If successful, its town meetings and board of selectmen and other officers (hog reeves, surveyors of timber, pound keepers, and the like) were thereby invested with the authority of the province or state, a representative could perhaps be sent to the legislature, and taxes could be collected and expended for public necessities such as road agents, schoolteachers, and a minister.

If the town was along the Merrimack or the Connecticut river, the first few dozen farms might be near the riverbank, the broad prehistoric flood plain. If the town was in the hill country between these rivers or to the north, the first farms of the town were usually on the highest elevations. This land was drier, more easily cleared because less brushy, freer of late and early frosts. A century or more later these same highlands were also the first areas to be abandoned to the forest; for by that time the lower lands, which had deeper, better soil and were more accessible to roads and buildings, were under control.

Having achieved a name and a political identity, the town was now a healthy adolescent, swiftly growing into a nearly self-sustaining and almost prosperous community wherein everything and everyone was closely connected with agriculture. Here, hard work, optimism, and self-reliance joined hands. Cities were necessary for some things—iron, salt, tea, schoolbooks, glass—and desirable for other things, such as markets for surpluses, but the key to the scheme was that the farm should supply raw materials for most of what was needed, the rest to be bartered in the village or in the local mill. There was little difference between the life and work of those who settled in, for example, Northwood at the beginning of the 18th century and those who settled 80 miles west in Goshen 80 years later. A letter written from Merrimack, New Hampshire, and published in the September 1821 *Monthly Magazine* in London said: "We have now a comfortable dwelling and 2 acres of ground planted with potatoes, Indian corn, melons, etc. I have 2 hogs, one ewe and a lamb. . . . I can assure you I have made every possible inquiry and can safely invite you to this happy country . . ." Prosperity was not at all unknown, a fact evidenced today in the many surviving specimens of "colonial" homes built around 1800 in hundreds of villages. In an essentially barter economy any cash crop—maple sugar, land, lumber, surplus livestock—was money in the bank. The town of Lyme may have been a bit unusual, but this is what the *Farmers' Monthly Visitor* said of it in 1839:

> The almost universal condition of the inhabitants of Lyme is the possession of abundance of good things of life. The difficulty is there that most of the farmers have money to let and there are few speculators anywhere with credit sufficient to hire it.

The basic frame of reference within which the farm communities developed and thrived was simply nature itself, not an economic system. The price of wool in New York or of rum in Boston simply did not matter. What mattered was that the millpond was full, that there was still more land and water in the hills, and still demand for it. Nature was the ally and the adversary. In 1792 Jeremy Belknap penned an eloquent summary of this sort of New Hampshire life. His idea of the happy society—and he spoke for his age—is entirely pastoral: man and nature in harmony, without alien intrusion. His sketch of New Hampshire husbandry is expressive of an image that has passed straight from the New England landscape into the American imagination, to become a permanent social and aesthetic resource.

> Were I to form a picture of happy society, it would be a town consisting of a due mixture of hills, valleys and streams of water: The land well fenced and cultivated; the roads and bridges in good repair; a decent inn for the refreshment of travellers, and for public entertainments: The inhabitants mostly husbandmen; their wives and daughters domestic manufacturers; a suitable proportion of handicraft workmen, and

two or three traders; a physician and lawyer, each of whom should have a farm for his support. A clergyman of any denomination, which should be agreeable to the majority, a man of good understanding, of a candid disposition and exemplary morals; not a metaphysical, nor a polemic, but a serious and practical preacher. A school master who should understand his business and teach his people to govern themselves. A social library, annually increasing, and under good regulation. A club of sensible men, seeking mutual improvement. A decent musical society. No intriguing politician, horse jockey, gambler or sot; but all such characters treated with contempt. Such a situation may be considered as the most favourable to social happiness of any which this world can afford.

By the next generation New Hampshire Governor Benjamin Pierce saw a cloud on the horizon. In his 1829 speech to the legislature Pierce worried about the growing dependence upon factory products, and he spoke of the dangers of trying "to support the style of modern days." He foresaw the old self-sufficiency beleaguered by the press of the industrial world, but he could not then foresee the competition to come from the American West. Hardly anyone foresaw what was to be: that every step away from self-sustaining husbandry and a barter economy toward commercial agriculture and a cash economy, and every step toward dependence upon manufactured merchandise and railroad transportation, was a stage in the slow disintegration of an entire social system. By the 1830s a garden of sorts had indeed been created within the wilderness. And the wilderness was hunkered down beside the garden—waiting.

Saving Wilderness

From the viewpoint of husbandry the forests of New Hampshire have usually been a problem—especially in the northern portions of the state. John Josselyn in 1672 had described Mt. Washington as encircled by "the infinite thick woods," and declared that the high country northward to the far horizon was "daunting terrible." When later loggers and farmers peered beneath those trees, the murmuring pines and the hemlock, they found a terrain likewise daunting terrible. Throughout most of the first two centuries of settlement the northern areas of New Hampshire stood as a physical and romantic challenge, more suitable for wonder and adventure than for agriculture. The mountains themselves—depending on whether one's perspective was aesthetic or mercantile—were either invaluable or

At the turn of the century the New Hampshire College of Agriculture and the Mechanic Arts practiced what it preached. It was a working farm. The dairy barn is on the left; the unmistakable profile of the towered Thompson Hall rises in the background. From the University Collection (UC). Courtesy, UNH Department of Media Services (UNH)

Opposite page: Temple has always been one of the smallest of the New Hampshire hill towns. In 1810 its population peaked at 941, plummeting by the turn of the century to one-third of that figure. Most of the cleared slopes depicted in this lithograph have since reverted to forest. Yet Temple had regular stage service throughout the 19th century, and the state gazetteer of 1856 listed "two stores, two sawmills, one gristmill, one tannery, and one hotel" in town. NHHS

This "farmer" is wearing a tie because he is an agriculture student at New Hampshire College of Agriculture and the Mechanic Arts. He is doing his homework on the college farm in Durham. The year is 1919, and the modern equipment is a double-disc harrow and a Fordson tractor. UC, UNH

When Roswell C. Osgood of Sullivan brought his "champion load of wood" through Keene's City Square on February 6, 1875, local photographer J.A. French wasted no time capturing the event. The ordeal for Osgood's oxen ended when they reached the nearby Cheshire Railroad Company. NHHS

In 1877 the Saunders Company laid rails to bring lumber out from the sawmills at Livermore. Lumbering made Livermore a boom town, and changes in the town's population reflect changes in the mills' productivity. The 1890 census counted 155 inhabitants (not including the transient population from the camps). In 1920 there were 98; in 1930, 23; and in 1940, only 4. Today Livermore has been reclaimed by the forest that was its genesis. From The Enterprise of the North Country of New Hampshire, *1983*

worthless. Adventurers and artists resorted to the White Hills, but the captains of enterprise went elsewhere. In retrospect, it appears that the most important of those who labored in the North Country in the early 19th century were the poets and artists. They went to work on the unconscious sensibility of the state, with effects that surfaced at the end of that century.

Husbandry was at its peak in 1831, though several hundred thousand acres of North Country land had never been granted in townships. The legislature that year, meaning to strike a blow for both farming and forestry, decided to sell all remaining state-owned lands. Up for sale went most of the White Mountains. Sargeant's Purchase, 25,000 acres near Mt. Washington, was sold in 1832 for $300; soon thereafter Chandler's Purchase, 10,000 acres nearby, went for the same amount. And so on. In 1867, 172,000 acres that included Mt. Washington were sold for $25,000—not quite 15 cents per acre. By 1876 all public lands had been sold.

There soon emerged throughout the state a kind of numbed puzzlement: Why on earth did we do *that?* By now railroads and pulp industries had penetrated the mountains, and the logger's ax, like a terrible swift sword, had struck even the remotest mountainsides. Across the White Mountains lay a depressing trail of erosion, forest fire, sawdust-clogged rivers, and general waste—sufficient to trigger a reaction on behalf of the land and the water. Having promoted northern timber cutting for half a century, the legislature in 1881 appointed a commission to inquire into "the extent to which the forests of New Hampshire are being destroyed by indiscriminate cuttings . . ." To a very large extent, the Commission Report stated in 1885. The report also stressed the interdependence of the transportation industry, the general economy, and the conditions of the forests.

Shortly, a conviction took hold in New Hampshire that certain traditional attitudes ought to be stopped cold and put into reverse gear. Fruits of this conviction were the Society for the Protection of New Hampshire Forests (SPNHF), founded in 1901, and the Weeks Act, passed by Congress in 1911, which initiated funding for the White Mountain National Forest. Since its inception the SPNHF, or the Forest Society, has been the leading conservation organization in the state. Saving the White Mountains was its initial crusade.

Founders of the Forest Society were among the political and financial heavyweights of the East Coast, and included New Hampshire Governor Frank Rollins (its first president), several soon-to-be U.S. Senators, the attorney general of Massachusetts, a bishop, and prominent newspapermen. Soon membership included other governors, senators, the president of the state university, the dean of the Yale School of Forestry, past and future U.S. cabinet secretaries, and the president of the Brown Paper Company. Theodore Roosevelt was the U.S. President; "conservation" (the famous ancestor of "environmentalism") was in the air and forestry was its major impulse. In New Hampshire books were written, commissions made ecological studies, committees made economic reports, corresponding committees of the Forest Society sprouted in towns, posters and editorials kept up a steady blast. Bills were drafted. The aim was to rewrite forestry law and provide a rationale for creating a White Moun-

In a state that is nearly 90 percent forest, forest fires periodically take on catastrophic proportions. The fires of the summer of 1953 were among the worst in memory, forcing Governor Hugh Gregg to apply for federal relief. The men above are building a fire line at the Grantham Mountain fire of that summer. SPNHF

tain Forest Reservation. Despite all the high-powered activity, progress was very slow. Many a politician dismissed the White Mountains project as sentimentalism: railroad and lumber interests were deeply entrenched. Eventually the Weeks Act of 1911 passed, and shortly thereafter the first national purchases were made in the White Mountains. By 1912 over 72,000 acres had been purchased at a cost of a bit more than $6 per acre. Sold as surplus wild land by one generation, they were bought back by the next generation as a natural resource, to become a national treasure. Late in 1914 Mt. Washington was purchased by the national government. Since that time New Hampshire lands owned by the national and state governments and by the Forest Society have grown to more than 750,000 acres.

The Forest Society was followed in 1914 by the Audubon Society and accompanied by the longer-standing interstate Appalachian Mountain Club. These were the conservation forerunners in the early 20th century. They remain the most influential conservation groups in New Hampshire today. In their wake have come dozens of similarly motivated local and statewide organizations, ranging from the Loon Preservation Committee (1979) and the Seacoast Anti-Pollution League (1969) to various kinds of environmental coalitions.

Lincoln was a tiny farming village when timber baron J.E. Henry moved his lumber company into town in 1892. By the time this photograph was taken in 1906, logs, shown filling the East Branch of the Pemigewasset River, were carried into Lincoln by Henry's East Branch & Lincoln Railroad. The White Mountain forests were accessible to major logging operations only by such logging railroads. NHHS

Once upon a time the King of England had simply said of New Hampshire: "This is my land; I give it to whom I will, to do with as he wills. These are my pine trees; I choose to keep them for myself." That was a long time ago. In the late 20th century, whenever the fate of the land or water is seriously at issue, three kinds of contenders are present. One is the array of various independent environmental organizations and ad hoc groups, ranging from the Forest and Audubon societies to the town conservation commissions authorized under a 1965 state law. A second is the cluster of governmental bureaus and officials charged with administering the laws. The third is the restless dynamic of economic interests, often driven to override public and long-term interests. In such a matrix laws must now be made and unmade.

Two major laws of recent decades illustrate that the kind of work initiated a hundred years ago by the first forest study commission continues and sometimes bears fruit: they concern "timber yield" and "current use." Until 1949 New Hampshire imposed an inventory tax on growing timber, thus encouraging owners to market even immature timber to avoid taxes. Efforts by the Forest Society and some legislators to change this began before 1920, and a Timber Yield tax—on harvested timber only—was eventually signed into law by Governor Sherman Adams in 1949. It has been a saving grace for the forests. A similar problem beset land taxes. For years tax assessments were legally bound to reflect the market value of the land, and though the law was widely ignored, the effect was to force some owners to sell land for development that was better left in field or forest.

The Current Use law passed in 1973 permits assessment of land based upon the purpose for which it is used (be it bird watching or cutting cordwood) rather than the price for which it could be sold.

An example of a contemporary portrait of rural New Hampshire is this 1982 photograph of a West Lebanon cornfield. Photograph by Tom Wolfe.

*   *   *

On January 20, 1961, Robert Frost, by then America's unofficial poet laureate, participated in President Kennedy's inauguration. He stood there on the platform, a venerable figure leaning against the breeze, speaking lines, slightly obscure, that yet touched the heart of the national experience and of New Hampshire's experience:

The land was ours before we were the land's.
She was our land more than a hundred years
Before we were her people.

New Hampshire settlers bought land, or got it as a gift outright, or somehow came to own it—to clear it, conquer it, ravish it, harvest it, have it. The land was ours. But *owning* it was chastened by time and the discipline of experience so as to become something more, something akin to *preserving*. So diverse were the forms of possession, and so open to predation and destruction were the natural resources, that defenses were necessary. There grew up a system of institutions, laws, and societies forming a zig-zag line of restraint against the worst assaults on the land. We became her people.

Opposite page: In late 1973 and early 1974 Governor Meldrim Thomson (left) promoted a plan whereby Aristotle Onassis (right) would build the largest oil refinery on the East Coast in Durham, with a tanker station at the Isles of Shoals. Local citizens rose in vigorous protest, and the project became a cause celebre. The issue was "home rule"—the authority of local municipalities. In the end home rule carried the day: when the citizens of Durham voted against the project at town meeting, the plan was dead. Photograph by Bob LaPree. Courtesy, New Hampshire Times

II

GOVERNMENT
AND PEOPLE

It took Franklin Pierce 49 ballots at the Democratic Convention of 1852 to win the honor of having his likeness placed on this Nathaniel Currier campaign poster. Oddly enough, he knew his opponents better than he knew his running mate. Whig Presidential candidate Winfield Scott had been Pierce's commanding officer in Mexico, and Free Soil candidate John Parker Hale was an old New Hampshire friend and political adversary. NHHS

CHAPTER FOUR

THE

DEVELOPMENT OF

GOVERNMENT

BEFORE 1784

A tale related by several early historians, beginning with Cotton Mather, tells of a Boston preacher who came to Dover and urged his hearers to be faithful to "the divine purpose for which this colony was planted," only to be interrupted by a New Hampshire voice, which declared: "Parson, we came hither to fish." At any rate, the earliest settlements around the mouth of the Piscataqua River were not parts of a religious movement or of a chartered colony. The King of England, through the Council for New England, had granted *land* to developers—Thomson, Mason, Gorges, Hilton, and others—while retaining political *authority*. The settlers were not expected to set up government: their mission in English eyes was not political or religious, but economic. From the King's point of view, early New Hampshire was just another piece of England, a remote province.

The First Four Towns

A little bit of England—that was the circumstance in the 1620s and 1630s for Dover and Strawbery Banke, two of the first four towns of New Hampshire. The other two original towns, Exeter and Hampton, lying to the south, had been primarily settled from Massachusetts, partially under religious impulses. John Wheelwright, a religious dissenter banished from the Bay Colony, had started Exeter by purchasing land from the Indians in 1638. Hampton, a Puritan political outpost in the wilderness, was a creation of the Massachusetts General Court between 1636 and 1639. During the same period, while England was distracted by civil war, Strawbery Banke had devised a government for itself and elected a governor; and Dover, just up the river, had put

together a three-paragraph compact (the 1640 Dover Combination) in which the inhabitants pledged loyalty to the laws of England "together with all such orders as shal bee concluded by a major part of the free men of our Society."

The Reverend John Wheelwright, who founded the town of Exeter in the 17th century, looked something like this in 1677 when he was 84 years old. Commissioned in 1947, this portrait is probably a copy of the John Wheelwright portrait in the Massachusetts State House. The original portrait showed a man with less hair and a trimmer mustache. Privately owned

It was a somewhat confused beginning for New Hampshire—in its land grants, in its religious assumptions, and in its political structure. By 1643 these four towns, awkward political orphans as they were, with a population of somewhere near one thousand, had come, one by one, under the political wing of the swiftly developing Massachusetts Bay Colony. Bringing this about involved considerable tugging and hauling. But the arrangement with Massachusetts gave to these four towns a focus of government closer to home than England, and it authorized their makeshift town governments.

Though the liaison with Massachusetts lasted nearly 40 years, until 1680, it was never a legal marriage from the mother country's point of view. But England was riven by civil wars and general upheaval, and too distracted to care. The tie with Puritan Massachusetts came to seem almost natural and, to all but the scattered Anglicans left in Portsmouth, it seemed permanent. But viewed from London, the expansion of Massachusetts' political influence was worrisome, as were the claims to ownership of New Hampshire by Robert Mason. Under pressure of an official inquiry by the Lords Chief Justice, Mason was bought off and Massachusetts backed off and "disavowed any right either in the soil or government thereof." This cleared the way for the King to establish New Hampshire as a Royal colony with a new government separate from Massachusetts. It went into effect on January 1, 1680.

A Crown Colony

This new "constitution" structured the New Hampshire government until the Revolutionary War. It called for an executive consisting of an appointed Council of nine men with a president, as well as an Assembly of representatives from the towns. In time, the Council presidency evolved into the role of Royal governor—sometimes called lieutenant-governor, sometimes governor-general. This Council, appointed by the English Board of Trade, is the historical antecedent of the present-day Executive Council.

The Council was designed to be far more powerful than the elected Assembly. The Council determined that voting rights for Assemblymen be restricted to Protestant males aged 24 and older with an estate of £20 or more. The Council and its president, or governor, at first initiated important legislation—tax levies, for example. The Assembly was invited to "concur." The governor called the Assembly into session and could dismiss it; he could veto its laws in the King's name, and he could determine its membership by controlling the process ("writs of election") whereby towns were invited to send representatives. The writs were issued in accordance with the political winds. Why invite representatives from troublesome towns? The governor also controlled major appointments to office—judges, justices, and administrators of shipping and masting contracts. In short, it was the governor and not the Assembly that became the locus of political authority in New Hampshire, though the "power of the purse" remained with the Assembly—and they used it.

These arrangements were not lost to the memories of those who forged new and very different governments for New Hampshire in a later generation. The little New Hampshire Assembly of 1680 and beyond, though politically weak, was symbolically mighty; it was a tiny democratic hairline fracture in the solid wall of monarchy, a crack that grew inexorably for 100 years, until finally the wall came tumbling down.

On the other hand, being governor of New Hampshire was not easy, and there were rival factions everywhere. Some cabal was usually ready to undermine the governor's authority, or to dispatch an informer to London to discredit somebody, or to rebut the normally self-serving reports the governor sent to the home office. A governor learned to pull strings all across the board, from town meeting to English court. Frequently, one tugged too hard or pulled rank too often and got into trouble. In 1717 Lieutenant-Governor Vaughan lectured the Council about "the arrogance and pride of those who do not consider I am a superior match, as being armed with power from my Prince, who doth execution at the utterance of the word." For this he was fired by his then superior, the governor of Massachusetts. To the degree that a governor was successful, it was perhaps because he was conciliatory, ruthless, personally ambitious, and public spirited all at the same time. It helped if he was also intelligent, well-born, religious, and had a sense of style. Even knowledge of government could be useful.

The Wentworth Dynasty

Between 1680 and 1741 sixteen governors served New Hampshire, under different kinds of political protocols, not easily summarized. For reasons of empire, the British government arranged for New Hampshire, Massachusetts, and sometimes New York to be nominally governed by the same person, while each province retained its legislative assembly and in some cases a local lieutenant-governor. This system, which lasted until 1741, enabled the Crown to coordinate both defenses and aggressions against the Native Americans.

But well before that, 18th-century New Hampshire was developing a gubernatorial dynasty that was to be unmatched in any of the American colonies. It consisted of three American born Wentworths, father, son, and nephew, and it lasted nearly six decades, from 1717 to 1775. John Wentworth was governor (technically, lieutenant-governor) from 1717 until his death in 1730; after a decade's interruption, he was succeeded by his son, Benning Wentworth, the most formidable of the three; and Benning was succeeded in 1767 by his nephew, John Wentworth II, who stayed until 1775. The Wentworths genuinely cared about New Hampshire—or at least managed to merge their own political ambitions with the ambition that the colony should prosper. Natives of the state, they understood local concerns; educated men, they were worldly enough to know they had to please the Crown without alarming the natives, and vice versa.

John Wentworth I, appointed as New Hampshire's lieutenant-governor when Vaughan was fired, a grandson of one of the earliest settlers of Exeter, New Hampshire, had risen through the ranks by serving a number of terms in the Council. A successful merchant and mast trader, he knew that as chief of state he would face border disputes in the south with Massachusetts as well as Indian raids on the north and east and financial problems in every section. But he had asked for the job. At that time, Massachusetts claimed everything west of the Merrimack River, and he instigated the opening moves against that colony by informing the Board of Trade in London that Massachusetts was both unneighborly and "strangers to all Kingly power." Manipulating kings of England became a Wentworth specialty.

Benning Wentworth

The central figure of the Wentworth establishment, Benning

Wentworth, was an amiably conservative aristocrat. He became governor in 1741 of a province much enlarged by the settlement of the boundary dispute with Massachusetts, and he also managed to get appointed Surveyor General of the King's Woods. His 26 years at the helm are unmatched by any American colonial governor. He grew wealthy by chartering scores of towns and reserving some of the best acres for himself, to be sold at a profit when the town was developed. As the most powerful and resourceful New Hampshire governor up to that time, he also managed to intensify some of the inherent problems of the political system. Like his father, he was good at playing off the appointed Council against the elected Assembly. Indeed, for a governor who preferred to rule by decree, a legislative Assembly was something of a nuisance: legislators could decline to grant funds, and they could lapse into the habit of initiating their own laws. Part of the time he dealt successfully with this kind of independence by giving Assemblymen huge chunks of land in newly chartered towns. He could also be liberal with military commissions, since he fell heir to the last and most bitter of the guerilla wars with the original Americans—the French and Indian War.

In fact, Benning Wentworth knew all the arts and wiles of patronage and practiced them to the hilt, sprinkling his tracks with Royal appointments, judicial offices, land grants, military commissions, and commercial preferments. His father, founder of the dynasty, had sired 14 children, and during Benning's years in power he arranged what his opponents called "family govern-ment." It worked better than one might have expected, and historians generally credit his "machine" with having established reasonably good, though imperialistic, government. His colony had to cope with extremely difficult terrain and climate, it had to accommodate a great deal of religious diversity, and it served as a battleground for the New World conflict between France and England.

One mark of his success as governor can be read today in the streets of Portsmouth. The port city with "safe harbor and rocky shore" was becoming a stylish provincial capital. There was wealth in masting, lumber, fishing, and land; and Portsmouth merchants and Wentworth relatives cornered enough of it to begin cultivating the tastes of those who, then and later, erected some of the finest Georgian and Federal homes in America. Nevertheless, Benning Wentworth's sumptuous and increasingly high-handed style triggered so much public disapproval, complaint, and conniving that he was in effect forced to retire in 1767, to be replaced by his nephew, John Wentworth II.

The Last Wentworth
Though he was run over by the revolution that he tried to slow down and was in some sense a failure, historians have given John Wentworth II a very good press. As much as any British official in America in the turbulent decade before the Revolution, he was ground up between the British Parliament and the American populace.

Returning to his native New Hampshire in 1767 as governor, John Wentworth was accepted with great enthusiasm, and for some time he maintained popularity with all levels of society. He took special interest in the interior of the state and in the conditions of the forests. He hiked to the hills, climbed one of the higher peaks in the White Mountains, visited logging camps, and promoted road building. In 1771, over the objections of many aristocrats in Portsmouth, he instituted the organization of the state into five counties and pushed the development of county government. He enthusiastically supported the founding of Dartmouth College in 1769. He liked New Hampshire's people and thought of them in heroic terms. Before becoming governor he had written: "At great expense of their whole fortunes . . . [the New Englanders] transported themselves to and purchased the country of the natives [this was largely a myth], cultivated with incredible labor, defended and extended it with their lives, entirely unassisted and for many years unknown." Especially at first, he was perceived as one who genuinely wanted to be a good governor.

But, of course, like his Uncle Benning before him, and his grandfather John before that, he ruled as a family oligarch. The relationship between the people of New Hampshire and the Royal governor, any Royal governor, was always an uneasy one—religiously, politically, and economically. On Sunday, the governor occupied an island of Anglicanism in a sea of Yankee Congregationalism. On Monday, the governor—through family, lackeys, and Council—controlled political patronage. On Tuesday, the governor—through the lumber and masting trade and town chartering—controlled the economy. But on Wednesday the governor could not control the sentiment of the people. Tensions in the system came to the breaking point in the years 1774-1776, two years of stress that undid the assumptions of nearly a century. In all the 13 colonies, Royal government collapsed completely during these years, and every colony had its characteristic mode of creative disintegration according to its own traditions and grievances. One major grievance in New Hampshire was summed up by Jeremy Belknap a few years after the Revolution as "the unequal representation of the people in the General Assembly."

As late as the year 1773, of 147 towns, 46 only were represented. . . . The towns of Nottingham and Concord, though full of people . . . had not once been admitted to the privilege of representation; and this was the case with many other towns; . . . No uniform system of representation had been adopted.

The governor wanted to broaden the legislative base, and feared what would happen if he did. In particular, he feared the influence of Massachusetts firebrands such as Sam Adams and Paul Revere. Of course, he had personal motives for blaming outside influence for internal troubles, but he also had good reason for writing to England that he did not expect to see law and order in the province "until they are effectually restored in the Massachusetts Bay." While he hesitated, local resentment grew: resentment of his manipulation of the Assembly; of patronage and nepotism in his "court"; of British authority.

Above: New Hampshire native John Wentworth was in many ways the most able of the Wentworth "dynasty," but his term as royal governor of New Hampshire (1767-1775) was cut short by the events of the Revolution. Wentworth was forced to flee his native province in September 1775, never to return. John Singleton Copley painted this portrait in 1769. Privately owned

Left: Mrs. Theodore Atkinson was portrayed by John Singleton Copley in 1765. Four years later, following the death of her first husband, Frances Deering Wentworth became the wife of John Wentworth, the last royal governor of New Hampshire. As such she became a Loyalist in the American Revolution. In August 1775, a month before her 30th birthday, she, her husband, and their infant son were forced to flee their Portsmouth home. From the Lenox Collection. Courtesy, New York Public Library

Opposite page: Theodore Atkinson, Jr., was prominent among the aristocratic Harvard-educated young men of Portsmouth before the American Revolution. Like his politically powerful father, he was closely allied to the Wentworth families and married a relative, Frances Wentworth. Atkinson became collector of customs at Portsmouth, secretary of the province, and a member of the Governor's Council. His career was cut short when he died of consumption at age 32. This circa 1757 portrait, long attributed to Joseph Blackburn, is now recognized as the work of John Singleton Copley. Courtesy, Museum of Art, Rhode Island School of Design

Above: New Hampshire residents commonly took part in public fasts to celebrate military victories, commemorate special events (particularly those pertaining to the royal family), or pray for deliverance from disease, famine, or oppression. The tradition began in 1680 with a fast for the good health of council President John Cutt (who died shortly afterwards); and evolved into a general day of thanks and school vacations. It continued as New Hampshire's annual Fast Day in April for over three hundred years, and was abolished in 1991 when the state created a Civil Rights Day in January, changed in 1999 to Martin Luther King Day. NHHS

Opposite page: From New Hampshire's earliest days the Piscataqua Harbor was protected by the strategically located Fort William and Mary, shown in the view from 1705. During the Revolution the fort was the scene, on December 14, 1774, of New Hampshire's first systematic act of aggression against British authority. Under the protection of Captain J. Cochran and only five men, the fort and its stores of gunpowder fell easy prey to an organized force of several hundred New Hampshire men who, having been warned by Paul Revere that a British ship was coming to remove the fort's gunpowder, gathered to take the powder for their own use. After firing on the "attackers," the six men were captured and "kept prisoners about one hour and a half," Cochran wrote, "during which time they broke open the powder-house, and took all the powder away... And having put it into boats and sent it off, they released me from confinement." Courtesy, the British Museum

Lady Wentworth, in a private letter to an English friend, happened to sum it all up: "They love The Governor as Mr. Wentworth, tho' they dislike him as Servant to the Crown."

During the year 1774, there were several turning points—and no turning back. In January Governor Wentworth asked the Assembly to combat the "infectious & pestilential disorders being spread among the inhabitants," but the Assembly just couldn't see the problem. In June, and again in July, he dismissed the Assembly shortly after it had convened in Portsmouth. The second time the Assemblymen promptly gathered at a nearby tavern and planned for a new "congress" to meet the next week in Exeter. At that gathering they appointed Colonel Nathaniel Folsom and Major John Sullivan as delegates to the Continental Congress in Philadelphia, and agreed to meet themselves again at Exeter. In December the New Hampshire patriots, prompted by rumors delivered from Boston to Portsmouth by Paul Revere, forcibly removed a store of guns and powder from Fort William and Mary. The governor called out the militia, but the militia pretended to be busy elsewhere. The governor wrote dolefully to his English patrons that of those who had led this attack "no jail would hold them long and no jury would find them guilty."

In the course of a year, the politicians and the citizen-soldiers of New Hampshire, acting separately, had developed together a devastating defense against British authority. They ignored it.

Seventeen Seventy-Five

After the battles at Lexington and Concord in April, revolutionary fever rose dramatically in New Hampshire. After the battle of Bunker Hill in June, there was no stopping it. Inevitably, much of the turmoil in New Hampshire swirled around the Royal governor, a symbol of wounded authority—forced out of his Portsmouth home and living under military protection at Fort William and Mary, unwilling to let the regular Assembly meet in Portsmouth, unable to stop the irregular Provincial Congress from meeting in Exeter. Stalemate, at a high level of chaos.

Then, on August 23, 1775, something stunning and unprecedented happened that baffled the entire colony. His Excellency, John Wentworth, Esquire, His Majesty's Captain General and Governor of New Hampshire, Surveyor of the King's Woods, not a rich man but the presumed owner of 27,000 acres of New Hampshire land, born and reared in New Hampshire, Harvard friend and classmate (1755) of John Adams, a New Englander to his fingertips, but alas, in the service of the King of England, packed his bags, climbed aboard the British man-o'-war *Scarborough*, and sailed out of Portsmouth Harbor toward Boston. It was really wonderfully simple and simplifying: the end forever of British rule in New Hampshire. Where once all political authority had been focused, was now—nothing. Of that vacuum, Belknap wrote: "All commissions under the former authority being annulled, the courts of justice were shut and the sword of magistracy was sheathed."

What to do? There was nothing to do—except devise a government and run it, raise a militia and support it, fight a war and pay for it, consolidate efforts with a dozen other disorderly colonies, and deal with pockets of perplexed Tories in scores of

scattered towns. It was the worst of times. True, the British governor was gone, but the situation was now more confusing than anything anyone had contemplated. It was also the best of times. For in fact, there in the autumn of 1775, New Hampshire stood alone of all the colonies, with no resident British authority. Without declaring it, without seeking it, and without fully realizing it, she was free and independent.

Of course New Hampshire was not really without government. The province, colony, or state—whatever it was to be called at this awkward moment—was really a collection of towns, and in the towns, officers and selectmen maintained authority by force of tradition, or exhortation. And town government itself rested on social bedrock: Belknap tells us that "habits of decency, family government, and the good examples of influential persons contributed more to maintain order than any other authority."

In the background, the Provincial Congress, which had started unauthorized meetings in Exeter the year before, had been constantly assuming more authority. Indeed, even before Wentworth's departure this Congress, ignoring the governor, had organized from its militia a New Hampshire "army" at Cambridge, Massachusetts, had sent delegates to the Continental Congress in Philadelphia, and had created a small executive group, the Committee of Safety, to act for the Provincial Congress between sessions. Then, in a meeting just after the battles in Lexington and Concord, it had petitioned the Continental Congress in Philadelphia for "explicit advice respecting the taking up, and exercising, the Powers of Civil Government." That fall (1775), still awaiting an answer, but now with all British authority gone, the New Hampshire patriots were far, far out on a political limb. They urgently pressed the Continental Congress again for "advice and direction . . . with respect to a method for our administering justice, and regulating our civil police."

Until this time the Continental Congress had had no occasion at all to tell a colony how to organize a government, or whether to do so. Pressured by New Hampshire, the Continental Congress did the normal thing: it formed a committee. Wisely, it put John Adams of Massachusetts on the committee, and Adams, sensing as usual the historic significance of an issue, grabbed the assignment. He had already made a speech on the need for setting up "state" governments. "State" was the Adams word of the hour; he taught a generation to dislike the words "province" and "colony." He had just urged "Congress to resolve on a general recommendation to all the States to call conventions and institute regular governments." Within a week the Adams committee reported and soon got the Continental Congress to pass the resolution that would lay open a new page in American political history:

> . . . that it be recommended to the provincial Convention of New Hampshire, to call a full and free representation of the people . . . [to] establish such a form of government as . . . will best produce the happiness of the people, and most effectively secure peace and good order . . .

The resolution was just what was wanted. Very general, but very definite: set up a form of government in New Hampshire. It was destined to be a beginning for America of *state* government—government to be based upon the will of a people and not upon the will of a king. And the transaction itself anticipated the intricate reciprocity that is now the heart of the federal/state system: New Hampshire's letters to Philadelphia had carefully deferred to the authority of the Continental Congress, and in the resolution of reply, the Congress had carefully validated the relative autonomy of New Hampshire.

Seventeen Seventy-Six

Immediately, a new Provincial Congress was called for and gathered at Exeter, nervous and exhilarated. No one dared call it a "state congress." Within little more than a week after getting the endorsement from Philadelphia and then voting solemnly "to take up Civil Government," the Exeter Provincial Congress had written and adopted a short state constitution, which specified the main elements of government. January 5, 1776—the day the positive vote was taken on the document—is the date that marks the real beginning of written constitutional government, not only in New Hampshire but in America. This constitution served the new state throughout the Revolutionary War. Like the old system it provided for an elected Assembly and also for a Council—not appointed but elected by the Assembly members. *This* Council is the ancestor of the present-day Senate, the "upper chamber." In this wartime constitution there was no provision for a governor. Of governors they had had enough.

Did the representatives fully know what they were doing? Yes and no. They were experienced sailors sailing political seas

Kingston's Josiah Bartlett was a physician, legislator, chief justice of the New Hampshire Superior Court, president and later governor of New Hampshire, and signer of the Declaration of Independence. Along with Matthew Thornton and Meshech Weare, Bartlett gave the state unspectacular but steady leadership during the American Revolution. His efforts delivered postwar New Hampshire from political and economic hardship. This 1790 drawing is the work of John Trumbull, who sketched the various signers' likenesses for his painting The Declaration of Independence. *It is believed to be the only life portrait of Bartlett. NHHS*

New Hampshire revenue and currency problems during the Revolutionary War were horrendous. Inflation was often rampant. The paper money shown here was issued in 1780 in many denominations and for a time was much in demand. But within a few months Meshech Weare, president of the Provincial Council, wrote: "The present situation of our currency makes me shudder." Shortly thereafter this paper money was withdrawn from circulation and punched to invalidate it. New Hampshire reverted to barter, to silver and gold, and to European currency. NHHS

uncharted. Many New Hampshire citizens were alarmed at the audacity of the venture. Ten towns sent protests to the Exeter Assembly almost immediately. A particularly impressive letter came from Portsmouth citizens: a New Hampshire constitution with no reference to Great Britain was going too far too fast, they said; it sounded dangerously like a claim to "independency" (i.e. treason); it was presumptuous to go far beyond what the other colonies had done, and also beyond what had been asked for by the New Hampshire citizens; moreover, it would cost money. Such protests were prompted by a thought too demoralizing to state: what if we Americans should lose this confusing war? New Hampshire will then be in terrible trouble; in English eyes it will be the worst province of the lot.

But the stronger arguments were on the other side. During the spring of 1776, all the frozen reluctance of the conservatives melted like snow, and by June it had evaporated completely. A New Hampshire constitution of sorts was in place. But the political air was now thoroughly heated by a new idea as bold as "constitution," and bigger. "Independency" was its name—only yesterday a cautious whisper and now the talk of the town. Why brood and bicker in Portsmouth about that makeshift government in Exeter when something so electrifying as Thomas Paine's *Common Sense* is in the wind? A drama far beyond Exeter was abroad, and like jagged lightning it was flashing up and down the Atlantic seaboard. New Hampshire, through a quirk of history, seemed to be out in front of it all—perhaps, for all anyone could tell at the moment, even leading it.

New Hampshire was not exactly leading, for it was independent in fact only, not theory. So on June 11, 1776, a committee of the Assembly was appointed to draft a resolution for "independence of the united colonies on Great Britain." Unknown to the New Hampshire Assembly, it was on that very day that the Continental Congress appointed a committee to draft a Declaration of Independence—just in case one would be needed. The New Hampshire declaration adopted in Exeter on June 15, a one-sentence masterpiece of 332 words with an array of rotund and eloquent "whereas" clauses, protested that New Hampshire was impelled to independence "by the most violent and

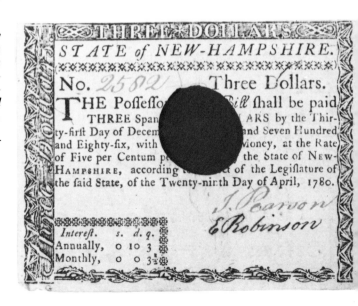

injurious treatment." The declaration was in the form of instructions to the New Hampshire delegation and included also a pledge of support for independence with "our lives and fortunes." The pivotal clause reads: "We do hereby declare that it is the opinion of this assembly that our delegates at the continental congress should be instructed, and they are hereby instructed, to join with the other colonies in declaring the thirteen united colonies a free and independent state." Josiah Bartlett and William Whipple cast the New Hampshire vote for independence along with the rest of the colonies' delegates on July 2, and also for the Jefferson committee draft of a declaration on July 4.

Writing a dozen years later, Jeremy Belknap said of New Hampshire's action at this time, "it relieved us from a state of embarassment. We then knew the ground on which we stood, and from that time everything assumed a new appearance."

Wartime Government

Throughout the Revolutionary War the legislature, elected annually under the new constitution, met in Exeter rather infrequently. It set general policy, or tried to, on matters concerning imports and exports, taxes, minting money, raising troops, handling deserters, appointing military officers, dealing with Tories, incorporating towns, corresponding with the Continental Congress, and the like. The legislators had to improvise every step of the way. But it was the Committee of Safety, which met frequently, that carried out the legislature's policies, and also a good many policies of its own. No such committee was provided for by the constitution. It was provided for by necessity: somebody had to be in charge. The Committee of Safety was a small group, usually less than a dozen, and it always included some of the ablest men in the state. Chief among them, both president of the Council (and thus sometimes referred to as the "President of New Hampshire") and chairman of the Committee of Safety throughout the war, was Meshech Weare of Hampton Falls, a pillar of strength in his own right. Weare is the unassuming and unsung hero of this difficult period. He was not theatrical like a Webster, or overpowering like a Washington, or flamboyant like a John Langdon or John Stark. No painting of him exists; his biography remains to be written. Yet during this entire time, as historian Frank B. Sanborn writes, "his hand is seen, energetic and unshaken by danger and difficulty, in all the measures of government."

Periodically the Committee of Safety called the legislature into session and gave it an agenda, such as raising troops and sending food in response to the urgent pleas of General Washington. The Committee also bought and deployed supplies on behalf of the state, punished Tories, and generally ran the war effort. It fell to the Committee, too, to administer the loyalty oath in the spring of 1776 as suggested by the Continental Congress. The Association Test, as it was called, required all adult males to sign a pledge to "oppose the Hostile Proceedings of the British Fleet and Armies." More than 90 percent of them signed.

But the New Hampshire Constitution of 1776 was a frail reed and it had a mortal weakness: there was no amending process. There was no way to deal constructively with such old sore spots as the question of representation in the Assembly. True, as soon

A physician by trade, Matthew Thornton had represented his town of Londonderry in the Provincial Assembly before the Revolution. As royal government collapsed in New Hampshire, Thornton was vaulted to statewide leadership, serving as president of the fourth Provincial Congress, chairman of the state Committee of Safety, associate justice of the state superior court, and delegate to the Continental Congress where he signed the Declaration of Independence. NHHS

as the governor had left, the Provincial Assembly had promptly given the vote to all adult male taxpayers, eliminating a property qualification. But that did not resolve the problem of apportioning representation to the towns, and neither did the constitution resolve it. Western New Hampshire towns especially felt discriminated against. The state fathers were obliged to consider redrawing their form of government from the ground up.

A New Constitution

Throughout these turbulent years, the state's leaders had to run the war and the state with one hand, and give to themselves constitutional sanction with the other. The United States Declaration of Independence in July, the official name change of New Hampshire from "province" to "state" in September, the Association Tests, gallantry on the battlefield—while all these rallied the people to sacrifices for the war effort, to loyalty to the Continental Congress, and to all the heady uncertainties of independence, they did little or nothing to bolster commitment to the state's own fragile constitution. Editorializing and pamphleteering against the government as unrepresentative and allowing too much power to too few—in particular, the Committee of Safety, mounted throughout 1776 and 1777, much of it emanating from Dartmouth College and surrounding western New Hampshire towns. The "college party" the critics were called. There was also sometimes an anti-Committee of Safety faction within the Assembly led by Representative John Langdon. In such a climate the authority of the Assembly itself inevitably eroded.

John Langdon, wealthy Portsmouth shipbuilder and successful privateer, later a delegate to the national Constitutional Convention, was Speaker of the House. Meshech Weare, Harvard class of 1735, lawyer, farmer, merchant, and jurist with legislative experience in the colonial Assembly going all the way back to 1745, was President of the Council, the upper legislative chamber, Chairman of the Committee of Safety, and the Chief Justice of the Superior Court. The New Hampshire legislative leadership was thus fortunately in superb hands. One or both of these men commanded the respect of nearly everyone in the state, sometimes even of each other. Together they piloted a resolution through both houses on February 26, 1778, calling for "full and free representation . . . in convention for the sole purpose of framing and laying a permanent plan or system of government. . . ."

Though the convention was held at Concord, a more central location than Exeter, the college party did not show up. A year's intermittent work under the presidency of Meshech Weare produced a new constitution—which was voted down by the towns in the summer of 1779. Weare continued as President of the Council, Chairman of the Committee, and Chief Justice, and John Langdon was renamed Speaker. Another Constitutional Convention was called in 1781 and instructed by the "legislature" (as the Assembly was now coming to be called) not to disband until a new constitution had been accepted by the towns.

The college party argued that every inhabited town, no matter if it were remote or small or unincorporated, should have at least one delegate to the House of Representatives. (As an indirect consequence of this view the New Hampshire House even today has 400 members, far more than that of any other state.) Ironically, when the new convention assembled on June 5, 1781, to draft a constitution, it was found that fewer than half the towns had bothered to send delegates. Clearly, New Hampshire was a politically distracted state. Small wonder. There was a war on. Inflation was rampant. Filling the ranks of the Continental Army was a terrible drain—economically, emotionally. The rural towns were made up of farmers still trying to subdue a wilderness, and roads to Concord from the interior were only trails. The war was always elsewhere. Would it soon be over? Would it soon be here? It was hard to get accurate news, hard to keep track of what was really going on.

Yet a constitutional draft emerged from Concord the next year and, like its failed 1779 predecessor, it proposed to put sharp curbs on the legislators' practice of appointing themselves to most of the civil offices. The draft was sent out to referendum in the towns borne on the wings of an eloquently argued letter signed by George Atkinson, president of the convention. The present legislators (meaning in particular the Committee of Safety) will not like this constitution, said the letter, for they have vested interest in all the powers and privileges they have accrued. "The love of Power is so alluring, we had almost said infatuating, that few have ever been able to resist its bewitching influence." In solemn irony, the letter added a thought for all ages: "A perfect system of Government is not to be expected in the present imperfect state of humanity. But could a faultless one be framed, it would not be universally approved unless its Judges were all equally perfect."

This version failed too. The proposed House of 50 representatives was not sufficiently representative, said the towns that had not troubled to send representatives to the convention. Each proposed version was dissected and debated in the pages of the Portsmouth New-Hampshire Gazette. A new version, submitted to referendum the next year, 1782, was also defeated—the word from the towns being that this one proposed too strong a chief executive. Even friends of the effort couldn't resist a jeer. Belknap wrote: "The hen has laid again. We have a Constitution as often as we have an almanac, and the more we have the worse." Indeed, it was a tiresome, exasperating, almost hopeless process upon which the delegates had embarked. In New Hampshire, which saw no bloodshed or battles on its own soil during the Revolutionary War, these were the times that tried men's souls—by trying their patience.

And yet. Through this very process, through referenda and revisions and decisions, through factions and compromises and blizzards of broadsides, New Hampshire was finding its own mind, forging in the midst of a disquieting, wearying war a political self-image that was to endure. Among its emerging features were: a larger, more widely representative legislature (officially styled the "General Court"); focus upon the town as the political unit in state government, and upon the people as the source of authority; a clear separation of judicial, legislative, and executive powers; prohibitions on office monopolies and conflicts of interest; a forthright and extensive bill of rights; and a rather weak and carefully circumscribed chief executive office. The next version, the fourth try, hit upon the combination of these

Merchant and ship captain, member of the Continental Congress, speaker of the New Hampshire House of Representatives, president and later governor of New Hampshire, delegate to the Constitutional Convention, and U.S. Senator, John Langdon was one of the most prominent figures in Portsmouth at the end of the 18th century. His house, built between 1784-1785, enjoyed similar status. When George Washington visited Portsmouth in 1789, he observed that there were "some good houses . . . among which Colonel Langdon's may be esteemed the first." The property is currently maintained by the Society for the Preservation of New England Antiquities. Photograph by J. David Bohl. Courtesy, the Society for the Preservation of New England Antiquities

features that, whether out of wisdom or weariness or wariness of alternatives, proved acceptable to the towns. In the autumn of 1783, shortly after the Revolutionary War officially ended with the Treaty of Paris, the local political war in New Hampshire also ended. On October 31 the announcement came that the draft had been accepted by the required two-thirds of the towns, and that the new constitution would go into effect on June 2, 1784.

Under the new constitution the principal appointive powers went to the chief executive, not to the legislature as before, and legislators were also excluded from holding most of the paid offices. It blithely thumbed its nose at the "college party" by barring from the General Court "any present professor or instructor in any college"—a prohibition since removed. Fortunately, it also built into the document a provison for amendment by giving the people, at least once every seven (now ten) years, a chance to call a convention "to revise the Constitution" if they so desire. Fourteen times during the last two centuries they have so desired.

In his introductory letter to an earlier, rejected, constitution, President George Atkinson had written eloquently about the need for a constitution more lasting than the one adopted in 1776: "When the people of this state first thought proper to assume government for themselves, it was a time of difficulty and peril. That form which was the simplest, and first presented itself to their view, in the perturbation of spirits that then prevailed, they adopted without that thorough discussion and calm deliberation which so important an object required. It was not intended to be lasting."

The 1784 constitution *was* intended to be lasting, and it has lasted.

CHAPTER FIVE

NEW HAMPSHIRE PEOPLE AT PEACE AND WAR

BEFORE 1784

In his 1628 report on a tour of the New England coast, Christopher Levett wrote that he reproached an Indian chief for having several wives, saying that even the King of England had but one, "at which he wondered, and asked me then who did all the king's work."

Most American Indians appear intermittently on the edges of recorded history, usually only as shadowy figures and not always in favorable light. In New Hampshire a few individuals stand out rather clearly from the shadows, and among these are Passaconaway (ca. 1575-1665), his son Wonalancet, and his grandson Kancamagus.

Passaconaway ("Child of the Bear") is a legendary personage; this has obscured the fact that he is also an important historical person. He was chief among Penacook tribes for at least a half-century and creator of the Penacook Confederacy against the Mohawks. When New Hampshire was first settled in the 1620s, his people were much diminished by a mysterious disease that had wiped out thousands of New England Indians before 1618 and by wars with the Mohawks. Passaconaway was greatly skilled in physical feats, juggling, swimming, handling the bow, sleight-of-hand, and the like; among both followers and enemies he was credited with supernatural powers. The personage overshadowed the person. One English observer, Thomas Morton, speculated in 1632 that his tricks were "done by the agility of Satan, his consort." Passaconaway said in later years that he had at first been unhappy with the Englishmen and had tried to relieve his land of them through sorcery. It hadn't worked.

Toward the English Passaconaway was always peaceful: in the 1620s, with an estimated 500 warriors at his command, he could

have wiped out the frail and scattered Piscataqua settlements, but he chose peace. From the Indians the English acquired the seeds and the techniques of New World farming—squash, pumpkins, cucumbers, beans, and especially Indian corn, which soon became English staples as well. The next decades record fleeting glimpses of Passaconaway struggling to help his people come to terms with the intruders: . . . handing over to Massachusetts authorities an Indian who had murdered an English trader (1632) . . . negotiating his son's release from Boston officials who had taken him hostage . . . acquiring English arms, later agreeing to give them up . . . officially submitting to the authority of the Massachusetts General Court (1644) . . . farming and fishing with his people along the Merrimack . . . petitioning the General Court for permanent land . . . meeting the Reverend John Eliot, "Apostle to the Indians" (1648) . . . being impressed with the Christian gospel. Eliot says that Passaconaway "purposed in his heart from henceforth to pray unto God, and . . . would perswade all his sonnes to do the same."

There is reliable evidence that about 1660, at a great gathering of Penacooks at Pawtucket Falls, Passaconaway, aged and beloved and venerated as near divine by his people, said his farewell. In the version reported secondhand from an Englishman present there, Passaconaway tells his people "never to contend with the English nor make war with them. . . . you will all be destroyed and rooted off this earth, if you do." By 1669 his son Wonalancet was sachem and living by his father's counsel.

Legend has it that the great Passaconaway did not die. He mounted a sled drawn by 24 prancing wolves, drew his bearskin about him, and then sped to the north. Over the treetops, over the lakes and rivers, up the slopes of Mt. Washington he rode at a furious pace, finally speeding up through the clouds and disappearing from sight. During his lifetime there had been peace between the Native Americans and the European intruders, and the Child of the Bear more than anyone had been responsible for it.

Wonalancet ("Fair Breather"), son of Passaconaway, had the pacific temper of his father, but was tragically caught in a clash of cultures. The Massachusetts General Court granted him a hundred acres "on a great hill about twelve miles west of Chelmsford, because he had a great many children and no planting grounds." Wonalancet and his tribe built forts near Pawtucket and in present-day Penacook for protection from the Mohawks. Like his father, he fished and planted along the Merrimack between these points, a man of peace. In May 1674, in response to a sermon by Eliot, he formally accepted the Christian faith, testifying that he had spent all his days in an old canoe "and now you exhort me to change. . . . I yield up myself to your advice, and enter into a new canoe, and do engage to pray to God hereafter."

The next year, when King Philip's War against the English began, all Indians became suspect to all the English. Philip, son of Massasoit, tried to draw Wonalancet, son of Passaconaway, into his plan to kill off the English. Wonalancet was trapped between his race and his religion. Desiring neutrality, he withdrew into the woods of New Hampshire to maintain it, and he spent some time with his followers far to the north in the Connecticut Lakes region. In 1676 he appeared at Dover to add his signature to a peace treaty.

Major Richard Waldron, the captain of the Dover militia who had helped arrange the treaty, was a man of few scruples. Having gained the Indians' confidence but wanting to punish some of the warmakers, he devised an elaborate farce whereby he took hundreds of Indians captive. Wonalancet and his people were released but others were sent to Massachusetts, where a few were tried and hanged, some escaped to return to New Hampshire, and dozens of others were sold into slavery in the West Indies. This betrayal the surviving Penacooks did not forget. For years after this Wonalancet was a vagabond leader: now and again back in Chelmsford . . . intervening to bury hatchets . . . withdrawing to the northern hills . . . residing in the upper Merrimack . . . back on the river island near his English protectors.

By 1685 Wonalancet was sachem of only the peaceful Penacooks, totaling perhaps a few dozen families, and his nephew Kancamagus ("Fearless One") was sachem of the war party of the Penacooks, a larger group. Kancamagus and his band conducted a savage raid on Dover in June 1689, burning houses and mills, killing 23 persons, and taking 29 captives to Canada. Settling an old score with Major Waldron, the Indians cut him to pieces on his own table. Kancamagus retreated north as Massachusetts put a price on his head. He continued raids and skirmishes in northern New Hampshire for several years and was presumably killed in battle about 1692. His uncle, Wonalancet, apparently spent most of his latter days among Christian Indians near the English settlements along the lower Merrimack, still referred to as "chief sachem on Merrimack river." He fades from record still faithful to his father's final counsel: "Never be enemies to the English but love them and love their God also."

Indian Wars

New Hampshire, located between the French in Canada and the English on the Atlantic coast, became one of the bloodiest battlegrounds in what was ultimately a struggle for control of North America. The French proved to be infinitely resourceful in exploiting the standing hostility between Mohawks and Penacooks. Thus, large international enmities and vague local terrors hovered over the New England landscape—under which conditions the daily life of ordinary people had to make its way. For nearly a hundred years, 1675 to 1763, there was intermittent random bloodshed and cruel guerilla raiding between English and Indians in New Hampshire. Periods of worst carnage, times when English settlers often feared for their lives whenever they were outside their garrisoned villages and when few Indians were safe at large, have been named: King Philip's War (1675-1678), King William's War (1689-1697), Queen Anne's War (1703-1713), Dummer's or Lovewell's War (1720-1725), King George's War (1745-1748), French and Indian War (1756-1763). The last of these proved in retrospect to be superb training ground for future officers of the Revolutionary War. In each war, hundreds died on each side. Time and again the astonishing human capacities for both savagery and gallantry were raised to a high pitch in all parts of New Hampshire.

One of the worst attacks of the early period occurred in July 1694, a few years after the Dover assault. Two hundred and fifty French and Indian attackers fell upon the Oyster River settlement (Durham), destroyed the buildings with fire, and killed and captured a hundred people. The survivors were dragged to Canada for slavery and ransom, in what became thereafter a regular pattern.

Massachusetts had put a bounty on Indian scalps in the 1690s. In 1711 New Hampshire followed with a bounty for one year only: £50 for a man, £30 for a woman, £15 for a child. When a new bounty law in 1722 offered £100 for an adult, Captain John Lovewell of Dunstable, Massachusetts, and others began hunting Indians for recreation and money. At first there was little money to be made, for most of the hostile Indians had left the eastern part of the state for the northern wilderness. One day in February 1725, near what is now Lovewell's Pond, Lovewell and his men came upon 10 Indians sleeping around a fire, and were soon £1,000 richer. Having turned in his trophies, Lovewell returned with his men to the north woods for more, and was promptly waylaid by Indians who put a violent end to his violent career.

After a truce was put together in 1725, settlers moved into the Merrimack Valley, lands claimed by both Massachusetts and New Hampshire, and new towns were started, literally on top of each other, at the site of present-day Concord. Free of Indian worries for a time, the settlers of the contended lands of Bow, Rumford (Concord), and Pennycook were, as an early historian remarked, at peace to fight amongst themselves.

In the 1740s at the instigation of the French in Canada, the entire Connecticut River Valley was beleaguered anew. Surprise

The Reverend Arthur Browne was for 37 years rector of Anglican Queen's Chapel (called St. John's Church after 1791) in Portsmouth. His parishioners there included the families of the Wentworth governors and many seacoast merchants. Robert Rogers, of Indian-fighting fame, and Samuel Livermore, a leading New Hampshire senator and jurist after the Revolutionary War, were Browne's sons-in-law. This somewhat routine, stylized portrait was done by John Singleton Copley around 1757. Courtesy, Historic Deerfield, Inc., Deerfield, Massachusetts

Indian attacks, massacres, and scalpings were frequent: on both sides it was capture or kill on sight. The New Hampshire bounty was now £50 per scalp; Massachusetts paid £75. Since English captives were taken to Canada to be ransomed by the French, Indians had a motive to take victims alive, the English to take victims dead. Raids continued around Keene, farther north around the fort at Number Four in Charlestown, and then spread inland to Hopkinton and Rumford (Concord). In one incident in August 1746 nine militiamen were ambushed near where the Concord Hospital now stands. Five were killed, stripped, scalped, and mangled; two were captured and taken to Canada. These were the days when the Reverend Timothy Walker of Rumford, the town's leading citizen, preached each Lord's Day with his musket in his pulpit. Such was the land where Passaconaway and Wonalancet had quietly walked.

Robert Rogers: Faded Laurels

Much of the agony and tainted glory of the Indian Wars is writ large in the life of Robert Rogers. At the time of the raid in August 1746, Rogers was a 15-year-old Rumford farm boy already studying the arts of wilderness hunting and survival. Ten years later he was captain of an elite scouting corps that roamed the frontiers in the service of the British army: Rogers' Rangers. Indian warfare was his natural medium but French adversaries served him well as relief. He had a knack for spectacular exploits and for initiating and surviving bloody raids. Fearlessness, cruelty, and generosity were dramatically compounded in his nature, and for a time all North America was his stage: he fought in Nova Scotia, Michigan, and South Carolina, but was usually in and around New Hampshire. Before the French and Indian War had reached its peak, word of his dash and daring had spread to England and fear of him to France. In one familiar exploit he led his men far to the north where at daybreak, on October 4, 1759, he fell upon St. Francis, the key Indian village of the region, destroyed its buildings with fire, and wasted its inhabitants—200 of them, he said in his journal. Other estimates put the number killed nearer 50; but in any case, this raid was the force that broke the French and Indian power in the Connecticut Valley. Final peace came at last in 1763 with the Treaty of Paris, and Rogers was sent to Michigan to receive the surrender of the French posts there. He then married the belle of Portsmouth, daughter of the Reverend Arthur Browne, rector of Queen's Chapel.

Peace was Rogers' undoing. At age 34 and out of wars he went to England, where he published his journals and a play, both to critical acclaim. Though he held several military posts in the colonies thereafter, he never oriented himself to American civilized life sufficiently to face the next crisis, the American struggle for independence. He was often deeply in debt. At the outbreak of hostilities with England, his actions were erratic and his position ambivalent. George Washington regarded him as a spy for the British and had him imprisoned. Upon his release the British gave him a command but relieved him almost immediately. His wife divorced him. Back in England before the war was over, he faded from view and died there years later in relative obscurity. So romantic and melancholy a career seems born of fiction more than life, and one part of it, the suffering and hardihood of his return to New Hampshire from the St. Francis raid, has been unforgettably rendered into fiction in Kenneth Roberts' *Northwest Passage.*

John Stark: "Unfaded Laurels"

Another scion of the Merrimack Valley, tempered in the fires of the very same wars, was John Stark of Derryfield. Stark and Rogers were two of about 5,000 New Hampshire foot soldiers who joined the 10 regiments of the colony between the years 1755 and 1763. Late in life it was still the French and Indian Wars about which John Stark reminisced—his capture by Indians in 1752 and his trip through wilderness to Quebec, his ransom and return—but all New England remembers him better as a hero of the Revolutionary War, and of two battles in particular, Bunker Hill and Bennington. Stark and Rogers grew up in the same region and served side by side in 1756 as captains of the Rangers. Parallel paths diverged in 1759 when, the southern Indian wars over, Rogers went north to attack St. Francis and Stark went home to farm.

It was from his Derryfield farm, more than 15 years later, that Stark answered the alarm from Lexington and Concord in April 1775. Arriving near Boston on April 20, he was appointed colonel of a group of New Hampshire volunteers. That June at the Battle of Bunker Hill, Stark and his New Hampshire troops brilliantly defended the rail fence on the American left. In the next two years Stark saw distinguished service in a number of operations in New Jersey and also in Canada, but he abruptly resigned his commission and returned to farming in March 1777, when Congress promoted a junior officer over him.

That same spring the British had worked out a definitive plan for winning the war before autumn. General Burgoyne was to land at Quebec, sweep south through the Champlain Valley, rallying the Loyalists, and take Albany, thus cutting off New England, consolidating the inland, and quelling the northern part of the Rebellion."

On schedule, Burgoyne headed south from Quebec in June with 3,700 British regulars, 3,000 German mercenaries, and a large assortment of Indians, Canadians, and American Loyalists. Northern New England had never seen anything like this, nor would again: a ponderous advance of color and power—English red, German blue, American homespun—sweeping out of the north and down the valley, gathering strength as it went, apparently as irresistible as a glacier. Indian scouts kept New Hampshire informed. Burgoyne's American recruiters fanned out into the countryside, enlisting hundreds of Loyalists to the cause. The descent from the north was like a refiner's fire, for suddenly Vermont farmers found the Loyalist/Patriot issue translated from ideas to actions, and neighbors were choosing sides against neighbors. Hundreds enlisted under Burgoyne's banner.

Sporadic groups of Patriots from New Hampshire and Massachusetts headed for Ticonderoga to lend assistance to the American forces, but it was too little too late. The American commander at Ticonderoga, with over 3,000 men, worried through July 4 and then evacuated in terror on July 5, some of his men

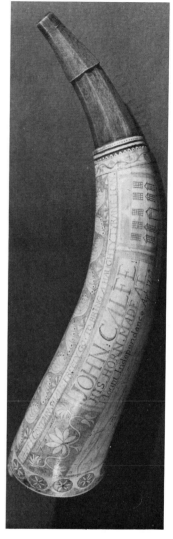

While stationed in the general vicinity of Fort Ticonderoga in April 1777, Hampstead's John Calfe exhibited both artistic flair and patriotic zeal upon his powder horn with the threat to the British "What I contain shall freely go: to bring a haughty tyrant low." In spite of such boasts, however, Calfe and his regiment were forced to retreat soon afterward. NHHS

being overtaken and attacked from the rear by Burgoyne's advancing troops. Dismay and alarm spread afar as the British laid seige upon the will of New England, just as they had planned. Burgoyne would need supplies for the final move upon Albany and would sidestep through New York and into Vermont for that detail: conscripting a few hundred oxen and horses and enough beef and cereal for the men would be fairly routine. The Vermont Council of Safety called to Boston and Exeter for help.

In immediate response, the New Hampshire Assembly met at Exeter on July 17, called John Stark from his farm at Derryfield, gave him the invented title "Brigadier-General of State Militia," and authorized him to raise and command an expedition to Vermont. The operation was to be executed in such manner "as shall appear expedient to you." But how would such an emergency action be financed? It was a state venture unauthorized by the Continental Congress and unknown even to General Washington. John Langdon, Speaker of the New Hampshire House of Representatives, is reported to have rallied his colleagues by pledging his own fortune:

I have three thousand dollars in hard money. I will pledge the plate in my house for three thousand more, and I have seventy

Brigadier General John Stark rallies his troops before the Battle of Bennington, August 16, 1777. NHHS

hogsheads of Tobago rum which shall be disposed of for what it will bring. These and the avails of these are at the service of the State. If we defend our homes and our firesides, I may get my pay; if we do not defend them, the property will be of no value to me.

In the atmosphere of general alarm over the Ticonderoga disaster and the emergency meeting of the Assembly, the appointment of Stark to lead the forces of rescue electrified the New Hampshire countryside. There was haying to be finished and the rye was ripe. No matter. Farmers dropped their scythes, picked up their muskets as if addressed by a supernatural command, and headed for Charlestown and the rendezvous at the fort at Number Four. One hundred and sixty-five were veterans of Stark's command at Bunker Hill. Within a week nearly 1,500 had volunteered and were ready to follow their leader into Vermont, into battle, and into history.

By Sunday, August 3, Stark had winnowed his troops, organized and equipped them, and pulled out of the fort at Number Four. A week later he had crossed the mountains, turned south, and was encamped at Bennington. It was not entirely clear just what this band of a thousand New Hampshire farmers stamping about in western Vermont was going to do that 3,000 American regulars entrenched at Ticonderoga had not even dared to attempt.

The issue, however, proved to be morale and strategy, not numbers or firepower. Burgoyne had sent a 600-man detachment, including many Vermont Loyalists, under Lieutenant Colonel Frederick Baum toward Bennington to seek out supplies. Meeting Stark's scouts, they encamped on a hill, built breastworks, waited out a day of rain, and then on August 16 had no choice but to face the New Hampshire musketeers, now strengthened by added forces from other New England states. Pointing to the camps across the valley, Stark is reported to have roused his men: "Yonder are your enemies, the redcoats and tories; if you cannot prove yourselves better men than they, let Molly Stark sleep a widow tonight."

The Battle of Bennington on August 16, 1777, was two battles, each brief and bloody: one from 3 to 5 p.m., in which Stark's troops stormed the hill from three sides and completely overwhelmed the foe, and the second when a surprise reinforcement of British troops arrived at 6 p.m., with the same outcome.

American losses were about 30 killed and 40 wounded. British losses were summarized in Stark's report:

> We obtained four pieces of brass cannon, one thousand stand of arms, several Hessian swords, eight brass drums, and seven hundred and fifty prisoners. Two hundred were killed on the spot; wounded unknown. The enemy effected his escape by marching all night, and we returned to camp.

One hundred and fifty-five of the captives were American Tories, many from nearby Vermont towns; many of the others were Germans. These all, together with wounded captives, were sent to Boston for Boston to handle as best it could. The total rout shattered Burgoyne's confidence, demoralized his troops, and effectively cut off his supplies. "The most active and rebellious race on the continent . . . hangs like a gathering storm on my left," wrote Burgoyne as he prepared for Saratoga. Stark could scarcely have known what a mortal blow he had inflicted. On October 17, instead of taking Albany and finishing the war, General Burgoyne, with Stark blocking his retreat across the Hudson, surrendered his entire army to the Americans at Saratoga. Two weeks earlier the Continental Congress had made the Derryfield farmer a brigadier general in the army of the United States. Some years afterward Thomas Jefferson put the victory at Bennington into the perspective it has since retained.

> This success was the first link in the chain of events which opened a new scene to America. It raised her from the depths of despair to the summit of hope, and added unfaded laurels to the veteran who commanded.

Life on the Farm

Lives of high drama becloud the fact that for most people most of the time life is more humdrum than heroic. It was for most early residents of New Hampshire. Matthew Patten was born in Ireland and came to Londonderry, New Hampshire, as a young boy in 1728. He later married and settled in the neighboring town of Bedford. Here he and his sons farmed along the same river plains where Passaconaway and his sons had farmed, and fished at weirs at the same Amoskeag Falls where they had fished. Besides farming and fathering 11 children, Patten worked as carpenter and cooper, surveyed land, lumbered, trapped for furs, fished, and was a judge of probate, a delegate to the New Hampshire Provincial Assembly in the crucial years 1776-1777,

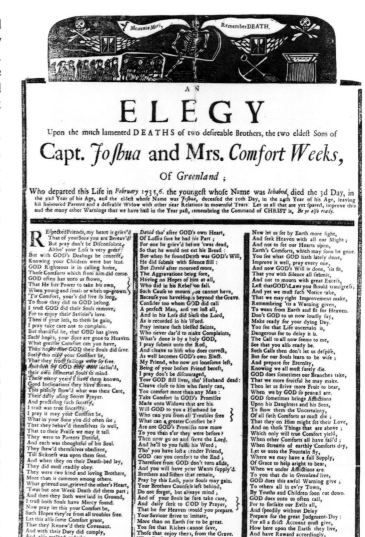

A cartoon of "Death" heads this broadside of an elegy, occasioned by the passing of two brothers in Greenland in 1735. "A warning given to wean from earth and fit for Heaven," the labored verse admonished: "Be ye also ready." NHHS

Thurſday, October 7. 1756.   THE   NUMB. 1.

New Hampſhire   GAZETTE,

With the Freſheſt Advices   *Foreign and Domeſtick.*

The Printer to the PUBLIC.

UPON the Encouragement given by a Number of Subſcribers agreable to printed Propoſals, I now publiſh the firſt WEEKLY GAZETTE, for the Province of NEW-HAMPSHIRE; depending upon the Favour of all Gentlemen who are Friends to *Learning, Religion* and *Liberty* to countenance my Undertaking, as this is the beginning of Printing in this Province, ſo that I may go on cheerfully, and continue this Paper in a uſeful and entertaining Manner.

Fondneſs of News may be carried to an extreme; but every Lover of Mankind muſt feel a ſtrong Deſire to know what paſſes in the World, as well as within his own private Sphere; and particularly to be acquainted with the Affairs of his own Nation and Country—Eſpecially at ſuch a Time as this, when the Britiſh Nation is engag'd in a juſt and neceſſary War, with a powerful Enemy, the *French*, a War in which theſe *American* Colonies are moſt nearly intereſted, the Event of which muſt be of the utmoſt Importance both to us and all the *Britiſh* Dominions, every true Engliſhman muſt be anxious to know from Time to Time the State of our Affairs, at Home and in the Colonies.

I ſhall therefore take Pains to furniſh my Readers with the moſt material News which can be collected from every Part of the World, particularly from *Great-Britain*, and its Dependencies: And great Care will be taken that no Facts of Importance ſhall be publiſhed but ſuch as are well atteſted, and theſe ſhall be as particular as may be neceſſary.

But beſides the common News, whenever there ſhall be Room, and as there may be Occaſion, this Paper will contain Extracts from the beſt Authors on Points of the moſt uſeful Knowledge, moral, religious or political Eſſays, and other ſuch Speculations as may have a Tendency to improve the Mind, afford any Help to Trade, Manufactures, Huſbandry, and other uſeful Arts, and promote the public Welfare in any Reſpect.

As the Preſs always claims Liberty in free Countries, it is preſumed that none will be offended if this Paper diſcovers that Spirit of Freedom which ſo remarkably prevails in the *Engliſh* Nation: But as Liberty ought not to be abus'd, no Encouragement will be given by the Publiſher to any Thing which is apparently deſign'd to foment Diviſions in Church or State, nor to any Thing profane, obſcene, or tending to encourage Immorality, nor to ſuch Writings as are produced by private Pique, and fill'd with perſonal Reflections and inſolent ſcurrilous Language. It is a great Abuſe of good Senſe as well as good Manners to employ thoſe Means which may be ſerviceable to the beſt Purpoſes, in the ſervice of Vice or any thing Indecent, or which may give juſt Occaſion of Offence to any perſons of true Taſte and Judgment. And therefore proper Caution will be always us'd to avoid all reaſonable Grounds of Complaint on that Score.   The

Printer Daniel Fowle gave New Hampshire its first newspaper in 1756. Before then news came largely from the Massachusetts press. Fowle promised that the New Hampshire Gazette *would carry not only the news, but "useful Knowledge, moral, religious or political Essays," and just about anything else of interest to readers in the Portsmouth area. NHHS*

Opposite page: Portsmouth remained New Hampshire's chief commercial port in the years after the Revolution, even though it relinquished its role as the provincial capital and center of government. In this circa 1778 view of Portsmouth from Badger's Island, the spire of Queen's Chapel (center) is flanked by that of North Church (right) and, at some distance, South Church (far left). NHHS

and a frequent member of its Committee of Safety. None of this was the least bit unusual. Somewhat unusual, however, was the fact that he kept a daily diary for over 30 years—basically a record book, noting most of his activities, travels, business transactions, but only rarely his thoughts. Two of the Patten sons, John and Bob, figure in the following passages.

In April 1775 the news from Lexington and Concord intruded upon the family springtime routines in the Pattens' Bedford household, but did not completely stop the normal activities.

> [April] *20th I Recd the Melancholy news in the morning that General Gages troops had fired on our Contrymen at Concord yesterday . . . We Generay met at the meeting house about 9 of the Clock and the Number of twenty or more went Directly off from the Meeting house to assist them . . . james Orr made me a great wheel Spindle of my Steel and he mended the Ear of a little kittle and finished the chain for my cannoe . . . And our john came home . . . and intended to Sett off for our army to morrow morning and our Girls sit up all night bakeing bread and fitting things for him and john Dobbin*

> *21st our john and john Dobbin and my bror Samuell two oldest sons sett off and joyned Derryfield men and about six from Goffestown . . . there was nine more went along after them belonging to Pennykook or thereabouts and I went to McGregores and I got a pound of Coffie on Credit*

There was probably but one musket in the family so there was no way to send the second son, Bob, to Massachusetts; anyway he was needed at home since on April 22 Matthew Patten "was wakened in the morning by Mrs. Chandlers comeing with a letter from the Comitee of the Provincial Congress for calling another Congress of the Province immeadeately and I went with it as fast as could to john Bells but he was gone to our army . . ." At this meeting the Provincial Congress voted, according to its records, to ask the Continental Congress meeting in Philadelphia for "explicit advice, respecting the taking up . . . of Civil Government." Back home on April 26, Patten went "at the desire of the town to Col Goffes and Merrils and MacGregores and Cautioned them to take Special care of Strangers and persons Suspected of being Torys Crossing the River to Examin and Search if they judge it needful and I got a pound of Coffie and nine flints from MacGregore . . ." A pound or two of "Tobacca" and a jug of rum were other staples frequently noted.

On April 28 Patten "began to Stock Capt Blairs Gun and I went and got jamey Orr to forge me a Screw nail for the breach of the Gun and I fitted it and cut the screws . . ." Any old gun barrel lying around was invaluable now. A 1773 census of New Hampshire shows that there were nearly twice as many adult males between 16 and 60 as there were muskets, and there were no gunsmiths in New Hampshire at the time. (Later, in 1775, when a town muster turned out 12 men and only 5 guns, Patten was put on a committee "to procure Guns for the men that goes out of this town but got none.") Again, on April 29, Patten "worked some at Stocking the Gun and the boys planted Potatoes." But things were not quite normal in May 1775 in

Bedford:

From the 15th to the 20th Inclusive I fished at the falls I got 106 Ells and how many shad I cant Remember on the 19th we finished planting corn on the 16th we had a town meeting in Bedford at which we Voted to Shut the meeting house against Mr Houston [their minister, who was suspected of Tory sympathies].

In early January 1776 the Provincial Congress was meeting to adopt a temporary constitution for New Hampshire, but Matthew Patten was in Cambridge, Massachusetts, with his second son: "I went out with a Slay to go to the army and Bob went with me to tarry a year . . . 3rd we arrived at the Camp and went and viewed the encampment at Cambridge and Prospect Hill and I lodged at Col Starkes Barracks in his bed."

That summer in early July, when the Declaration of Independence was adopted, the Provincial Congress and the Committee of Safety were meeting in Exeter, and Patten was with them. He started home on July 20 with "2£ of tobacca a rub ball for my breeches and a Declaration for Independance."

Matthew Patten arrived home with a copy of the Declaration to show his wife, and his wife had a document to show to him. Independence had been dearly bought. On the way home on July 21:

I got an account of my johns Death of the Smal Pox at Canada and when I came home my wife had got a letter from Bob which gave us a particular account it informed us that he was sick of them at Chambike and that they moved him to Saint johns where they tarried but one night when they moved him to Isle of Moix where he died on the 20th day of June the Reason of moveing him was the Retreat of the army which was very preceipitate and he must either be moved or be left behind

whether the moveing hurt him he does not inform us but it seems probable to me that it did He was shot through his left arm at Bunker Hill fight and now was lead after suffering much fategue to the place where he now lyes in defending the just Rights of America to whose end he came in the prime of life by means of that wicked Tyranical Brute (Nea worse than Brute) of Great Britain he was 24 years and 31 days old

Three weeks later word came that son Bob was sick near Ticonderoga. On August 6, "my bror borrowed ten Dollars for me and lent me four himself and we had sixteen dollars and 2/6 among us in the famely and I set out for Fort George to see Bob." On August 16, "I arrived at Tyconderoga and tarried at Col Starke and his other field officers untill the 22d in the morning which time I set off for fort George and Bob [who had recovered] with me on Furlow We were two days comeing over Lake George and September first we arrived home I was 27 days from home." During Patten's absence the family and neighbors had harvested the "Rie." On October 15 Bob returned to the army so "our women folks all helped us husk" the corn and later dig the potatoes—"we have 165 bushell in the wholl this year." Potatoes at this time were no longer simply an Irish crop, for English Americans had now accepted this once-curious ethnic food.

Life went on, the banal and the dramatic, the trivial and the sublime, side by side throughout the long years of the Revolutionary War. The year 1778 closed out thus:

[Dec.] *30th WAS A CONTINENTAL THANKSGIVING BY ORDER OF CONGRESS and I got a copy of the plan of government from my bror and I copyd a considerable part of it*

31st I finished Copying the Plan of Government and Shed made nails to set the shoes on my horse

CHAPTER
SIX

THE ROLE OF
GOVERNMENT

AFTER 1784

The New Hampshire Constitution does not envision political parties. Framers of constitutions in the early American states feared the party spirit, as did the framers of the U.S. Constitution, and would do nothing to encourage it. The rift during the Revolutionary War between the Dartmouth-based "college party" and the rest of New Hampshire had been a cultural and regional squabble that came within inches of destroying the state as a political entity.

Party Politics

There were good reasons to worry about party politics. The New Hampshire Constitution of 1784 emphasized that the three branches, legislative, executive, judicial, "ought to be kept . . . independent," but it failed to assure this independence. It did not define the jurisdiction of the higher courts, and did not even expressly create a "supreme court." As a result, throughout the 19th century the courts were periodically "reorganized"—sometimes by a wholesale dismissal of judges—by the legislature on partisan grounds. The solution to this problem was a long time coming and lay not in squelching political parties, but in adopting constitutional amendments (1966, 1978) to protect the courts.

Generally speaking, it has turned out that political parties are very natural and usually valuable instruments of political expression. A bare-bones sketch of party life for 19th-century New Hampshire is this: the first half of the century belonged essentially to the Democrats, who did very well both in New Hampshire and beyond; the last half-century belonged essentially to the Republicans, who did less well both in New Hampshire and beyond. That skeleton needs to be fleshed out a bit on both sides and then made more complicated.

The Democratic Party

The heirs of Thomas Jefferson largely dominated New Hamp-

shire politics almost up to the Civil War. They were the Democratic-Republican party, after 1830 called simply the Democratic party. The opposing Federalists, the party of Washington and Adams, prevailed early in the century: John Taylor Gilman was the Federalist governor from 1794 to 1804, the only person to serve in that role for 10 years. The Democratic party (sometimes also called "Jeffersonian Republicans" at the time) took its rise from John Langdon's election as governor in 1805, though he was elected by personal popularity more than party politics. Langdon had been the chief executive also in the 1780s, before the advent of parties. Generally, the Democratic party stood for the common man, for curbing vested money interests, and for progressive social action on a wide range of issues: stopping the slave trade; building a state prison (1812) and a State House (1816); revising the criminal code and expunging the whipping post and the pillory (1812); separating church and state (1819); abolishing debtors' prisons in principle (1820) and totally (1840); and developing a hospital for the insane (1840).

From the Democratic party came outstanding leaders, many of them distinguished far beyond New Hampshire. Even a short roll call is long on achievement. Governor John Langdon was a leader from the earliest Revolutionary days, eight times chief executive between 1785 and 1812, delegate to the national constitutional convention, many times Speaker of the New Hampshire House, and for 10 years a U.S. Senator. William Plumer had dominated the 1791 convention, had then been a leading Federalist, joined the Democrats in 1808, and was subsequently elected U.S. Senator and three times governor during the next decade, after which he retired to write biographies of several score of his contemporaries and to help found the New Hampshire Historical Society, becoming its first president. Isaac Hill was editor, after 1809, of the *New-Hampshire Patriot,* and turned it into an eloquent and powerful voice of the Democratic party after which he went on to become a U.S. Senator and governor, and also to edit the *Farmers' Monthly Visitor,* the paper that kept the entire New England countryside in touch with the social mainstream. Levi Woodbury moved with ease from governor to U.S. Senator, to Secretary of the Navy, then of the U.S. Treasury, and finally to the U.S. Supreme Court. A onetime law student of Woodbury, Franklin Pierce of Hillsborough and Concord was U.S. Senator, Mexican War general, astute party organizer and spokesman, and in 1852 was elected President of the United States.

These were men of stature. Through them, and others like them, New Hampshire continued to be a vigorous participant in the national dialogue up to the eve of the Civil War. Through them the validity of New Hampshire rural impulses—dedicated, independent, righteous—and the success of its institutions as expressed through the Democratic party, were vindicated and thoroughly woven into the larger national fabric. The election of President Pierce in 1852 appeared to consolidate and confirm all this. The one worrisome cloud on the horizon, at first no bigger than a man's hand, was the inability of the Democratic party to face the issue of slavery without ambivalence.

The Republican Party

New Hampshire Republicans of the Civil War time were a gathering of remnants of the dying Whig party (which, after the Federalists disappeared, had been the main alternative to the Democrats), of the anti-slavery Free Soilers, of the Know Nothing party, of rebellious Democrats, and miscellaneous others. New Hampshire Republicans, legislators especially, became closely allied to the booming affairs of capitalist adventure in textiles, lumber, and railroads. They were usually more in tune with business entrepreneurs than with common farmers, who were leaving their hillside farms in droves. Democrats inherited the thinning countryside and Republicans dominated the growing cities—except for the immigrant ghettos, which tended to be Democratic. For nearly two generations after the Civil War, Republicans called the shots and Democrats tried to imitate them. Meanwhile, New Hampshire seemed to withdraw from the great national conversation: in contrast to the Democratic heyday, almost no distinguished national leaders went forth from the state. In the last half of the century William E. Chandler, Secretary of the Navy and then U.S. Senator from 1887 to 1901, stands out almost alone as a national voice with a clear New Hampshire accent. On the slavery issue, the Democrats in their day had lived under a cloud, not of their own making, which eventually broke on their heads; the Republicans in their day, half a century later, had in the railroad monopolies a serious canker of their own making.

The Dartmouth College Case

The summary of party affairs just given needs to be complicated by facts that blur its simple symmetry. One of these facts is the career of Daniel Webster, New Hampshire's greatest gift to the nation during this era, ever a man apart. Like England's Winston Churchill, whom he most resembles, Webster greatly complicates any picture he enters. Among other things he turned par-

In the 19th century Concord took advantage of its central location and its role as state capital by building some of New Hampshire's finest hotels. Abel Hutchins opened the first Phoenix (or Phenix) Hotel, built on the site of his burned house, with this announcement in the New-Hampshire Patriot *of January 19, 1819. Before it burned in 1856, the Phoenix had been a "pleasant asylum" for such visitors as Abraham Lincoln, Daniel Webster, Horace Greeley, and actor Edwin Booth. In 1857 a new Phoenix Hotel rose from the ashes. NHHS*

After Dartmouth College's 1773 commencement and trustees' meeting, President Wheelock apologized to his guests about the unfinished condition of his house, about his lack of table linen, and about the cook's getting drunk again. Nevertheless, at that meeting the college got its seal, a gift from Trustee George Jaffrey. The seal showed American Indians responding to a "voice calling in the wilderness" and striding upward toward the halls of learning. In the 18th century most people who saw the seal probably knew that "Hant" is the abbreviation for the Latin translation of the Old English word that in modern English became "Hampshire" (simple for scholars, but it drives cooks to drink). Courtesy, Dartmouth College Archives (DCA)

tisan oratory from mere politics into theater and literature. His political roots lay in the New Hampshire countryside, and he entered national life as a Federalist congressman from Portsmouth in 1812. For 40 years he was the pride of New England before the world, though he was not an intrinsic part of New Hampshire's party politics. Webster moved his base of operations to Boston in 1816, and though he kept a home in New Hampshire, it was as a lawyer, Whig Senator, Secretary of State, and force of nature from Massachusetts that he was known across the world.

The "Dartmouth College Case" cast Webster in his most characteristic role and demonstrated how difficulties nurtured in the spirit of partisan politics sometimes mature into genuine achievements of state.

In 1815, for a variety of reasons, the Trustees of Dartmouth College (mostly Federalists) replaced President John Wheelock, son of the founder. In June 1816 the New Hampshire legislature, controlled by Democrats and led by Democrat Governor Plumer, passed a law that revised the college charter of 1769 and created around the college an additional entity, Dartmouth University, with a governor-appointed Board of Overseers with veto power over the college trustees. The legislature then named college ex-President Wheelock as president of the university. Many Democrats had wanted a state university anyway, and now they had one, acquired by a novel process of creative theft. However, having done the deed, party leaders Plumer and Hill conducted a brilliant justification for it through pamphlets and the pages of the *New-Hampshire Patriot,* arguing that Dartmouth was, after all, chartered by and for the people of New Hampshire and that its trustees had been turning it into a sectarian preserve for the wealthy.

Affairs in Hanover were a little odd for the next two years. Though it was a bizarre nuisance, the university didn't amount to much educationally, and the college trustees, though threatened with fines by the legislature, did not cooperate with the university overseers (all Democrats). Amid the confusion

John Wheelock, president of the alleged university, made a clarifying contribution by dying in April 1817. The college trustees brought suit against the offending law of 1816, lost in the New Hampshire Supreme Court (all of whose members were Democratic appointees as a result of a recent legislative "reorganization"), and appealed to the U.S. Supreme Court with Daniel Webster as their chief advocate. There, history and histrionics converged.

The basic question as to the meaning of the growing clamor must be answered from at least three points of view. Viewed from Hanover, the issue was whether the president or the trustees should administer the college. (A valid question: the college had had just two presidents, the Wheelocks, father and son, who tended to regard the college they had created as property they owned.) Viewed from Concord, the question turned on the rights and prerogatives held by the people of New Hampshire in their only chartered institution of higher learning. (A valid question: this was a time when the distinctions between public and private education had not yet been historically expressed.) Viewed from Washington, D.C., the issue turned on the question of the constitutional powers of a legislature over a corporation it had created. (A valid question: in days when towns ran the churches they had organized, it might naturally be supposed that the state should run the college it had chartered.)

Thus, crucial collegiate, state, and constitutional issues surfaced one after the other, and as they did the heat of partisan politics melded them together. The case was made for Daniel Webster, a Dartmouth alumnus who was handed the opportunity of a lifetime to make of it what he could—which, being Daniel Webster, is what he did. The rather slim legal basis of the appeal was the U.S. Constitutional clause forbidding states to pass laws "impairing the obligation of contracts."

The case, which opened before the U.S. Supreme Court in March 1818, ultimately brought the rights of state-created corporate entities under the protective wing of the U.S. Constitution, and it was a major instrument of judicial self-assertion for the Supreme Court of Chief Justice John Marshall. It became the landmark case throughout the United States in the freeing of education from party politics, and after more than 150 years, it still has enough potency left to launch a flock of legal footnotes every year. Not incidentally, the case also etched into New England memories the phrase that still raises warm smiles—"It is, sir, as I have said, a small college, —and yet there are those that love it"—the words with which Webster began the climax of his four-hour spellbinding presentation before the U.S. Supreme Court judges.

Webster's logic and rhetoric swept the day. The court voided the action of New Hampshire's legislature as unconstitutional. At age two Dartmouth University folded up in March 1819, Dartmouth College thrived, and party politics in New Hampshire turned from education to other turf. Other kinds of corporations—railroad companies, with powers then undreamed of—would haunt the politics of the state at a much later date.

Democrats and Slavery
In 1800 there were but eight slaves in New Hampshire. The

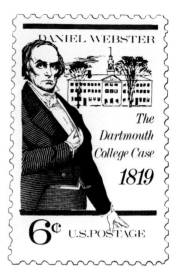

In 1969 a U.S. postage stamp commemorated the sesquicentennial of the celebrated Dartmouth College Case, in the course of which Daniel Webster (then age 36) became a national figure. An alumnus of Dartmouth's class of 1801, Webster represented the trustees of the college in the power play between the New Hampshire legislature and the school. DCA

Daniel Webster's later career tends to eclipse his New Hampshire beginnings. Born in Salisbury in 1782, he graduated from Dartmouth in 1801. After studying law in Salisbury for several years, Webster was admitted to the Boston bar in 1805. Shortly afterward, however, he was recalled to New Hampshire by family matters, "dropping from the firmament of Boston gayety and pleasure, to the level of a rustic village, of silence and obscurity." In 1807 Webster settled in Portsmouth, where he launched his national political career. In 1816 he moved to Boston, after which point he belongs to Massachusetts history. Webster's 1824 portrait was painted by Joseph Wood. NHHS

Above: This William H. Kimball daguerreotype of Franklin Pierce shows the future President as a Mexican War general. Pierce's superior officer was General Winfield Scott, his unsuccessful Whig opponent in the 1852 Presidential election. NHHS

Opposite page: An 1853 view of Concord included the State House, the opera house, mercantile blocks, banks, and homes. Lyford's 1903 History of Concord acknowledged that Concord "may not equal Portsmouth and Exeter and other coast towns in aristocratic traditions and old memories of foreign trade, and . . . may have a less exclusively intellectual tone than a village dominated by a college." However, the work asserted that "there are probably few places . . . where the general social life is so agreeable . . . due, in a measure, to the large proportion of official society." NHHS

institution was being denounced from many pulpits—following the example of Jeremy Belknap, who strongly condemned slavery in the last chapter of his *History of New Hampshire* in 1792. The 1820 census indicated there were "786 free persons of color" and no slaves in New Hampshire. In that year the legislature, led by Portsmouth Federalist Jeremiah Mason, declared unequivocally that slavery was "morally wrong" and that nothing could justify the "extension of this great evil to newly formed States." But after that, resolutions of the Democratic legislature were bland, as were speeches on the subject by a string of Democratic governors unbroken until 1846, when Whig Anthony Colby of New London was elected. Colby promptly denounced slavery in his inaugural address, stating flatly that it was "at variance with our declaration of liberty and equal rights, and repugnant to our moral sense"—sentiments Democratic party leaders would neither disavow nor declare. In 1834 a chapter of the new American Anti-Slavery Society was formed in Concord, one in Dover the next year, and within a decade many others in other towns.

John P. Hale, a faithful party organizer and New Hampshire Congressman, came to fame in mid-career through his courageous opposition to slavery. As a Democratic Congressman, he wrote an anti-slavery letter to his constituents in 1845. In response, the Democrats, led by Franklin Pierce and his clear vision of a national, unified Democratic party, promptly dealt Hale out of the party by removing his name from the party ticket. The next year Hale was elected to the U.S. Senate by a coalition of Whigs and anti-slavery Democrats, and became then the most outspoken opponent of slavery in the U.S. Senate. After that, it took all of Franklin Pierce's very great talents as state party leader to keep the Democrats together. Hale and his cause were too deeply rooted in morality and principle to be held comfortably within the accommodating mentality of the Democratic party. Of course, the whole tangled tragic fact of slavery and the national agony it generated from plantation to battlefield went beyond all party, but in New Hampshire it was scattered Whigs, Free Soilers, and assorted splinter parties of abolitionists whose moral outrage raised the anti-slavery standard. The Democratic position was essentially the states' rights position: let the states and territories themselves decide. Democrat Franklin Pierce disliked slavery intensely and disliked unctuous abolitionists too, but he was an acceptable Presidential candidate in 1852 partly because he had made few enemies in the South. Copious evidence can be marshalled for each of two opposing verdicts: either the Pierce Democrats rightly helped to hold off the war to a time when the Union but not slavery would survive it; or the Pierce Democrats were too acquiescent for too long with an institution they knew to be evil.

"Young Hickory of the Granite State" was elected as the United States President in 1852: a good man in the wrong place. Historians have not considered Pierce notably successful as President, but the whole period between Andrew Jackson and the Civil War is occupied by forgettable presidents. Pierce's management of complex foreign affairs was adequate and, in the Perry mission to Japan, outstanding. Domestically, the slavery problem stained every issue, and with the Kansas-Nebraska Bill in 1854 the Great Compromise of 1850 seemed to be coming apart.

It is unlikely that anyone could have been a great President in these years. The trick was to avert calamity, and Pierce did that. Personally, the Pierce family had suffered the agony of seeing their only surviving child killed in a train accident just after Pierce's election. They went to Washington in 1853 without joy, managed four years without disaster, and returned to Concord without triumph.

Republicans and Railroads
Early in the 19th century the decline of the Federalist party and the rise of the Democrats corresponded with the rise of a statewide agricultural society. Later in the century the decline of the Democratic party and the rise of the Republicans corresponded with the decline of agriculture and the rise of industry. The Republican party, though born in Wisconsin, was conceived and named at a meeting in Exeter, New Hampshire, called by Amos Tuck in 1853. In 1857, with the Industrial Revolution going full blast, the new Republican party elected its first New Hampshire governor, and for a hundred years thereafter only three Democrats were permitted to occupy the chief executive's chair.

Ichabod Goodwin, the second Republican governor, typifies the new Republican era: he had once been a Whig; he was a bank president and for 24 years president of two railroads; he was a forthright opponent of what he called in his inaugural address "the curse of slavery." In March 1860 former Illinois Congressman Abraham Lincoln visited New Hampshire, made four triumphant speeches (Concord, Manchester, Dover, Exeter), and suddenly became a leading candidate for the Presidency. Nevertheless, under Republicans after the Civil War, New Hampshire political life tended inward. Industrial development was the consuming passion, and Republican legislators were very compliant. Railroads reached in every direction, and state forest land was sold for change to lumber companies. Before the Civil War national issues had been common currency in New Hampshire, and Democrats sometimes left office in Washington, D.C., to assume office in Concord, leavening the local discourse with national concerns. Republican governors usually came from the business community and returned to it. However, one, Charles Bell (1881-1883), was a scholar and historian, and 18 years president, not of a railroad but of the New Hampshire

Historical Society; another, Moody Currier (1885-1887), wrote poetry which, said historian Everett Stackpole, "lacks fire, inspiration and moral vigor." So did most of the governors.

The governorship was something of an honorary office, probably unavailable to anyone with real pretension to govern. But bland and honest governors were providing a face of decency for a pattern of corruption that was getting harder and harder to hide. By 1907 critic Frank Putnam would write: "The true capital of New Hampshire is the North Union Railroad Station in the city of Boston," adding that no matter who sat in the governor's chair, the man who really governed New Hampshire was "the president of the Boston & Maine Railroad."

William Chandler, later a U.S. Senator, owner of *The New Hampshire Statesman* and the *Concord Evening Monitor,* had predicted it in the early 1880s. Enough was shady in the system then for a wise man to draw a dark conclusion: free railroad passes for the chosen; low tax assessment for the railroads; heavily lobbied legislators; evidence of votes being bought in statewide elections. Chandler warned that if too much economic power flowed to too few railroad corporations, then they

will rule New Hampshire with a rod of iron. They will debauch and control both political parties, subsidize and destroy every newspaper, retain every lawyer, nominate every legislator and fill his pockets with free passes of mileage books, select the presiding officers of both Houses; name the Committees and secure the legislative action or non-action needed.

Matters did go almost that far: the free pass and retainership for lawyers became open bribery.

For a time Chandler, who enjoyed a fight (they called him "the stormy petrel"), battled the interests of the railroads almost single-handedly, much in the way his father-in-law Senator John Parker Hale, who did not enjoy a fight, had battled the interests of the slaveholders in an earlier day. In one memorable case in the early 1890s, Chandler published a brilliantly devastating analysis of the state supreme court's conclusion that the state had no equity in the Concord Railroad. Chandler argued that this "morally dishonest" decision, supported by "irrelevant and unintelligible verbiage," cost the state's people $2 million, and made likely a complete Boston & Maine monopoly. He was

When the state fair came to Concord, it was time to decorate the town, as shown in this 1902 photograph of Main Street near the corner of Pleasant. NHHS

As the postwar economic slump worsened throughout America in 1919, the nation's immigrants were blamed for joblessness and social unrest. One solution, a common sentiment, was deportation, represented in this Albert Reid cartoon from the Concord Evening Monitor *of December 1, 1919. One month later hundreds of Russian and Polish immigrants were rounded up and jailed throughout New Hampshire. NHHS*

right; the Concord/Boston & Maine merger was railroaded through.

In 1887 the New Hampshire House Judiciary Committee investigated Democrat Frank Jones, a Portsmouth brewer and railroad man, on charges of attempted bribery of legislators. His testimony, published by Chandler, included this revealing statement:

> *I say I could take a hundred Republicans tomorrow and in two years 90 of them will vote just about as I do. That has been my experience. . . .* Men are a good deal like hogs; *they don't like to be driven, but you* throw them down a little corn *and you can call them most anywhere.*

Progressivism in New Hampshire

The wan smile and the bright remark that after all "the Boston & Maine gave New Hampshire pretty good government" were wearing thin by 1905. There was truth in the remark, bitter though it be, but reform was overdue. It came from within the the Republican party, though it soon caught the political winds coming from Robert LaFollette's Wisconsin and Teddy Roosevelt's Washington.

A young writer named Winston Churchill, at the time America's best-known novelist and least-known politician, first mobilized the citizenry against the "corporation," as the Boston & Maine Railroad and its political machine were known. He had served two terms in the legislature and poured his observations into a 1906 novel, *Coniston,* which brilliantly depicted the power and manipulations of a political machine. A citizen's group persuaded Churchill to run for governor as a reform candidate. Such a thing was unheard of—but not for long. With help from wise old ex-Senator Chandler, the reform group put together a program of specific proposals: laws against free railroad passes to government officials; public election of railroad commissioners; reassessment of the property of railroads and other public-service companies; a corrupt practices law to deal with corporate campaign funding; public registration of lobbyists and their fees; direct primary election of party candidates; general tax reform; enforcement of liquor and anti-gambling laws; and the like. The New Hampshire group called themselves Lincoln Republicans, but the collection of ideals and attitudes that linked proposals such as these came to be known nationally as Progressivism. It was the time, shortly before World War I, when New Hampshire seemed to rejoin the national political conversation. A main theme of that conversation was retrieving political leverage from corporate and party machines and restoring it to the people.

Churchill was attractive, sincere, and certainly seemed to know what he was talking about. Thousands were persuaded that David had a chance against Goliath. The September 1906 Republican convention was a brawl: Churchill led in the eighth ballot, then lost when the other candidates united against him. His dramatic campaign clearly indicated that reform was in the air, and new legislators soon responded. Indeed, the very next year, 1907, the first legislative curbs were put upon the free railroad pass.

One of the new legislators was Robert Bass, a wealthy, upper-class Peterborough farmer and forester who had come to the state from Chicago through Harvard. His own interest in conservation and his work on the State Forestry Commission, which was then working on rescuing the White Mountains, helped to add a new theme to New Hampshire Progressivism. In 1909 he sponsored legislation creating the direct primary system for the selection of candidates for state office—hitherto the party convention had selected candidates. The next year the Republican party nominated Bass for governor and he was subsequently elected. Thus by 1910 the movement, started long before by Senator Chandler, focused and made popular by Churchill, and consolidated and deepened by Bass' experience as forester and legislator, was in ascendancy.

Under Bass there was soon a new regulatory body for utilities and monopolies (now the Public Utilities Commission), and new laws covering campaign contributions, workmen's compensation, child labor, corporate tax assessments, factory inspections, forest protection, and the like. Historians Elizabeth and Elting Morrison summarize thus:

Between 1910 and 1912, New Hampshire achieved a place in the national consciousness that it had not held since the great days of Jacksonian Democracy. . . . New Hampshire in two years more nearly fulfilled the stated and promised objectives [of Progressivism] than any other state in the Union, with the probable exception of Wisconsin. And what in 1910 seemed radical in New Hampshire became, in not so many years, commonplace throughout the nation.

The Winant Years

William Chandler, who had long warred against the railroads and a host of other vested interests in Concord and Washington, died in 1917, and his Concord funeral was appropriately graced by a roaring snowstorm—nature itself saying farewell to a long, tempestuous career. That same year a young history teacher from St. Paul's School in Concord had spent his first term in the New Hampshire legislature, a man of utterly different temper, quiet and unassuming, but destined to become the heir of New Hampshire Progressivism. He was John G. Winant, three times elected governor (1924, 1930, 1932), at 35 the youngest man to serve in that office and the first since John Langdon to serve in it for six years.

No New Hampshire public servant of modern times had so sure and favorable a grip on the imagination of the citizenry as John Winant. One attributes this in part to his personality, a compound of ambition, utter sincerity, and a humility unknown in politicians—stuff of which martyrs are sometimes made; in part to the fact that he was New Hampshire's Depression governor, heir to the tangled emotions that attach to ennobling leadership in dark times; in part to his later distinguished wartime role as Ambassador to Great Britain, beloved and admired by all of Europe, an intimate of Churchill and Roosevelt; in part to the fact that he died tragically by his own hand (1947) after his wartime service was over. Those who knew Winant were constantly put in mind of Lincoln, whom he uncannily resembled in more than one respect.

In 1924, with considerable help from a powerful ally, former Governor Robert Bass, John Winant was elected governor, and did a novel thing: he laid out a specific and detailed legislative program and got much of it passed (though two of his favorite measures—a better workmen's compensation law and a 48-hour week—failed). In an ironic twist for Progressivism, he successfully opposed efforts of the Boston & Maine Railroad to drop one-third of its trackage. In 1930 Winant was elected again, and reelected once more two years later, running against the Democratic Roosevelt tide. Remarkably, he led the state along two parallel paths at once. One involved increasing the efficiency, administration, and organization of state government, a course based upon an extensive 1932 Brookings Institution study of New Hampshire, which he had initiated. The other path involved relief efforts to lift the burden of the Depression: food, housing, and work projects, such as the State Unemployment Committee, the National Civilian Conservation Corps, and even the League of New Hampshire Craftsmen. These activities were spearheaded by the most activist, accessible, and visibly involved governor the state had known. Here was a man devoted to the common weal. In his State House office he often ran an open-door policy, admitting all who wished to see the governor. To some, Winant seemed to be New Hampshire's Republican Roosevelt; indeed, by 1935 he was familiar and sympathetic enough with the New Deal to be appointed by President Roosevelt as head of the International Workers Organization in Geneva, Switzerland.

Winant replaced Joseph P. Kennedy in 1941 as Ambassador to Great Britain—to international sighs of relief—and came in remarkable degree to symbolize in his own person and action the supporting American presence to the beleaguered nation. His unusual resources of benevolence and fellow-feeling surfaced in wartime England as they had in Depression New Hampshire. The Prime Minister and the Ambassador often toured England together, a memorably reassuring combination of resoluton and compassion amid the storms of war. At a farewell dinner for Ambassador Winant, Churchill spoke of him as "always giving us that feeling, impossible to resist, how gladly he would give his life to see the good cause triumph. He is a friend of Britain, but he is more than a friend of Britain—he is a friend of justice, freedom, and truth."

Returning from England in late spring 1946, Winant gave the

New Hampshire Governor John Gilbert Winant is also remembered as the U.S. Ambassador to Great Britain during the Second World War. Seen here in 1943, Winant managed to squeeze his lanky frame onto a light railway car with British Prime Minister Winston Churchill in order to inspect coastal defenses in Sussex. Courtesy, Wide World Photos

President Dwight D. Eisenhower received a hero's welcome when he visited New Hampshire in 1955, the state that launched his 1952 campaign with its primary, traditionally the first in the nation. Sitting next to him as the car swings through downtown Concord is New Hampshire Senator Styles Bridges—a Taft supporter in 1952. NHHS

main eulogy at the belated Joint Congressional Memorial Service for President Roosevelt. Then, freed of the pressure of the public's distresses for the first time in 15 years and cast back upon himself, he set about to write his memoirs—but found the reflective effort excruciating and emotionally disastrous. His was a public life of strangely compelling impulses, gifts, historical moments, and quietly magnificent achievement.

The Primary State

In the early 20th century New Hampshire shook its political insularity and, through the Progressive movement, rejoined the national political discourse. How much that spirit of adventure prevailed after World War II is difficult to measure. Politically, it appears that the state's major engagement with issues of national concern is not through ideas or powerful figures or progressive institutions but through something more exotic—the "first in the nation" Presidential preference primary, held in New Hampshire every four years since 1952.

Like many political institutions, the primary came to significance more by inadvertence than by design. There had been a direct primary vote for Presidential convention delegates in New Hampshire since 1913, and few realized in 1949, when the primary law was sponsored by Speaker of the House Richard Upton, how drastic was the meaning of the switch to voting directly for the candidates. Whether or not it now represents the best way for the nation to conduct its political business, it is one of the best ways now available for New Hampshire to draw attention to itself. The state has found the national spotlight thoroughly addictive, and the primary has become a national institution—a circumstance enhanced by the fact that for forty years no one was elected President without first winning his party's primary election in the Granite State. The primary enhances tourism, and it has also become the pliant instrument of considerable political patronage from the party in power in Washington. The eventual significance of the patronage factor was not foreseen in 1952. It was, however, in that year that Sherman Adams, a popular and effective governor of New Hampshire, joined the campaign of General Dwight D. Eisenhower and went on to become an extremely powerful chief-of-staff in the Eisenhower White House.

Curtailing Authority

In the late 20th century two conspicuous features of New Hampshire government are its enormous House of Representatives (400 members versus 24 Senators) and its weak chief-executive office. Written into the New Hampshire Constitution and attested in popular attitudes, both of these bespeak a long, deep distrust of strong central authority—a distrust extending back to the Wentworth governors of colonial days. The House, for example, has been bloated for a century: in 1876 it had 391 members, was then cut to 280, but blew up again by 1942 to 443 and was then constitutionally restricted to a maximum of 400. The salary of legislators has been fixed by the same constitution for more than a hundred years as $200 per term. A "citizens legislature" is the favorite self-description of the House of Representatives.

One problem that faces an extremely large state legislature is that of getting everyone into the official legislative photograph. In 1877 there were 393 members of the New Hampshire House of Representatives; yet, notwithstanding the variety of precarious perches, not everyone made it into this W.G.C. Kimball picture. NHHS

The Constitution gives the governor but a two-year term, just as it did a hundred years ago; and it surrounds the governor with an Executive Council, just as did two hundred years ago. Traditionally, the Council approves all major appointments and expenditures. Many appointments extend years beyond a governor's term; so each governor inherits a "team." In colonial days the governor also had to barter with a Council, but usually he controlled appointments to it, thus selecting his own adversaries. In early New Hampshire the Council was elected from the legislature, but today's Councilors are independently elected and have formidable constituencies of their own. Attempts through constitutional conventions from 1850 onward to restrict the Council's essentially negative authority (as in Maine and Massachusetts, the only other states with this colonial leftover) or to abolish it completely, have uniformly failed. The sheer force of the impulse to baffle central authority, force of tradition more than of thought, is felt on every hand. For example, in 1982 the voters rejected a legislature-proposed constitutional amendment to give the governor a four-year term. Another example is older and subtler: many New Hampshire statutes that establish an executive office vest its authority in the "Governor and Council," even though the constitution would not require the Council's participation.

Inevitably these attitudes and arrangements affect the course of New Hampshire's political history, and affect too its idea of political leadership. Tepid leaders have been more common than forcefully effective ones. While bluster, veto, and threat of veto can produce a kind of negative strength, positive strength requires a rare combination: a cooperative Executive Council, persistent diplomacy, imaginative staff work, legislative initiative, and considerable personal prestige. New Hampshire traditions and institutions make it difficult for the democratic process to cast up a John Langdon or a John Winant.

The New England institution of the town meeting has continued in New Hampshire. Traditionally held on the second Tuesday in March, it is the annual occasion when the affairs of the town are deliberated—at length. A farmer wrote in his diary on March 13, 1860, "Went Town Meeting some in wagons, some in sleighs." On March 16 he continued: "went Town Meeting haint got through yet." Pictured are the citizens of Webster meeting in 1979. Courtesy, New Hampshire Times

CHAPTER
SEVEN

PEOPLE OF PLACE,
PEOPLE OF
MOVEMENT

AFTER 1784

At home in Concord, the family of the Reverend John Atwood sit for their portrait in 1845. Having served 18 years as minister of the Baptist church in New Boston, Atwood was appointed chaplain of the state prison at Concord in 1843. In 1850 he ran unsuccessfully for governor, returning afterward to New Boston with his family. This portrait is the work of artist Henry F. Darby, then only 16. In later years Darby recalled that he spent three months in Concord "to paint the Atwoods all on one canvas. The father was represented . . . expounding his Bible." From the M. and M. Karolik Collection. Courtesy, Museum of Fine Arts, Boston

Although some New Hampshire families occupy an ancestral home or work land farmed by generations of forebears, already in 1830 Alexis de Tocqueville, visiting from France, found Americans to be restless people. New England, famous for images summoned by the phrase "sense of place," was settled and nearly unsettled, by people who moved from place to place to an extent unknown to European contemporaries. The Fogg *Gazetteer* of New Hampshire said that in 1870, when the resident population was 318,000, there were 125,000 natives of New Hampshire living outside that state. Something similar holds true today: one-half of the more than one million residents of New Hampshire were born elsewhere.

This chapter highlights the vision of those who tended to stay put, those who focused upon the recurring and enduring things, be they as banal as the ever-returning mud season or as sublime as the hills: people of place. The chapter then turns to reports of comings and goings, of nomads and tourists, of soldiers of fortune and soldiers of war: people of movement. This chapter sticks close to the people by sticking close to their own words. Their words extend from the homes and hearths of the 18th century to the United Nations of the 20th century.

Interior Places

The domestic hearth—whether fact, symbol, or cliché—remains a vivid image. By means of it, two diarists, widely separated in time, temperament, and outlook, unintentionally sum up more than a century of New Hampshire experience. Francis Parkman, a young Harvard student, later a famous Harvard historian, tramped through the Granite State in 1842 and jotted into his journal a classic description—the hearth as locale. "We spent that evening about their enormous cavern of a fire place, whence a blazing fire gleamed on rows of suspended stockings, the spinning wheel, the churn, the bed, and walls covered with an array of piled up cheeses, plates, milkpails, and clothes; all clean and all in order; while the older children were dodging about the furniture of the crowded room and the younger ones venting precocious snoring from a box under the bed."

In 1902 Clara May Hurd, elderly and unknown to fame, was writing to her daughter in Massachusetts from her village home in Washington, New Hampshire, and contemplating the bric-a-brac and the busy Victorian decor in the house whose hearth she had first known as a child in the 1830s.

Sitting here and resting this p.m. I went back to my mother's life in this same house—and—it seems at this day and generation to be a life devoid of comforts and plenty. . . . The house was very cold—and how bare and wanting in all the cosiness that more modern furniture and the many pretty little accessories of living as books, plants, pictures, that go to make a home, were not in evidence then and there. And yet these were not missed because they had never been possessed. So their want was not known or felt. She had the home of her day and generation. I have the home of my time.

Rural Places

Normally it is the resident, not the passerby, who claims the authoritative word on the natural environment—the seasons of the year, for example. Summertime activity is put into perspective by Kate Sanborn, a New Hampshire woman writing in the 1890s: "Haying is a terrible ordeal. There's real poetry about emerald-tinted dewy grass, and the waves of growing grain, and the tall and blithely nodding oats, and the stalwart bronzed haymakers, and the merry sun-kissed maidens in broad brimmed hats. But the real man in actual prosaic haying is like a woman on washing day—so outrageously and unreasonably cross and irascible that the very dogs dart out-doors with tails between their legs."

Ellen Rollins, a gifted and forgotten writer of the 1880s, mused on one of her neighbors who was "tied to the soil" and "whose speech was jagged as its rocks." He himself "was almost as stolid as the oxen he drove." She wrote that "he chewed tobacco in meeting-time, and spit into a box filled with sawdust in a corner of his pew." "Uncouth yet honest," his speech like that of his neighbors was "homely, but not coarse," and full of "figures drawn from the soil and devotion to it."

No better orators or writers have ever spoken or written, in this country, than certain ones whose wits were sharpened in the stimulating atmosphere of this quaint, figurative New England tongue. It was truly born of earth and toil, hence its healthy ruggedness. Hence, also, that underlying imagery, borrowed from sun and winds, field and forest, from all forms and aspects of Nature. There was a marrow to it often, inside an outer crust of homeliness, a sweet-meat of sentiment. When the farmer told you that his wife was a "good critter to work," he

This Christmas gathering took place in the Manchester home of Franco-American photographer Ulric Bourgeois in 1907. From the Manchester Visual History collection, Dimond Library, UNH, and Manchester Historic Association (MVHC)

Boston artist Frank H. Shapleigh spent most summers of his professional career living in and painting the White Mountains. At the time he painted this kitchen scene in 1883, he was artist-in-residence at the Crawford House, one of the most famous of the area's "grand hotels." Although best known for his landscapes "full of facts and sentiment" (as a contemporary put it), Shapleigh also moved indoors to paint traditional scenes centered around an open fireplace. Privately owned

compared her to his mild-eyed oxen, which he loved, and which to him were the type of patience and meekness. When he said he was having "a hard pull" in life, his words were shaped by the tugging of these same oxen at his rocky farm.

Whether it was a sense of place within a New Hampshire natural environment giving birth to a "quaint, figurative" and eloquent tongue, or whether it was a combination of other reasons—it is clear that a remarkable lot of New Hampshire women writers of the latter 19th century gave especially apt expression to the integrity and the values of life within small New Hampshire communities: Lucy Crawford, Kate Sanborn, Sara Josepha Hale, Edna D. Proctor, Ellen Rollins, Celia Thaxter. Coincidentally or not, it was no less eloquent—though less literary—female voices that also took up in sequence the major social causes of the day: anti-slavery, temperance, women's suffrage. While men excelled in industry and raw politics, women excelled in literature and social causes. Indeed, it came to be widely assumed that, for those capable of it, a woman's "place" was to be a spokesperson for, if not a guardian of, social values. In 1903 a New Hampshire journalist wrote that "the progress of women has proved . . . that the larger the voice women have in affairs the higher are the moral ideals entertained by the community." Not everyone believed this, but no one undertook to demonstrate that it was untrue.

Working Places

In some urban environments a very different sense of place developed. Raymond Dubois reflected on life in Manchester at the turn of the century, "I was brought up in the area of the mill. All our people were mill people, and we didn't know anything else but mills. . . . We lived near the mills, we carried dinners for our parents, and we just were accustomed to the mills. It seemed like this was where we would fall in when we got old enough. I went in a few months after I became sixteen. . . . I didn't like it and I don't think too many people in there liked it either."

Many urban children knew all too well the meaning of the working place: child labor was standard, with sometimes predictable results. *Foster's Daily Democrat* for August 1, 1874, reported: "Accidents happened to a couple of boys in the mill yesterday. . . . One of them. . . . aged 12 years got his hand caught in the doubler, a machine used in the card room, which stripped the skin and muscle from the wrists to the finger ends. . . . Soon afterwards another boy put his hand into the same machine and came off worse still. Two of his fingers had to be amputated."

The Manchester Coal and Ice Company, which according to its city directory ads sold "coal, wood and Massabesic Ice," delivered its products throughout Manchester in horse-drawn wagons. The employees of the company, with their ice tongs, are shown here about 1915. The photograph is probably by Arthur Boulanger of Manchester. MVHC

Families worked at the Amoskeag Mills, lived in Amoskeag housing, and wore Amoskeag-made cotton. For a long time and for many families it was a satisfactory life. This couple was photographed in 1920, two years before a long bitter strike against the company began. MVHC

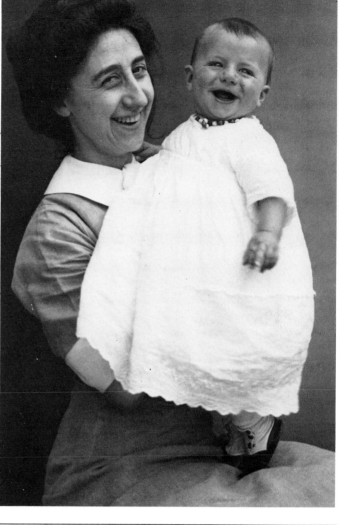

When photographer Ulric Bourgeois migrated from Quebec to Manchester near the turn of the century, he began the process of documenting the city of Manchester and its working-class people. Nevertheless, many of his best photographs were shots of his own family, which provide the viewer with insight into both family life of the period and the Franco-American experience in New Hampshire. The photographer manages to include himself in both 1910 family photographs on page 70 and in the 1915 photograph, above left, with his wife and daughters. This portrait of mother and daughter, above, is from 1907. MVHC

Cora Pellerin of Manchester said: "I came from Canada in 1911. I started working in 1912 when I was eleven . . . my father had a birth certificate made for me in the name of my sister Cora, who died as a baby, because you couldn't go to work unless you were fourteen. . . . I worked in Canada during the strike of 1922, . . . but I never would go back there to live. It was paradise here because you got your money, and you did whatever you wanted to with it."

In some circumstances a sense of place was connected with certain other intangible qualities. The gloom of the Depression hung over the land in 1931 when John Winant gave his inaugural address as governor: "I feel very strongly that certain essential spiritual qualities are needed in order to restore confidence." Winant told his audience that "neither over-optimism nor fear are safe guides . . . in maintaining economic stability. We can do more . . . by undramatic and unselfish effort combined with hard work and quiet faith than through legislative panaceas." This is vintage New Hampshire talking to itself.

That year historian and journalist Bernard De Voto traveled through New England to discover how these tribes had adapted their heritage and the needs of the hour to their own sense of place within the social order. His report appeared in *Harper's*

Manchester's ethnic groups have maintained a degree of cohesiveness over the years. Pictured (above) is a Greek coffeehouse in 1978 (photograph by Gary Samson) and (top) a Greek coffeehouse in 1910 (MVHC).

Magazine in March 1932, "New England, There She Stands." These people, he wrote, have "never thrown themselves upon the charity of the nation. . . . from this frigid north, this six-inch soil sifted among boulders, has come no screaming for relief. The breed has clung to its uplands, and solvency has been its righteousness and independence has been its pride. . . . here are people who have mastered the conditions of their life." At this time New Hampshire had not yet seen the worst of the Depression, and the WPA, the CCC, and the REA all lay in the future, as did the closing of hundreds of New Hampshire mills. But De Voto saw or thought he saw the qualities that would see New Hampshire through.

Their ancestral religion told them that the world is a battleground whereon mankind is sentenced to defeat—an idea not inappropriate to the granite against which they must make their way. By the granite they have lived for three centuries, tightening their belts and hanging on, by the sense of what is real. They are the base of the Yankee commonwealth; and America, staring apprehensively through fog that may not lift in this generation, may find their knowledge of hard things more than a little useful.

Movements Out and In

The temptation to romanticize the achievement of those who stay put and acquire knowledge of hard things is nearly irresistible. The other side of social life, its sense of coming and going, is kaleidoscopic, impressionistic—and subject to its own idealization.

By the middle of the 19th century so many New Hampshire natives had moved to Boston that there were celebrations of remembrance. "Festival of the Sons of New Hampshire" one such affair was called, and of course Daniel Webster was the orator. No one in America could recreate heroic origins like this son of New Hampshire, who had moved to Massachusetts in 1816. People of his native state, he said, were "given to the chase and to the hunt in time of peace; fitted for endurance and danger and when war came, they were ready to meet it. It was in the midst of these vicissitudes that they were formed to hardihood and enterprise, and trained to military skill and fearlessness. . . When the march from Boston to Lexington and Concord had spread the flames of liberty, who answered to the call? Did New Hampshire need to be summoned to Bunker Hill? She came at the first blaze of the beacon-fires. None were earlier, none more ready, none more valiant."

In Webster's time many natives of Massachusetts were also traveling north. In 1839 Henry David Thoreau and his brother rowed up the Merrimack River to inspect the New Hampshire interior. Specimens from the Granite State met them coming down: "another scow hove in sight, creeping down the river, and hailing it, we attached ourselves to its side, and floated back in company, chatting with the boatmen. . . . They appeared to be green hands from far among the hills, who had taken this means to get to the seaboard, and see the world; and would possibly visit the Falkland Isles, and the China seas, before they again saw the waters of the Merrimack, or perchance, not return this way forever. . . . What grievance has its root among the New Hampshire hills? we asked; what is wanting to human life here, that these men should make such haste to the antipodes?"

For his part, Thoreau liked the New Hampshire he saw: riverbank farmsteads "more pleasing to our eyes than palaces or castles" that were "surrounded commonly by a small patch of corn and beans, squashes and melons, with sometimes a graceful hop-yard on one side, and some running vine over the windows." Such dwellings appeared to him "like bee-hives set to gather honey for a summer. I have not read of any Arcadian life which surpasses the actual luxury and serenity of these New England dwellings." Thoreau knows that he sees these New Hampshire homes with the eyes of a poet and an idealist, and he yields to the fancy that "the employment of their inhabitants by day would be to tend the flowers and herds, and at night, like the shepherds of old, to cluster and give names to the stars from the river banks."

A few years later, Bostonian Francis Parkman took a coach to Lake Winnipesaukee, and then hiked from Alton Bay around to Center Harbor. In his 1841 journal Parkman wrote that for the first hours of the walk "we passed no dwellings but a few log-cabins, with a little clearing in the forest around them. But, alas, the little pathway was widened by the junction of others, and farm houses began to appear, first singly, then in clusters, with clearings extending for miles." Parkman was amazed to see so much of the lakeside wilderness cleared. He was also annoyed: "It was almost noon and we toiled up the scorching road, sweating and grumbling at the folly which had deprived us of shelter and comfort by ridiculously burning the forests, in the zeal for making clearings." In his eyes "the burnt lands lay utterly waste and the sole effect of the operation is to ruin the scene and lay the road open to the baking sun."

Above: Milford's Union Square seems unusually quiet in this late 19th century photograph. Throughout the century Milford was a thriving manufacturing town along the Souhegan River, where mills churned out cotton and woolen cloth, furniture, rugs and rug yarn, ladies' woolen hosiery, plows, and a number of other goods. In addition, Milford's granite quarries provided substantial employment during the second half of the century. NHHS

Top: A few carriages, pedestrians, and cyclists work their way up lower Main Street, Peterborough, in this 1899 photograph. The cleared fields and stone walls on East Hill in the background belie the fact that Peterborough's prosperity in the late 19th century rested upon commerce and a highly diversified manufacturing base. NHHS

Left: Their stylish riggings unbuttoned, this party posed to be photographed on their ascent of Mt. Monadnock. An earlier climber wrote in 1838, "After something of a strain we reached the top of the first peak. As we looked upward we saw another peak at the distance of a mile. So down we go . . . and up we toil to the height of the second peak. To our surprise and disappointment there is a still higher peak beyond . . . So down we go again and up we toil again. Quite exhausted we reach the height of the third peak. We look beyond and upward, and lo! another still higher and more difficult of access . . . We perform another go-down and go-up . . . We look again and the summit is far off still. . . ." NHHS

This group of soldiers from Company F of the Third New Hampshire Regiment had yet to see combat when they posed for New Hampshire photographer Henry Moore near Hilton Head, South Carolina. Before the war was over, however, they would experience their share of combat: the regiment suffered a 54 percent casualty rate. NHHS

Henry Moore's photograph of the regiment's cooks' galley, Company K, suggests that Civil War army cuisine may not have met gourmet standards. Taste aside, however, the cooks of the Third New Hampshire Regiment deserve some credit: the Third was one of the few New Hampshire regiments for which death from disease was less common than death in combat. NHHS

The next year Parkman was tramping around in the old Indian Stream Republic in Pittsburg. Following the common practice of hikers, he and his friend stopped at a house "and asked for lodging and a supper. . . . We went in to supper, which was served in rough style, but had the virtue of cleanliness, as did the whole place—children excepted. There were some eight or ten imps of both sexes." Their host was "a rough-hewn piece of timber enough, but his wife was a perfect barbarian, as far as the entire absence of all manners can make one, but both were equally open and hospitable."

Dr. Albert A. Moulton was brigade surgeon of the Third New Hampshire Regiment when he, his wife, and their young son posed for this Moore photograph in 1862. Moulton, a native of Meredith and a graduate of the Dartmouth Medical School, had been joined by his wife and son in March 1862. NHHS

Tourists and Migrants

Older forms of travel often brought different classes of people abreast of one another—where they could size each other up with a sidelong glance. Nathaniel Hawthorne traveled to the White Mountains, stayed at Crawford's Inn, and formed the plan—never carried out—to spend extensive time there "for the sake of studying the yeomen of New England"; he would mingle with the drovers, lumberjacks, and farmers in their own settings "to see how sturdily they make head against the blast." Later Hawthorne caught a glimpse of New Hampshire people when they were themselves on the move: on the Isles of Shoals in 1852, waiting for Franklin Pierce to arrive so they could discuss the Presidential campaign, Hawthorne watched people arrive by boat from Portsmouth. The first troupe was "apparently from the interior of New Hampshire." Among them "country traders, a country doctor, and such sorts of people, rude, shrewd, and simple, and well-behaved enough; wondering at sharks, and equally at lobsters; sitting down to table with their coats off; helping themselves out of the dish with their own forks; taking pudding on the plates off which they have eaten meat." No doubt he would have preferred these people in their own setting, for people "at just this stage of manners are more disagreeable than at any other stage. They are aware of some decencies, but not so deeply aware as to make them a matter of conscience."

The Civil War brought a new form of travel for New Hampshire's young men. Fourteen regiments went south, probably at least 35,000 men, more than one-tenth of the population. In an 1861 letter published in the Keene *Sentinel* a member of the Second New Hampshire Regiment told of his stop in Reading, Pennsylvania: "I strolled about a while to see the place and people. This is a German city. The name upon every tradesman's sign is a jaw-breaker, and *'lager beer'* is everywhere." He admitted he had tasted that "nauseating beverage in New England, with very wry face, but when I drank in Pennsylvania the real

Dutch brew, I did not wonder that the Dutchmen love it." At this time New Hampshire was hooked on hard cider, and a temperance movement was gathering momentum. Later, better New Hampshire beer probably helped the temperance cause by providing an alternative to "ardent spirits."

"Go West, young man," said New Hampshire native Horace Greeley, editor of the *New York Tribune.* One knows from his autobiography what he was advising these young men to leave: "Picking stones is a never-ending labor on one of those rocky New England farms. Pick as closely as you may, the next ploughing turns up a fresh eruption. . . . youngsters soon learn to regard it with detestation. I filially love the 'Granite State' but could well excuse the absence of sundry subdivisions of her granite." Many who heeded his advice went west in the vigor of youth, dropping the past like a worn shoe, but many others went dolefully. Ziba Crane wrote home to New Hampshire from his stopping point in New York: "Yes, dear brother, I never expect to see you or any of my friends again on earth, nor my native land. I bid farewell. We expect to start next Monday for the west . . . and whether I shall live to accomplish that long journey, it is more than I can say."

Traveling implied meetings and separations and recollections of them: the stuff of nostalgia. A coach which at the time was hot and dusty and jarring is seen in retrospect serenely "wending its course." Already a hundred years ago dozens of town historians were sighing the sigh of the 1878 author who said that the railroad brought a new order of things. "The numerous teams and stages . . . disappeared forever. From that day to the present, no ponderous wagon, with white canvas covering, drawn by eight stalwart horses, has been seen wending its course along [the Fourth New Hampshire Turnpike]." The old stagecoach, he said, with its "passengers, and mountain of baggage, has rolled along the road, leaving a cloud of dust behind: all have gone,— nor will they ever be seen again."

Above: Vigneault and Pigeon's bar and retail liquor store did business in Manchester from approximately 1914 to 1917. The short-lived firm disappeared from its Manchester Street location just before the 18th Amendment and the Volstead Act would have closed its doors. MVHC

Top: One look at Horace Greeley's rustic birthplace in Amherst suggests why he may have advised young men to "go west" in the years before the Civil War. Greeley, founder of the New York Tribune and Presidential candidate, was one of many New Hampshire natives who found fame and fortune somewhere else. His family deserted their New Hampshire hill farm when Greeley was a boy and went west, first to Vermont, and later to Erie County, Pennsylvania. NHHS

Tramping

Always with the coming of hard times came new forms of vagabondage. The "knights of the road," as tramps were called, appeared from nowhere and were going nowhere. "Any person going about from place to place begging and asking or subsisting upon charity" is a tramp, said an 1878 New Hampshire law, and to be "punished by imprisonment at hard labor." This didn't stop the tramps, but it encouraged them to offer to work for a meal. In the New Hampshire countryside itself there was more understanding and sympathy than the state law implied. Many, perhaps most, towns had a tramp house—a roof and usually one meal guaranteed by the town—intermittently active from the Civil War to World War II.

Haydn Pearson's memories of Hancock, which go back to the early 20th century, sum up the experiences of hundreds of communities: "I used to lie awake at night in my small room under the eaves and wonder about them. 'Tramp' was a word we learned to fear." Pearson recalls that "tramps drifted into town from the cities south of us." (If you lived in the country tramps always originated in the city.) "They were ragged, unkempt, and bearded. They plodded up the road on the way to the big orchard farm."

> *They would come to the ell door and ask Mother if she could spare a bite to eat. If Father was around Mother sent the tramps to him. That was an inflexible rule. The other rule was, when we children were young, that if we saw a tramp coming up the road the girls were to go into the house and Mother was to lock the doors and not answer a knock.*

True, the bearded fellow was probably not Parkman or Thoreau or Longfellow doing research and offering to buy a night's lodging. True, tramps were said to be petty thieves, and often unseen tramps were blamed for otherwise unexplained fires; but the basis of these beliefs was usually gossip, not evidence, and fears usually dissolved. Pearson writes:

> *By the time I was ten I knew the tramps for what they were. With rare exception they were broken, dispirited men. Most of them blamed liquor for their sorry condition. All who came to Hancock were men well along in years. It seemed silly to be afraid of such specimens of humankind.*

Some tramps were simply perpetual travelers; some were seasonal and turned up in the same village in the same week, year after year. Sometimes an apple farmer or potato farmer looked over the tramp crop and hired the best of the lot for the picking season. One tramp who stopped at the Pearson farm and stayed the winter as a hired man was college-educated and past middle age, and full of yarns about faraway places. By spring he was uneasy and confided his dark secret to young Haydn: "I don't want you to tell your parents this until after I've left," he said. "I wish I could stay, but I can't. When I have been in a place just so long I get restless and moody. I haven't touched liquor for years, but I've got a disease worse than that. I have to travel."

The biggest hit at Concord's Bicycle Parade of 1896 was the Big Trike from Nashua. Made by the people at Vim Tire, the tricycle weighed 1,900 pounds, and its wheels were 11.5 feet in diameter. It took the muscle of eight men to peddle the contraption to Concord from Nashua—scaring horses the entire way. A punctured tire had to be repaired in Manchester, and, according to newspaper accounts, it took an hour to refill the tire with air. NHHS

For about three decades, from approximately 1880 to 1910, bicycle clubs flourished throughout the state, and cycling was a very stylish sport for both men and women. This carefully posed photograph of the Dartmouth Bicycle Club was made about 1888. DCA

Other itinerants added a regular color to the landscape: the tailor who boarded with a family for a week, made a suit of clothes for each member, and then moved on to the next household; the painter who came to stencil the halls and parlors of the village mansions; the traveling photographer who distributed the family, the horse, and the sulky in front of the homestead and produced in, say, 1890, a wonderfully sharp print, such as is not easily matched even today.

Wheels and Wars

Trains taught Americans that it was possible to move fast and survive, so other forms of high-speed transportation were designed and put on the market. Bicycles were the rage of the 1880s and 1890s, catching the fancy of the public the way snowmobiles did 80 years later. In the 1890s Frank W. Rollins, later governor, dreamed of "skimming like a swallow along perfectly kept bicycle paths." New Hampshire Senator William Chandler developed a reputation in Washington, D.C., for the way he careened through the United States capital on his bicycle, swallowtailed coat streaming in his wake, the terror of horses, dogs, Democrats, and other denizens of the capital city. Back in New Hampshire, Chandler promptly went in for the latest contraption: he bought an automobile. A diary entry for 1902 tells a story many others of the time could tell: "All went well to Warner, when the chain flew off. Got it on again, but within half a mile it flew off and broke. Oscar hauled me home with horse

William Stark of Manchester specialized in domesticating wild animals. At the 1866 state fair held in Nashua, Stark and his elk were the highlight of the day. Henry W. Herrick, a Hopkinton native, sketched and engraved scenes of New Hampshire for New York clients, and this one of Stark and his elk appeared in Harper's Weekly. *Residing in Manchester, Herrick in his later years painted in watercolor and became a distinguished author and landscape artist. NHHS*

Just eight years after the Wright brothers' initial flight Manchester hosted an aviation meet on September 23, 1911. To the surprise of some spectators this flying machine actually got off the ground. NHHS

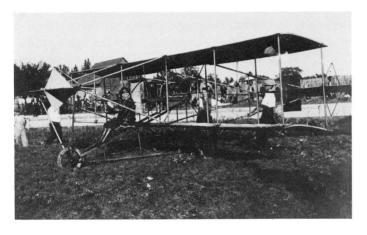

and wagon." As usual, Senator Chandler was too far ahead of his time. He sold the troublesome auto and went back to a bicycle.

For many a remote town the real age of the automobile began when the 1911 Sears Roebuck catalogue arrived: there on page 1266 were four automobiles displayed in all their glory. Sixty-five years later Caroll Farnsworth recalled bringing the first auto permanently to the town of Washington. It was July 6, 1911, when he, his father, and brother went to the freight office in Hillsboro "to assemble our new Sears auto. The wheels were gotten on, and gas in the tank and then we cranked it up. I then took the seat at the steering-bar and headed across the railroad and on to the fair-grounds. Then three laps around the race track for my first driving lesson, then headed for home. Got there safely." In similar ways a new era of mobility came to hundreds of towns.

Just as the Civil War had opened America to New Hampshire eyes, so World War I brought Europe into the consciousness of the Granite State. On May Day, 1915, the Portsmouth *Daily Chronicle* said that "every year large numbers of travellers go abroad and scatter their money lavishly among the people of foreign countries," a practice which is unpatriotic since many of these tourists "have never seen their own country" and also now dangerous: "There is war in the Old World, earnest, bitter and cruel war, and it is the part of wisdom for Americans who are not obliged to go there to keep as far away from it as they can." The war came closer and in May 1916 the Laconia *Democrat* reported proudly on "the biggest civic parade in American history" held in New York City "in favor of preparedness." New Hampshire was represented "by the largest American flag in existence, measuring 100 feet long and 52 feet wide and weighing 500 pounds. It was made, every stitch of it, by the Amoskeag Manufacturing Company." In March 1917, one hundred and eighty towns passed resolutions of support for the national government, and in less than a month the nation was officially at war with Germany. Twenty thousand New Hampshire men served in the armed forces; 697 of them gave their lives.

World War II supplied the pressure by which the New Hampshire outlook merged with the national perspective: it happened to a degree unprecedented then and unequalled since. Most of the familiar, self-consciously New Hampshire terms of reference were suspended: sense of local identity and of place receded, and the dynamics of movement were all related to the war effort. Sixty thousand Granite State uniformed men and women were dispersed to every corner of the earth; 1,600 did not return. Dozens of organizations popped up to guide the war effort, diverting the local will into the mainstream of the national will. Success was imperfect, of course. The *Hillsborough Messenger* reported that Frank Cutting, country store owner, protested: "Mr. Cutting recognized the necessity for regulation and control of business as a war measure, but being an Individualist and never having been used to taking orders and to absentee management, he decided to close the store for the duration."

In the New Hampshire hills a hundred mica mines were opened; on the coast the Portsmouth Naval Shipyard churned out a new submarine every two weeks throughout the war. Like caissons rolling along, the symbols of that time come to mind, each one heavy with memories: victory gardens, the USO, sav-

Military launchings have been common in the history of the Piscataqua—the first warship built at Portsmouth was commissioned in 1690, the last in the 1960s. To bolster American defense in response to World War I, the Atlantic Corporation was founded in 1918 and contracted with the Emergency Fleet Corporation to produce 10 steel cargo vessels. Completed in record time, the Babboosic was launched at Portsmouth in 1919, the second ship off the line. From the Historic Photograph Collection of Strawbery Banke, Inc.

ings bonds, gold stars, V-mail, draft boards, scrap iron, ration books, the home front, the GI Bill. But they are one and all national emblems and part, not just of the state's, but of the nation's experience.

Some actions stand out as uniquely New Hampshire's. Chief among them was the resolution debated at the March 1945 town meetings, one that suggested a link between the security of New Hampshire hearths and the peace of nations, a referendum no other state put before its people:

To see if the Town will vote to support United States membership in a general system of international cooperation . . . having police power to maintain the peace of the world.

By more than a two-to-one margin New Hampshire people urged the United States to join the proposed United Nations organization.

On October 24, 1950, a block of New Hampshire granite was laid as the cornerstone of the United Nations building in New York City.

III

ECONOMY
AND
INDUSTRY

The legendary Granite State reveals something of itself in outcroppings of gray stone. Veins of granite abound, but at Concord a ledge of superior stone was recognized by 1819 to have quarrying potential. In this circa 1910 view of the New England Granite Company quarry, workers remove granite blocks. Concord granite has been used in the construction of important buildings throughout the country. NHHS

BEFORE
THE
INDUSTRIAL
REVOLUTION

Before the coming of the railroad the workhorse of Great Bay commerce was the Piscataqua gundalow, in which cordwood, hay, boards and planks, bricks, and other cargo traveled the tidal waters of Great Bay and the Piscataqua River to Portsmouth. By 1900, however, the unique Piscataqua gundalow had seen its day, victim of the railroad and Portsmouth's declining importance as a coastal trade center. The Piscataqua Gundalow Project commemorated the gundalow by constructing one. The Captain Edward H. Adams, *seen here at its launching in Portsmouth Harbor on June 13, 1982, took two-and-a-half years to build, at a cost of over $100,000. Photograph by Gary Samson*

For 100 years after New Hampshire was first settled, the main businesses were fishing, lumbering, and the associated trades, including extensive shipbuilding. For the next 100 years, the 1730s to 1830s, the main occupation was farming and its allied trades, including extensive small-time manufacturing to supply farm needs.

Ships and Farms
Shipbuilding was a significant New Hampshire industry throughout most of the 200 years that led up to the Industrial Revolution. Small vessels for the Boston lumber trade, built on the Piscataqua as early as the 1650s, were soon followed by more and larger ships. There is record of 34 vessels with an average size of 30 tons built on the Piscataqua between 1687 and 1695. Before 1700 larger warships were also built there for the British Navy, one, the HMS *Falkland,* of 776 tons. The lumber and ship

building businesses, although at first dependent upon the fluid capital produced by the fisheries, soon provided a well-developed economic base for the coastal colony: carpenters and coopers, shipwrights and sailmakers, and a dozen other craftsmen set up business and thrived. The merchants thrived most of all.

Shipbuilding continued to grow after 1700 and so did the size of the ships. In one five-year spurt, 1722-1727, 94 vessels with an average carrying capacity of 60 tons were built at dozens of different Piscataqua shipyards. With the mast trade in full gear, the ships were getting larger and larger: "Masters" had a capacity of 400 to 600 tons. In another five-year spurt, 1740-1745, 142 vessels were built on the New Hampshire coast. On a typical day in the 1750s one could have seen at least one cargo ship enter and another leave the Portsmouth harbor.

Mast shipments to England were halted, of course, by the Revolution, but shipbuilding was only slowed. After the Revolutionary War, shipbuilding in and around Portsmouth continued, with a trend toward still larger ships. By 1790 production was in high gear again, 20 vessels being launched from the Piscataqua that year. Between 1800 and 1860, 575 sailing vessels were constructed at or near Portsmouth. Though this represents fewer vessels per year than during the high point a century earlier (10 per year as compared with 25), because of the ships' increased size it represents more capacity than ever before. The Portsmouth ships of the 1850s averaged over 1,000 tons. But by the time of the Revolutionary War, and certainly by the 1850s, the shipyards were representing a smaller and smaller percentage of an economy that had become increasingly agricultural.

Before the Revolutionary War many of the best forests near the coast had been cut down, the waters around the Isles of Shoals were being fished out, and, indeed, the rivers of the coast were so polluted with sawdust that fish could scarcely spawn here. At the same time, population pressures from Massachusetts and abroad were increasing. By the middle of the 18th century, the interior of New Hampshire, increasingly freed

of Indian troubles, was being rapidly opened up for development by deliberate government policy and by the skillful programs of speculative land merchants. There was land, free or cheap, for anyone who wanted to try his luck subduing it. It took a long time, but before the Revolution the New Hampshire frontier had moved away from the seacoast, and a basically agricultural society had planted roots in the thin and rocky soil of the interior. As measured by the amount of land under cultivation and by the percentage of the state's economy and population tied to the farm, the high point of New Hampshire agriculture came sometime in the 1830s. It had taken 200 years.

From Rural to Industrial Economy

Lumbering, fishing, shipbuilding, and finally and most importantly, farming—these were the premises of the New Hampshire economy from the beginning until well into the 19th century. But by the 1830s the picture was changing. From one point of view—the view that takes the rural yeomanry of Jefferson and Belknap as its ideal—New Hampshire was clearly on the skids before the middle of the 19th century. Town after town in rural New Hampshire reached its peak of population and of rustic, small-town self-sufficiency some time between 1820 and 1850 and then began to shrink as the population escaped to the city or the West.

From another point of view, however, New Hampshire was just getting going. Industrially, the beginnings of modern New Hampshire date from precisely the period when the agricultural economy crested. Looking back from today's standpoint, it is easy to see that after the 1830s all the major social and economic reference points had changed—though not everyone noticed it at the time. Some noticed it then and rejoiced. With their own eyes they had seen the humming factories of Manchester rise suddenly out of pastureland. Daniel Webster, a New Hampshire farm boy who had blazed a path to the centers of power, stood on the brand new railroad tracks in Lebanon in 1847, hailing a new day:

From earliest times the one flaw in the Portsmouth harbor had been Henderson's Point (also known as "Pull-and-Be-Damned Point"), a projection of rock 500 feet into the river's mouth that created vicious crossgrain currents hazardous to navigation. When the Portsmouth Navy Yard was expanded in 1905, the point was removed. First, a dam was built around it, and the layers of rock were hammered and blasted loose and carried away on freight cars. Then it was decided to finish the job with one massive dynamite blast—the largest ever executed. Hundreds of holes were drilled up to 80 feet into the rock and 50 tons of dynamite were deposited. The blast itself was the major tourist attraction of the season. Special trains ran to Portsmouth on July 22, 1905; at 11 minutes past 4 p.m., 18,000 spectators saw Henderson's Point disappear. Courtesy, Dimond Library, UNH

It is an extraordinary era in which we live. It is altogether new. The world has seen nothing like it before. I will not pretend, no one can pretend, to discern the end; but everybody knows that the age is remarkable for scientific research. . . . The ancients saw nothing like it. The moderns have seen nothing like it till the present generation.

Some perhaps heard his words and felt their depth and truth—if only because the great man said them with such force and majesty—yet without really knowing what he was talking about. Had not soothsayers been saying time out of mind that the old way is going or gone, that we live in a new age? Many expected that their sons would farm the same homestead, with the same tools, pretty much as their fathers had—and they were right. Yet vast changes were sweeping through the economy of New England, and social trends were afoot in New Hampshire that would completely alter the state.

Certain symbols of the new age saluted by Webster in the 1840s stand out: water and turnpike had been the basic means of commercial transportation, now it was to be rail; iron had been the basic strong metal, now it was to be steel; the household shop, and local mill had been the locus of industry, now it was to be factory and corporation; the farmer had always stood out as the representative American, now he was to be flanked by the businessman and the factory worker. New England would still be, numerically at least, a rural region for another century, but it was now to be more and more the city that would focus the ambitions of its youth. As a city, Manchester encapsulates the whole story. It is New Hampshire's representative 19th-century city as Portsmouth is its 18th-century city. Portsmouth, created by politics and a seacoast economy, is an artifact of colonialism; Manchester, created by the railroads and the mills, is an artifact of industrial development.

More generally, the significant economic facts for New Hampshire gather round three major 19th-century themes, in each of which new technology was the decisive element: railroad transportation, textiles, and lumbering. They are stories of risings and fallings. Behind these developments, however, lay the colonial struggles with the challenges of transportation.

Province Roads

In the middle of the 18th century, one could get about fairly well in the seacoast towns, but travel in the rest of the province was difficult and painful. The Portsmouth-to-Boston post road was an exception: it accommodated a weekly round-trip stage and the more frequent mail riders well before the Revolution. Inland most of the roads were bridle paths or cart trails that wound over ledges, around stumps, and through brooks. The first major road authorized by the New Hampshire Assembly was in 1722—6 miles to Lake Winnipesaukee to build a fort there "for the annoyance of the Indians." The roads themselves annoyed the citizens. Lady Wentworth, writing in 1770 from the governor's Wolfeboro summer home, worried about the trip back to Portsmouth: "I dread the journey, as the roads are so bad."

Until 1770 western New Hampshire was joined to the eastern part by only the most haphazard system of individual town roads—adequate near the villages, then petering out. Selectmen were mandated by the New Hampshire Assembly to keep the town roads in repair, but enforcement was another matter. Towns sometimes complained to the Assembly about their neighbors. The town of Camden (now Washington) wrote in January 1773 to the Assembly about "the greait Deficulty we the inhabitance of Camden, Labour under by Reason of the Roades being So bad in the Township of monadnick No. 7 or Limbrick [Goshen] so Kalled that it is Allmost imposable for a teem to Pess there and Dangorous for a Hors Nothing has Ben Done."

There was good commercial reason for New Hampshire to work for something better. In 1761 the Assembly had noted "...the place called Cohass [Haverhill] ... represented to be in great forwardness, where great quantities of Corn will soon be raised which will be transported down the Connecticut River for sale, unless a good Highway can be made ... into this Province." Accordingly, the Assembly decided to unite the province by constructing a public road northwest to southeast: from Coös to the sea. It was a sound idea, but ideas do not build a highway the way money does.

The Assembly record for January 16, 1770, says: "The Question was put, Whether the Province should be at any Expense for opening and clearing said roads, and it passed in the negative." Let the towns that get the road pay, thought the Assembly. Let the Province pay for what the Province mandates, thought the towns—a refrain that still echoes today. The Assembly prevailed: the road was built, Dover to Cohass (Durham, Barrington, Strafford ... to Haverhill), 100 miles, much of it only bridle path, and the towns were charged through a "Province Road Tax" levied on property holders—10 shillings per 100 acres.

Was this an early version of "home rule" controversies in which home rule lost? Not exactly. Siding with the towns, the governor and his Council (which included Portsmouth merchants with land investments) wanted the Province, not landowners, to pay for the road through towns where they owned much land. Gilmanton, for example, had the longest mileage on the new road, the steepest hills, and a lot of acreage held by the governor and his Portsmouth friends. By laying the tax on the landowners in the towns, the Assembly had also laid the tax on the governor—an opportunity not to be missed.

Nevertheless, Governor Wentworth was a doer, and road building was a thing to be done. The Indian wars were over, the interior was being settled rapidly, lines for supplies and surpluses were needed everywhere. So the "college road" was put through from Dartmouth via Plymouth to Wolfeboro; also the "Governor's road," 60 miles from Wolfeboro to the sea. A new road from Hanover through Concord to Portsmouth was started. A road—or at least a "road"—was put through Crawford Notch. In the early 1770s there was fortnightly mail service across the state from Hanover to Portsmouth. Indeed, the public roads promoted by Governor Wentworth just before the Revolution turned out to be of major importance for keeping the colony united during the Revolutionary War.

Turnpikes and Canals

In the burst of democratic enthusiasm following the War for

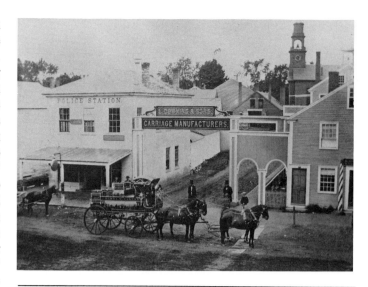

In 1813 Lewis Downing, wheelwright, advertised a Concord shop where he would sell "small waggons . . . as cheap as can be bought." From this beginning came the empire of the Concord Coach. In 1826 Downing hired J. Stephens Abbot, and the next year they formed a partnership. By 1830 they had perfected the design of the coach (distinguished by a flat top, rounded bottom and, most importantly, "thoroughbraces" which served as shock absorbers). In 1847 Abbot and Downing split: Abbot continued in the old shops, and Downing set up an operation elsewhere in Concord. Then in 1865 the two firms were rejoined and remained in partnership until the company closed in 1925. Through the years no other coach rivaled the Concord Coach, and the name of Abbot-Downing became known around the world. NHHS

In the summer of 1896 workmen began replacing the old covered bridge at Cornish with a modern steel bridge. At the New Hampshire end of this bridge over the Connecticut River, the steel span was already in place (far right) when this photograph was taken. The roof and siding of the old bridge were removed, exposing the heavy, wooden truss members held together by wooden pins. The unusual frame pictured here served as a crane and derrick in the rebuilding. NHHS

Above: Concord's Abbot-Downing Company was a big business when this picture was taken around 1890. At its height, the company employed about 250 men and turned out about 2,000 coaches and carriages annually, with sales throughout the United States, South America, and Australia. NHHS

Right: This snow roller packed roads in the Hanover area near the turn of the century. DCA

In this lithograph from the mid-19th century, a coach clatters from the "flats" toward the Free Bridge at Concord. Spring flooding made spanning of the Merrimack an expensive proposition: the bridge shown here was the third to be erected at the site. This approach to Concord off Interstate 93 is still called "Bridge Street." NHHS

Independence, it appeared to many that what the government had only halfheartedly achieved in the way of public road building could be swiftly accomplished by free enterprise. It was a venturesome thought, backed by conviction and energy, but not by evidence. Turnpike corporations were formed to build public roads, pay for them from tolls, and return a profit to the investors. By the time the plan had proved to be basically unprofitable, New Hampshire had a fair start on a public road system.

"Proprietors of New Hampshire Turnpike Road" incorporated themselves in 1796 to build a 36-mile road from the Piscataqua bridge, then under construction near Portsmouth, to the Merrimack near Concord, linking nine towns with an almost straight line. Other corporations formed quickly: for the Second New Hampshire Turnpike (Claremont to Amherst) and for the Third (Walpole via Keene to Massachusetts), both in 1799, and for the Fourth (Merrimack River at Boscawen to the Connecticut River at the White River), in 1800. Incorporation automatically conferred right of eminent domain along the proposed

routes. The company was typically empowered to lay out a road four rods wide on a route best combining "shortness of distance with the most practical ground" between the designated end points. Affected towns and the resident farmers almost never objected to their land being bisected by a turnpike—indeed there was usually competition for the honor. By law, toll rates were to be lowered if profits exceeded 12 percent. No problem.

Entrepreneurs of every sort immediately clambered aboard the turnpike bandwagon: 50 corporations were chartered by 1810. More were chartered during the next half-century, but after 1820 the early roads tended to lapse into public freeways.

about the same rate new ones were opened elsewhere. Parts of the First New Hampshire Turnpike, for example, were being sold to its host towns by 1824, and in 1821 Keene appropriated money to maintain its part of the Third New Hampshire Turnpike. Still, nearly 600 miles of road were constructed in New Hampshire by corporations. One such road, aslant Mt. Washington, still operates as a toll road, as it has for more than 100 years.

Though turnpikes brought poor returns for their investors, they were a boon to the farmers, for they diverted the flow of New Hampshire produce from the Connecticut River toward Boston markets. Farmers went to the seacoast with their own teams in the winter, carrying produce and returning with sleighs full of supplies. As the toll roads became town-owned freeways, public ownership conquering private enterprise, their use and value to enhance free trade increased.

By far the best highway in the state in the early 19th century was the Merrimack River. Before the first turnpike was started, men of Massachusetts were digging the Middlesex Canal from Charlestown, Massachusetts, to the Merrimack near Lowell. This kindled the dream of a direct Concord-to-Boston waterway—though of course only a fanatic would project a canal around the Amoskeag Falls. Judge Samuel Blodget, already past 70 years old, was the required New Hampshire fanatic: in 1793 he bought the land and started digging. Blodget, a noted inventor who had also developed coach lines, traveled through Europe, and raised sunken ships, built along the east bank of the Merrimack a novel system of locks which, when first tried in 1799, were promptly smashed to bits by the river current. Altogether he sank most of a fortune and 14 years of love and labor into the mile-long canal. The state finally authorized a lottery to help pay the bills, and Blodget lived to oversee the completion of the canal and to ride in triumph through the new locks on May Day, 1807. He died in heroic peace just a few months later.

It required, then, but a few short canals in Bow and Hooksett and there it was: a smooth highway from Boston, 85 miles into the heartland of New Hampshire at Concord. By 1815 traffic was heavy and getting heavier every year. The Boston and Concord Boating Company paid for the locks and paid dividends from 1826 to 1842. Long boats, 75 feet by 9 or 10 feet, were poled, two men to a boat, up and down the river, sometimes aided by a square sail, bringing supplies one way and produce the other. Typically, the trip was five days up and four days down. Granite from Concord was one of the main products—down the Merrimack River to all the major seaboard cities, day in, day out. By 1825 the industry of the capital city had given the state a nickname: the Granite State.

Floating the inland freight downstream to the cities on the sea—one is struck by the ageless simplicity and charm of the idea, just as one knows instantly that the Merrimack was finished as a highway as soon as the iron horse sauntered up the banks of the river in the 1840s. Daniel Webster, en route to Lebanon for that speech in 1847, would have glanced out the train window as he careened along at 30 miles per hour, would have watched the freight boats adrift on the Merrimack, and may have suddenly sensed how quaint were all the old ways and how extraordinary the new.

As the old shipping trade declined, most industry moved inland. By the middle of the 19th century, however, the Portsmouth wharves began to see new traffic. The inland transport of coal to the mills of Manchester and other towns began at Portsmouth, where great piles of coal were unloaded from coal packets onto waiting railroad cars, illustrated in this circa 1885 lithograph of the Concord Railroad Wharf. NHHS

At Portsmouth the Piscataqua passes to the sea under a lace of bridges that connect the harbor islands and bind New Hampshire (on the right), to Maine (on the left). Photograph by Bob LaPree. Courtesy, New Hampshire Times

CHAPTER
NINE

GETTING AROUND:
ROADS
AND TRACKS

Imagine the lucky citizens of Wakefield, New Hampshire, on January 8, 1833. Not only would they get to see one of their fellow citizens drawn about in a "Rail-road Car," but they would get a firsthand look at a machine which, according to this broadside, was capable of "annihilating distance" and "beautifying our little globe, which to a great extent, has so remained a moral waste." NHHS

Time was when the railroads filled that niche in the public imagination now occupied by super highways, jet airlines, and space travel—fantastic and routine at once.

At first only fantastic. A worn story, nearly forgotten a century ago, has an old-timer visiting the new railway station for his first glimpse of the enormous locomotive. It stands, big as a barn, 50 tons of iron and steel eating piles of hardwood, belching and hissing. Awestruck by the monster, the old-timer confides solemnly to his neighbor, "They'll never get it going." In due course the great iron horse roars out of the station, bells aclang, trailing clouds of smoke and flatcars, takes the bend at easy stride, and, fast as a racehorse, disappears beyond the hill. Old-timer shakes his hoary head and says, "They'll never get it stopped."

If the story died as a joke as railroads became routine, it survives as a metaphor. Who was to suppose in 1800 that the jagged New Hampshire landscape would be trussed up within the century in 1,000 miles of steely bars? How get something so fantastic going? When it was completed at century's end and railroads were *the* mode of transportation, it seemed a permanent achievement: a way of life was then in motion that one could hardly imagine being stopped. Fourteen hundred cars a day passed through Concord. It turned out to be even easier to stop than to start.

In New Hampshire railroad building began in the 1830s. The first railroad charter, granted in 1832, represented a grandiose pipe dream of the Boston and Ontario Railroad to connect Boston—and, incidentally, New Hampshire, Vermont, Massachusetts, and New York—to the Great Lakes. It was never built. In 1835 the first three effective charters were issued, and in 1838 the first trains crossed the southern border and entered Nashua. The charters of 1835 set the pattern for future development: they were independent lines, and in a few decades there were dozens of other railroad companies operating in the state, mostly short lines connected to other lines. Gradually the other lines bought or leased the short lines, as other short lines were built, and were then rapidly absorbed in turn. Just as with the toll roads 50 years earlier, local entrepreneurs wanted to get in on the action, and after a time they wanted to get out. In a few more decades there were essentially only two major companies operating all the lines. And then there was one. In 60 years the Boston & Maine had achieved a monopoly in New Hampshire.

Building Railroads

The first chartered lines of 1835 were these: the Nashua and Lowell Railroad (from Nashua to Lowell, Massachusetts), which opened in 1838; the Boston & Maine Railroad, which opened from Boston to Exeter in 1840, to Dover in 1845, and the next year got to Portland, Maine, by absorbing the Boston and Portland. The Concord Railroad Corporation opened its road on September 6, 1842, with the locomotive *Amoskeag* and three passenger cars roaring into Concord while cannons were fired in the background. It was a death knell for the Boston and Concord Boating Company, which paid no dividends after that year.

Fifteen miles of New Hampshire track in 1840 grew to 900 by 1870, and Concord was the central point in the developing system. From the capital city railroad lines reached toward the interior and through it to Vermont, Canada, and Maine, sometimes meeting other lines coming in. The Northern Railroad Company reached from Concord 69.5 miles to White River Junction; the Boston, Concord and Montreal Railroad went more directly north toward Canada. These lines and several others were chartered in 1844 within weeks after the legislature had temporarily settled the recurring question of what kinds of powers of eminent domain were to be granted to railroad companies. The first charters, which were essentially permissions granted by the legislature to build and operate railroads in the state, had not fully addressed the problem of how to get the farmers to permit the running of a railroad track through one man's back pasture, through his neighbor's potato patch, and past the third farmer's barn door—which was where the needed straight and level lines just happened to go. The people of Dorchester, in the west central part of the state, instructed their Representative in 1842 to "endeavor to prevent, if possible, so great a calamity to our farms as must be the location of any railroad passing through." The 1844 statute created a Board of Railroad Commissioners with power to authorize railroad land-taking and to determine compensation. This Board was a focus of politics for many generations and is the ancestor of today's Public Utilities Commission.

In 1848 the bridge across the Connecticut River at White River Junction was completed, Keene was connected to Boston and Peterborough was connected to Concord. So it went, year after year, farther north, farther inland. The White Mountain Railroad went to Littleton in 1853, and in the same year the Atlantic and St. Lawrence Company completed their line from Portland, Maine, to Island Pond, Vermont, slicing through 52 miles of northern New Hampshire.

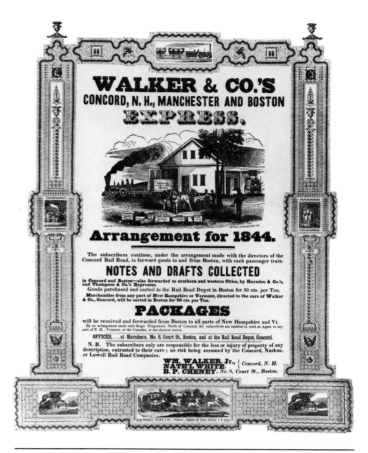

In 1844 the Walker Express offered to ship freight from Concord to Boston in one day instead of four for 50 cents per ton, a fraction of river freight cost. The broadside pictured is itself a work of art, the wood engraving in the center an early piece by the renowned engraver Henry Walter Herrick. Shown is the Concord railroad station, built in 1842 and replaced in 1847. The printing, including the virtuoso border, was the work of Morrill & Silsy, whose fancy print shop stood opposite the station. NHHS

Sylvester Marsh made his fortune in the Midwest processing and selling grain, but made headlines when he returned to his native New Hampshire to build a "cog railway" up the side of Mt. Washington. Born and raised in the "primitive environment" of a Campton hill farm, Marsh claimed never to have seen a wheeled vehicle until he was nine years old. Yet by 1869 he had designed and built one of the engineering marvels of his time, a two-and-a-half-mile railroad up the side of New England's highest peak, whose average grade was 1,300 feet per mile. NHHS

A car so crowded with excursionists (above) might test any locomotion, but ascent of Jacob's Ladder (above right) gave proof of Marsh's novel railway. Kilburn Brothers photographs, NHHS

It was not unusual to see a variety of Concord coaches pulling into Marshfield Station in the 1870s, each carrying a load of tourists bound for the train ride to the summit of Mt. Washington. Newspaper publisher and White Mountain aficionado Henry M. Burt described the rustic depot as "an ungainly, unclapboarded, three-story building with a tiny waiting room for passengers and bedrooms for the railway men." It was destroyed by fire in 1895. NHHS

Briefly, the Civil War quieted the railroad boom: it diverted the adventurous spirit of the state, depleted its manpower, and curtailed the textile industry by cutting off raw cotton supplies. But not for long. Before the war was over the railroad business was in full stride again. In 1869, the year the golden spike was driven in Promontory Point, Utah, to complete the transcontinental railroad, the Cog Railway, 2.5 miles to the top of Mt. Washington, was also completed. Together these events (both engineered by New Hampshire men: Sylvester Marsh of Campton designed the Cog Railway, and Samuel Montague of Keene was the chief engineer of the Central Pacific) seemed to certify the faith of the many who supposed that the nation's destiny, and New Hampshire's destiny in particular, was tied to the railroads.

The theory was that all this wondrous technological development would better country life. The fact was that the railroads eventually had the opposite effect. They hastened the breakup of the self-sustaining, community-based husbandry so effectively developed after the Revolutionary War, and the ironic side of progress was soon showing through.

In the 1870s, with 900 miles completed, the railroads kept sprouting and spreading. New Hampshire would be wrapped in rails, come hill or high water. Bridges, trestles, grades unthinkable in neighboring states, were built—if for no better reason than that they could be. Frank Jones, the Portsmouth brewer, adventurer, and politician, brewed up a plan to span Little Bay at Dover Point, and so it was done—with a spectacular 1,646-foot bridge, which opened in 1874. Surely such an achievement would never be superseded. For exactly 60 years it carried the freight and arched the skyline over the water that had borne the freight of an earlier generation. But a relentless logic was now loose in the land: just as the railways had put the inland waterways out of the transportation business, so the highways later would put the railways essentially out of it. In 1934 a parallel highway bridge opened, proclaiming the ascendency of cars and trucks, and the railway bridge across the bay was dismantled and stored away among heroic memories.

Also in the 1870s the railroads opened up the White Mountains: Boston had found a vacationland. Engineers had found a

stunt just as preposterous as putting a railroad up Mt. Washington or putting a freight train on a quarter-mile bridge over the Dover tides. The new idea, too exciting to resist, was to put a railroad right through the heart of the White Mountains, trestle over treetop, up through Crawford Notch. By 1875 it was done, the track rising more than 1,000 feet for the last nine miles on the ascent from Conway to the Crawford House.

Consolidating Tracks

When in the 1850s it had first become possible to travel by rail from Boston to Montreal, six changes of cars were required, for seven companies owned the rails. The "through ticket" had to be invented, but the bookkeeping was so complicated that mergers were not far behind. Sometimes companies merged when their lines joined; sometimes the company of the longer line leased the shorter line. Frequently a branch line was independently chartered and built, failed to turn a profit, and was absorbed by the main artery. Some unprofitable lines—Suncook to Candia, and North Weare to Henniker—were abandoned already before the Civil War. By the early 1880s, with over 1,000 miles of track within the state, charters had been granted to 108 different companies, 35 of which were then in operation, many only as lessors.

Mergers, leases, sales, recharterings, and other complicated adjustments were an inevitable part of this curious kind of "noncompetitive" free enterprise. Competition there was, of course, but two sets of tracks were rarely laid parallel along the same run to compete for the public's business. There *were* competitive routes, Portland to Boston, and Manchester to Boston. But for the most part competition assumed darker forms, involving talents such as these: lobbying the legislature for special favors; anticipating traffic flow and controlling it by pricing; exploiting monopoly situations; extracting subsidies from towns for tracks to their doors; attracting Boston investment capital; cajoling stockholders; and generally exploiting the "double your money" mentality of those with loose cash to invest. All the high spirits

Above left: The Portland & Ogdensburg Railroad through Crawford Notch offered spectacular views of the White Mountains. Frankenstein Trestle, shown here in 1878, was one of the high points of the trip. Guidebook author Moses F. Sweetser described the trestle in 1879: "For 500 feet the line is thus suspended in mid-air, sustained by the spidery network of striding piers, yet as firm and secure as if it rested on a prairie of mid-Iowa." NHHS

Above center: The "gate" of Crawford Notch had to be widened in the 1870s to make room for the Portland & Ogdensburg Railroad. In this photo from a B.W. Kilburn stereograph circa 1880, the famous Crawford House is visible in the background. The P&O served primarily as a tourist railroad, taking sightseers through the Notch to the hotels beyond. NHHS

Above right: Another highlight of the P&O excursion through Crawford Notch was the trip across the Willey Brook Trestle. Mt. Webster looms in the background of this 1880s B.W. Kilburn photograph. NHHS

and middling motives of speculative capitalism and boosterism went into the laying and consolidating of rails.

Within the spreading web of the rail network, the New Hampshire countryside was irrevocably changed. Butter and eggs were suddenly going fresh to market each day; bulky produce like potatoes now had a city market; locomotives were browsing cordwood from the hillsides so greedily that woodcutters could make a good living. For a time it all looked like progress. What was happening was that a secure and self-sustaining husbandry was becoming a market-based agriculture, with all its vulnerabilities. Beneath that impressive fact was the further fact that bringing to the countryside factory-made goods of every sort, from socks to hayrakes to horse collars, at prices below those at the local mills, systematically laid waste a thousand small village manufactories—but slowly, so it was hard to tell just what was

happening. Even so, most towns directly tapped by railroads
flourished for a time, even while their neighbors didn't. A
further fact, inscrutable and profound, was that the railroads
brought contact with the outside world, and with that grew ideas
of an alternative life in the big city with a regular pay check, or
life in the Midwest on farmland known to be smooth, deep, rich,

In this circa 1925 photograph the
horse-drawn dump truck is still
necessary for repairing the streets in
Lisbon, although the streets themselves are evidently being readied for
automobiles. NHHS

Function and flair are sometimes blended in New Hampshire roadside architecture. This Manchester Esso Station was a well-known landmark when it was photographed in the early 1950s. Photograph by Laurier Durrette. Courtesy, Gerald Durrette.

and cheap. Everything tangible and intangible in the life of the New Hampshire countryside was eventually touched by the railroad.

The End of the Line

Were there pots of gold at the ends of the tracks? Only for the few. Building railroads may have been an engineering adventure, but running and consolidating them was an adventure of politics and business tycoons. The major tracks having been laid, the drama shifted from engineering to economics and power politics. By the late 1880s buying, leasing, and merging had, practically speaking, narrowed the field to the two companies which always had the best routes, the Concord Railroad through the state's midsection and the Boston & Maine along its coast.

The Concord Railroad Corporation made money from its beginnings. Its track, running along the level banks of the Merrimack, had been built inexpensively. It had strong feeder lines from northern and western New England, and the granite quarries of Concord themselves originated a considerable freight traffic. Twenty-two hundred flatcars of granite went from Concord to Washington, D.C., to build the Library of Congress. With all the business it could handle, this line had more profits, quite literally, than it knew what to do with. Since developing equitable taxes on profits was beyond the skills or the will of the heavily lobbied legislature, and since lowering the freight rates was beyond the imagination of the owners, there was little to do to relieve the cash problem but to drastically overpay the owners and executives of the railroad.

In one sense the high point of the railroad business in New

Hampshire came only after the Boston & Maine Railroad had achieved a monopoly—in the 1890s and thereafter. Additional track was laid each year, though at a slower pace, until 1920, when there were 1,250 miles in use within the state. But by that time both the drama and the grosser forms of politics had been drained from the network, and the railroad had become a routine form of transportation, suffering increasing competition from the trucking industry. In 1905 a state highway department was created, and the first 125 miles of state roads were adopted. Within a decade 10 cross-state roads had been marked out as state highways, and the annual railroad reports were alluding to competition from motor trucks. By the 1920s New Hampshire was firmly committed to a regular state highway construction program and, inadvertently, the railroads were sent down the long road to ruin.

Gone forever were the days just a generation earlier when the Concord Railroad Corporation had entertained itself by tearing down and building railroad stations in Concord. The fourth and last of these, constructed in 1885 in the grand style of that transient species, was a transportation station befitting a capital city: in 1900, 25 passenger trains left that Concord station daily. The structure served its city well, adding a tincture of nobility to the slightly wild capitalism of that era, and it stood thereafter, when railroad passengers had wandered away, as a fitting monument to an age that was gone, awaiting some other form of service. It was not to be. After the highways and trucks had bankrupted the Boston & Maine Railroad, this fine old building was beaten to dust with a wrecker's ball and buried beneath a shopping mall. An era had ended.

New Hampshire tourism, which relies on the natural beauty of the state, does not always promote beautiful roadways, evidenced by these billboards from the early 1960s. Photograph by John Karol. SPNHF

CHAPTER
TEN

MAKING THINGS: DEVELOPING INDUSTRIES

Had you been shopping for a fire engine between 1859 and 1877, you might have taken note of this ad displaying the various products of the Amoskeag Manufacturing Company's subsidiary, the Amoskeag Steam Fire Engine Works. During its 18 years the company turned out 550 fire engines, selling them in the United States, Canada, South America, England, Russia, Japan, China, and even as far away as Australia. NHHS

In the early 19th century textile mills in New Hampshire were mostly woolen mills, though Londonderry had been producing Irish linen since the middle of the 18th century. Benjamin Pritchard erected a small mill on the west bank of the Merrimack River in 1805 near where Samuel Blodget was digging his canal around the Amoskeag Falls. The mill was incorporated as the Amoskeag Cotton and Woollen Manufacturing Company in 1810, the same year Derryfield was renamed Manchester in what seemed an absurd imitation of the great English textile manufacturing city. In the 1820s sizeable textile mills were developed in Dover, Somersworth, Nashua, and Exeter—while Manchester remained a typical small town with a typical mill on a rather atypical site.

The site caught the eye of Boston entrepreneurs who assumed control of the mill in the 1830s, reincorporated as the Amoskeag Manufacturing Company, and started building on both sides of the river. Nothing was typical after that. A huge mill complex and a supporting city (modeled roughly on Lowell, Massachusetts) was laid out on paper, and in less than two decades was transferred to the countryside. Millions of bricks were made in Hooksett—Thoreau, who was there, reports this—and floated down the Merrimack to build Manchester (incorporated as a city in 1846) and its mills. An early branch of the textile company started producing locomotives and steam fire engines. Later, in the 1860s, a new company, Manchester Locomotive Works, took over production of steam engines, and soon the flatcars that took Concord coaches to the West were being pulled by Manchester locomotives. Indeed, between 1850 and 1900 the new city produced steam locomotives and steam fire engines at a rate of nearly one a week—a kind of local sideshow to the main business of Manchester. The main business was cotton cloth.

By 1851 Amoskeag textiles were winning prizes in England's Crystal Palace exhibition; in a few more decades the mills of Manchester, New Hampshire, had surpassed those of its namesake—in size, number of employees, and production. By the turn of the 20th century (when several nearby mills had been consolidated with the Amoskeag) New Hampshire claimed the largest set of textile mills in the world: a stunning mile-long brick row along both sides of the Merrimack River, employing as many as 17,000 workers and turning out cotton fabric at a mile-a-minute clip from 24,000 looms.

The Amoskeag mills lasted just a century—the 1830s to the 1930s. Their creation was a great industrial adventure and their demise was a great economic disaster. During that century the headquarters were in Boston and the board members and shareholders were mostly Bostonians. Though the mills were managed by a hired New Hampshire agent (three generations of the Straw family during one long stretch), the real boss was the Boston-based treasurer of the board, through whose hands passed all the important company decisions.

The Triumph of Amoskeag

In the early mill years, the 1840s, most of the mill operatives were girls from rural New England. Following the Lowell pattern, the Amoskeag company built special housing for the operatives—substantial brick and hardwood structures, some of which are still standing—and sent its agents throughout the state to recruit girls. The mills offered farm and village girls an ambiguously attractive life: secure work in a protective environment, the taste of independence that comes from earning one's own wages, a benign community of one's own kind, life in the city, long hours of regimented work, but also an escape from the boredom of remote hill towns. And the girls came—not only daughters of farmers but daughters of the middle class, too. In the 1840s, 1850s, and 1860s, they came not only to Manchester, but also to Nashua, Dover, Somersworth, and Exeter, where mills offered similar working and living arrangements. Some girls worked to finance a brother's education, or to save for their own; some to support aging parents or to pay off a family mortgage. Many worked in the mills only part of the year, returning to their home villages for the summer work or to teach school. For most, the years in the mill were an interim between school and marriage.

By the 1850s the mills required larger cadres of workers, and waves of foreign immigrants headed for Manchester. First came the Irish families, fleeing the desperation that followed the potato famines in their homeland; Swedes, Germans, and Scots added their skills; then French Canadians were recruited and guided down the new railways from Montreal to set up a new life in Manchester. Later came Greeks and Poles. The Amoskeag mills provided jobs for the whole family, including children. There were 750,000 humming spindles to be tended.

As the recruiting of immigrant families became established policy, various additional paternalist structures were developed: the company providing conveniences and acquiring loyalty in return. By the early 20th century welfare and social programs of all kinds were taken for granted. The mill community had its tex-

The Great Falls Manufacturing Company, founded in 1823, made Somersworth one of New England's leading textile manufacturing centers in the early 19th century. In 1830 Somersworth was New Hampshire's fifth-largest community, surpassing the future manufacturing centers of Nashua and Manchester in population. This engraving of the company's Mill Number One (right) and Mill Number Two (left) was probably made about 1835, prior to the arrival of the Boston & Maine Railroad. Unfortunately, this otherwise excellent look at an early New England textile factory is backwards. NHHS

The Amoskeag Manufacturing Company was almost a society unto itself with its own clubs, social life, athletic teams, newspaper, and educational efforts. Although this 1916 issue of the semi-monthly Bulletin *reported that the "English Class is Going Good," it was apparently not going quite so well as it might have. NHHS*

tile club, shooting club, baseball team, cooking school, workers' playground, visiting nurse service, company picnics, musical shows, rental privileges in corporation apartments, language classes, concerts, and a company newspaper, the *Amoskeag Bulletin.* Workers and management became bound in a common *esprit,* carefully nurtured by managers, usually accepted with gratitude by the workers. In Manchester itself the different ethnic groups congregated in their own communities: the melting pot was the mills and whatever was allied with them.

For a long time it worked extremely well: raw cotton was cheap, transportation was convenient, production was high, the market for gingham and calico was good. Workers were not notably dissatisfied; if they were, there was not much to do with their dissatisfaction: there was no point in going back to Poland. The Industrial Revolution took a heavier human toll in England's Manchester than in New Hampshire's, but it took a toll here too. The hours were atrocious: 11 hours a day, six days a week, was normal as of the 1860s, and child labor was simply taken for granted. Company profits accruing to the absentee owners were always substantial, sometimes enormous, and during World War I extravagant even by wartime standards.

Opposite page: Photographer Lewis Hine captured images of Americans at work from around 1905 to 1930. The conditions that Hines' work documented made a nation self-conscious and helped lead to some reforms. Hines' photographs of children at work—like these two from the Amoskeag millyards (top) and the workers' district of Manchester (bottom) in 1909—helped to change child labor laws. From the Manchester Collection (MC), UNH

The Amoskeag Millyard complex, looking south from the Notre Dame Bridge in Manchester, is pictured in 1980. Photograph by Gary Samson

The Amoskeag strikers dramatized their cause with a parade across the Merrimack River on April 10, 1922. MVHC

Opposite page: In 1860 Concord streets were already lighted with Concord-made gas. The handsome round brick gasholder on the right was built in 1888 and stored gas until 1957. In the foreground—partially shielded by trees—are some of the outbuildings where gas, tar, and coke were made from coal until 1952. The original gasholder and its indescribable modern successor on the left, built in 1921, operate on the same principle: a heavy steel tank in tracks holds the gas and with its own weight applies the pressure that discharges the gas into the mains and throughout the city. The old gasholder had a complex water seal system and the building was designed to protect the tank and seal from the elements. Though the 1938 hurricane knocked the cupola askew, the building remains the only completely intact gasholder of its kind in the country. Photograph by Gary Samson

The Fall of the Amoskeag

Wartime profits were barely banked when disaster loomed. Relatively high wages, old machinery, excessive production capacity, and Southern competition all pushed the New Hampshire mills from the wartime high to an early version of the Great Depression. Three significant events occurred, and that was the end.

First, in 1922 the Amoskeag company abruptly announced an increase in working hours from 48 to 54 hours per week and a corresponding 20-percent cut in wages. Thousands of workers, by now unionized and united, were immediately alienated from the company which they and their parents had proudly identified with for all their lives. There followed a major strike, lasting nine months and leaving economic and moral wounds that never healed. There were similar strikes for similar reasons in other New Hampshire mill towns.

Second, in 1925 the board of the Amoskeag Manufacturing Company transferred to another corporate entity—the Amoskeag Company, an investment corporation with nearly the same board members—$18 million in assets drawn from company profits. Judgments differ about the meaning of this maneuver. One line of thought offers the blunt verdict that "they took the money and ran," and emphasizes the unwillingness of the parent company to invest in retooling antiquated machinery and in new marketing strategies—the money having been invested instead, through the new corporation, in Southern

textile mills. The other line of thought sees the transactions as an astute business move in the face of the inevitable decline of New England textile milling. At any rate, the parent manufacturing company was economically much weakened, though the severity of the problem was not then evident to the public. What was evident by the late 1920s was that textile mills throughout New England generally were in trouble, and with them most of the New England economy.

The third event (foreseeable from Boston but not foreseen in New Hampshire) was the sudden closing of the Amoskeag mills in 1935, coupled with a promise to reorganize and reopen. Instead of reopening, the Amoskeag Manufacturing Company was ordered to liquidate assets under the bankruptcy law. Nearly 11,000 people in Manchester were jobless, and the economic base of the city was destroyed. (The investment corporation thrived: in the 1970s it had controlling interest in a large Northern railroad and a large Southern textile mill, and though no longer incorporated in New Hampshire, its assets in 1980 totalled more than $80 million.)

A group of Manchester citizens formed Amoskeag Industries to salvage the mills. Public Service Company of New Hampshire bought the electrical plant and, thus financially fortified, Amoskeag Industries borrowed money, bought the mill buildings, and began luring new and smaller businesses to occupy the vast spaces. World War II gave the project a boost and by the late 1940s there were a hundred businesses in the buildings where the Amoskeag mills had been.

All the hardy drama of the Industrial Revolution is to be found in the career of the Amoskeag Manufacturing Company, and all its moral ambiguities too: the story is exhilarating and depressing in turn, and even rather awesome in its full dimensions. Like the Boston & Maine Railroad, Amoskeag was, for the state of New Hampshire, a fatally flawed partner in progress. The company itself roared out of nowhere into the bucolic New Hampshire countryside with eager and vital energy; it burned with a furious and often equivocal glow for a full century; and then it crashed headlong into the Great Depression to sink from sight forever. Echoes linger to this day in poignant published reminiscences, of those who lost jobs at the mills many years ago.

If our old parents, who worked so much in these mills, if they'd come back today and see how these mills are, it would really break their hearts.

Other textile mills in dozens of other New Hampshire cities and towns followed somewhat similar patterns, though none of them had the size or dramatic contours of the Amoskeag story.

CHAPTER
ELEVEN

LUMBER, TOURISTS, AND TECHNOLOGY

Ben Houston's sawmill in Barnstead, photographed in 1905, was typical of the portable steam sawmills found in most New Hampshire towns during the first half of the 20th century. Courtesy, William R. Brickett

Opposite page: Two aspects of New Hampshire's North Country are juxtaposed in this late 1970s photograph: the majestic Presidential Range in the background, and the James River Corporation mills of Berlin in the foreground. The former symbolizes the state's natural beauty, the latter New Hampshire's industrial base. Continuing the symbolism in this world of mergers, ownership of the James River Corporation (formerly the Brown Company, formerly the Berlin Mills Company) went to Crown-Vantage Corporation in 1995 and to Pulp and Paper of America in 1999. Photo by Bob LaPree. Courtesy, New Hampshire Times

During the half-century of the most rapid development of the New Hampshire manufacturing industry—roughly 1840 to 1890—the state's agriculture was completely transformed. First the frontiers disappeared (so far as tillable land was concerned), and the railroads created upheavals in the rural economy; then the cities growing round the manufacturing centers siphoned the youth from the land; to thousands of others the call of the West and of far horizons proved irresistible. Trains that brought New Englanders to Indiana and Wisconsin returned with reaper-harvested grain that sold in Concord more cheaply than the scythe-harvested grain grown in Merrimack County. Some said that instead of grain they might better import soil from the West. In a hundred rural New Hampshire towns, the population dropped steadily decade after decade.

Portable Sawmills

By the 1870s one could take a train to Michigan and find employment for a dollar a day and decent land for a dollar and a half per acre. Why fight rocks in New Hampshire? Meadows lapsed to pastures, and pastures relapsed to young pine seedlings. During the last half of the 19th century a new crop of timber was growing swiftly to maturity on thousands of acres of abandoned farmland in southern New Hampshire. Inevitably, the farms that remained and remained successful were oriented not so much to rural self-sufficiency as toward markets—milk for Boston, potatoes for the entire East Coast, wool for the mills, and lumber for the cities.

Thus the stage was set: the abandoned farm and the portable sawmill—two memorable New Hampshire symbols moving in tandem across the historical landscape. The settlers of the first generation cleared the land, walled it, and farmed it; their sons and grandsons relinquished it, and *their* sons harvested lumber from it once again.

With their massive steel boilers and powerful circular saws, portable sawmills were exciting contraptions, and they easily eclipsed the small water-powered mills that had straddled the streams for a hundred years. From about 1880 to 1950 the new mills were a kind of moveable fixture in the countryside. A mill operator with his small band of "rounders" (woodsmen who went round from mill to mill) would set up shop on a favorable spot for a year or more, hire additional local hands and teams and then, when supplies were exhausted, would move on to the next town. Since growing timber was taxed at market value until 1949, there was tremendous incentive to sell to the mill operators.

The efficiency of these operations soon raised eyebrows. Joseph B. Walker, president of the State Board of Agriculture and descendent of the Reverend Timothy Walker, wrote that when "a portable sawmill locates in a forest, it is liable to consume all the trees around it for a mile or more, every one of them." Forty bushels of sawdust poured out of a mill for each 1,000 feet of lumber; and mills located, said the 1889 Fish and Game Commission *Report,* "so as to run the refuse into some stream to avoid the bother to take care of it. The greatest injury to our streams by mill refuse is the destruction of the spawning beds and young fry." That had been a New Hampshire rivermouth problem for 200 years: the difference was that it was now happening further up streams, in trout pools and bass ponds.

As portable sawmills multiplied, so did worries concerning them—worries about tax laws that encouraged clear cutting, about the appearance of cutover hillsides, about sawdust, about fires in the slashing. Every Arbor Day elicited public pleas to choppers to spare seed trees. So it went—on into the 20th century.

Stern economic facts had to be weighed against the qualms. The portable sawmill came to the hillsides during a period of prolonged rural decline, and between 1880 and World War II New Hampshire rural communities needed an economic cushion, needed ways to ease the transition to a more varied economy. The cushion came from the woods first of all, for even in the worst of times there were logs to saw, maple trees to tap, and markets for the products: employment for man and team in winter and early spring. Best of all, the crops renewed themselves naturally and time healed the scars on the hills. In dozens of New Hampshire communities the lumber business, although marginal, held disaster at bay. Inadvertently, the forests that crept back to the fields from the inaccessible slopes and valleys to which the first settlers had driven them, had created there a hedge against hard times.

North Country Lumber

Meanwhile, the Industrial Revolution itself—having transformed the countryside and having built cities at Manchester, Nashua, Concord, Somersworth, and Dover—invaded New Hampshire's North Country.

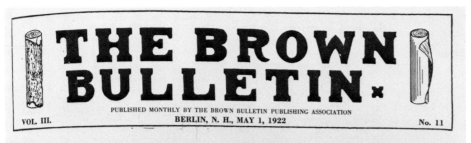

THE BROWN BULLETIN

PUBLISHED MONTHLY BY THE BROWN BULLETIN PUBLISHING ASSOCIATION

BERLIN, N. H., MAY 1, 1922

VOL. III.   No. 11

Left: Throughout the 20th century, the industrial giant of New Hampshire's North Country has been Berlin. The Berlin Mills Company began making paper in 1888, and in the years before World War I operated the world's largest chemical pulp mill. (In 1917 the company changed its title to the Brown Company, casting off the name of the capital city of America's wartime enemy.) NHHS

Opposite page, top: In July 1919 the Brown Company began publishing The Brown Bulletin, *which documented social life, sports, company news, and other items of general interest in the company town. NHHS*

Above: In the 1920s untold numbers of pulpwood logs found their way down the Androscoggin River to Brown Company mills. The logs were cut from company-owned lands totaling about 6,000 square miles— an area somewhat larger than the state of Connecticut. By the Brown Company's standards, the amount of lumber pictured is quite small. NHHS

"The North Country"—it stretches from the southern edge of the White Mountain National Forest northward, to encompass essentially the entire upper half of the state: all of Coös County, and most of Grafton and Carroll as well. It is 2.5 million acres of forest land and a few thousand acres of farmland, and its population hovers around 150,000, about 15 percent of the state's. Only a small percentage of the timber in this land had been harvested before the Civil War—along the Connecticut river on the west and along the Androscoggin River and Lake Umbagog on the east—but once serious lumbering began in the North Country, it accelerated swiftly.

Several things made these northern timber operations possible, probably inevitable. The first was the transfer of large tracts of public timberland into the hands of private corporations: lumbering was now to be not just an individual but a corporate business. Another was the railroad—to the lumberman a double blessing in that it provided access to markets at one end and access to the remote valleys at the other. The Atlantic and St. Lawrence line, for example, reached north from Berlin to the otherwise inaccessible regions of North Stratford in 1853; on the other hand, spur lines from main tracks could poke into a dozen remote valleys where the rivers had been too steep or swift or small to ferry the logs. At last the loggers could take genuine satisfaction from Ethan Allen's maxim that even God

cannot make two ranges of mountains without a valley between. The third fact was the development, after 1880, of papermaking processes from pulpwood, which itself transformed the northern timber industry. Trees once disdained as too small for lumber were now salvaged for paper: entire mountains of spruce that might have been left were swept into the pulpwood mills.

In the beginning of the 20th century, when the world's largest textile mills were operating full tilt in Manchester, the world's largest newsprint paper mills were operating full tilt some hundred miles north in Berlin. The northern "infinite thick woods" of earliest legend were being thinned at last.

Many elements combined to make 1907 a notable year in the annals of the New Hampshire timber industry: the science and the technology of papermaking had been fully developed; railroad spurs and reached into most of the wooded valleys; the legislature had not yet seriously restricted either railroading or timber cutting; the first pine growth on the pasturelands of southern New Hampshire had come to maturity; and the technology and economy of portable steam sawmill operations had been worked out. 1907 was the all-time record year for timber harvesting in New Hampshire.

Toward the end of the 20th century there were more acres

Above: The city of Berlin, home of the Brown Company, was photographed early in the 1920s. NHHS

Opposite page: Whitefield was the lumber capital of New Hampshire at the end of the 19th century. When this picture of the city was taken in the early 20th century, small concerns like the Whitefield Manufacturing Company, shown here, still operated as sawmills, and in this case, also as a manufacturer of bobbins for the state's textile mills. A lone employee was photographed surrounded by logs in 1925. Courtesy, Forest Service, White Mountain National Forest, U.S. Department of Agriculture

of woodland in New Hampshire than at any time in the previous 200 years, and more professional foresters per acre than in any other state. Besides several hundred thousand cords of pulpwood, several hundred million board feet of lumber were harvested each year—less than the annual new growth and also less than the normal harvest a generation or two ago. Seventy-five thousand or more gallons of maple syrup also came from the woodlands each year, also less than a couple of generations ago. But forests remained a major economic resource, in addition to being a great treasure of botanical, biological, aesthetic, and recreational diversity.

Hotels, Farms, Tourists

A very different kind of influence upon the New Hampshire economy came from the tourist industry. Like the lumbering industry, tourism once meant different things to different regions of the state. In the North Country, in and around the White Mountains, the principal symbol and locus of the tourist industry was the "grand hotel"—elegant structures in mountainous settings that catered to the well-born, the well-connected, and the well-heeled.

The first tourist stops in the North Country, well established already by the 1840s, were simple inns, and the most famous of them were run by the Crawfords in the notch that bears their name. These taverns were superseded in the 1850s by much larger establishments. In the last half of the 19th century dozens of major hotels were built in the North Country, confirming the

White Mountains as the major recreation area of the Northeast, a role they have increasingly occupied ever since.

Whereas the earliest taverns had been accessible only to coach or foot travelers, the grand hotels were built for the railroad era. Each of the major establishments, such as Crawford House, Fabyan House, Profile House, The Maplewood, The Waumbek, The Glen House, had its own train station or livery service, and its own versions of comfort and elegance: gas lighting, fancy dining, lawn tennis, coaching parades, mountain guides. Each of the above houses—the largest among many others—had a guest capacity of 400 or more, each was built entirely of wood, and each was eventually destroyed by fire. The last to be built of the truly grand hotels, one of the largest and one of the few still operating today, is the Mount Washington in Bretton Woods. It opened in 1902, in an era when New York corporate executives commonly sent their families to the White Mountains for the summer months and trained in to visit them on weekends. Presidents and foreign dignitaries came too—a way of seeing America. Mrs. Pullman came each summer in her own private railroad car.

By the beginning of the 20th century the recreation industry was well underway in the southern part of the state as well, actively promoted by state officials. In a few areas of the south— the seacoast, the Jaffrey-Peterborough-Dublin areas, the Cornish-Plainfield regions—summer visitors had been present in substantial numbers as soon as the railroads came. But around

the turn of the century the "summer industry," as it was called took on major economic significance and, outside cities, i formed a place beside lumbering and dairying as one of the three or four staples of the rural economy. While White Mountain tourism was primarily sponsored by Eastern seaboard money and catered to people of means, tourism in the south, with some few notable exceptions, was more a middle-class phenomenon Hotels began to show up on the edges of village greens in dozen of small hill towns.

The summer industry was welcome in rural New Hampshire where the last decades of the 19th century had been depressing The journals of that day regularly carried articles whose titles are indicative: "A Good Farm for Nothing" (1899); "The Decadence of New England" (1890); "The Deserted Homes of New England" (1893); "The Doom of the Small Town" (1895) "The Rural School Problem" (1896); and dozens more. In 188 the New Hampshire Department of Agriculture produced a booklet titled *Price List of Abandoned Farms in New Hampshire* This represented a break with past policy—which had indulged the pretense that nothing was wrong with New Hampshire farm ing that a little Yankee resolution could not cure. The aim wa now to advertise the fact, throughout the country and abroad that cheap farms were available in New Hampshire. In 1891 new booklet bore the upbeat title: *Secure a Home in New Hampshire—Where Comfort Health and Prosperity Abound;* it listed an described farms for sale town by town. In that same year a New

Above: Plymouth's second and most famous Pemigewasset House was built in 1863 by the Boston, Concord, & Montreal Railroad. Pictured in a John H. Bufford lithograph shortly after it opened for business, the Pemigewasset House became a favorite resting place for tourists on their way to the White Mountains. It was here that Nathaniel Hawthorne died in 1864 while traveling to the mountains with his old college friend Franklin Pierce. The hotel burned in 1908. NHHS

Opposite page: The Notch House, located just to the north of the gate of Crawford Notch, was built by the Crawford family in 1828 and run by Thomas Crawford until it burned in 1854. This particular print appeared in the book American Scenery *(1840) and is based on a drawing by William H. Bartlett. NHHS*

Left: The 1893 Baedeker guide informed potential tourists to the White Mountains that hotels varied "from the large and fashionable summer caravan-serais down to small, unassuming, and inexpensive inns and boarding houses." The writer especially praised "the waiting of the students (male and female) at some of the larger hotels." The starched staff of Fabyans line up to receive guests circa 1895. NHHS

Late each summer throughout the 1880s and 1890s, hotels in the White Mountains sent their decorated entries to the Bethlehem Coach Parade. Gaudily dressed Concord Coaches, pulled by gaudily clad teams of matching horses, made their way up and down Bethlehem's main street to the sound of bands, coach horns, and the applause of passengers and spectators. NHHS

These four unidentified gentlemen, photographed around 1910, were guests at the Crawford House. Bridle paths for sure-footed burros were common throughout the White Mountains. NHHS

Above: Salt haze and languid air are fused in a summer day at Wallis Sands, circa 1890. New Hampshire's coast on the Atlantic is just short of 18 miles. But the attraction of the beach has been no less because of its brevity. By the third quarter of the 19th century cottages and grand hotels on the beach were catering to a major tourist trade; and with the advent of the automobile, daytrippers began to come as well. Courtesy, John P. Adams

Left: There are various kinds of "camps" in New Hampshire's past. Along with military camps, church camps, children's summer camps, and sportsmen's camps of various descriptions, there were the lakeside summer camps to which urban Americans migrated annually. Harry Jones' cottage on Sewall's Point, Wolfeboro, was typical of many lakeside camps in 1908. From the Wolfeboro Collection. UNH

Hampshire woman, Kate Sanborn, wrote a how-to book, *Adopting an Abandoned Farm*. The book sold well, but not quite so well as did her next book, *Abandoning an Adopted Farm*.

The emblem of the new summer business became Old Home Week—instituted by Governor Frank Rollins in 1899. He caught the nostalgia then adrift in the New Hampshire air and focused it upon a simple and seductive idea: spruce up the town and invite the wandering sons and daughters back to the villages for a week of remembrance and celebration of rural values; they may reclaim an interest in their roots, may even buy up the family homestead before it falls down, perhaps endow a school or library or put up a cottage on the pond. After all, it was an era when nearly everyone—the president of Harvard and the captains of industry included—was making the most of the fact that he too had been schooled in a village and reared on a farm, sprung from the communities of virtue.

It worked extremely well. Hotels, inns, and guest houses

The automobile brought a new class of tourist to New Hampshire's White Mountains in the years after the First World War. This group from Connecticut is in Franconia Notch viewing the Old Man of the Mountains. NHHS

cropped up; farmhouses were remodeled into guest houses. Many towns of 500 people listed a half-dozen guest houses in the *Guide* Rollins published in 1902, and many other farm families made it a practice to take in city guests, a week or two at a time, during the summer. The New Hampshire Department of Agriculture started to sponsor "workshops" on how to attract and serve the summer guests. In 1925 the state legislature first appropriated money ($25,000) for publicizing the attractions of the state for tourists. A few years later the state began publishing booklets, such as the 1930 *New Hampshire by Motor*. Such publications were more successful than those of an earlier generation, which had tried to rescue the abandoned farms by attracting immigrants to the hill country.

Since the beginning of the 20th century tourism has been a central element in the state's economy, though the coming of the automobile changed its forms significantly. The grand hotels of the north began dying out slowly early in the century—as soon as automobiles in numbers reached the mountains. A few carried on the grand tradition: the Mount Washington in Bretton Woods, the Balsams in Dixville Notch and, until quite recently, the Mountain View House in Whitefield and even faraway Wentworth-by-the-Sea in New Castle. The latter two closed for business in the 1980s, but both have very recently developed restoration plans (or at least hopes) for the 21st century. Elsewhere in the state the guest house tradition lasted until the 1930s, and after World

Above: Recreational skiers are shown on Mt. Moosilauke in the 1930s. Mt. Moosilauke has a special place in the history of skiing in America. On March 12, 1933, the Mt. Moosilauke Carriage Road was used for the first U.S. National Downhill Championship. Of the 80 contestants, only 69 finished the 2.8-mile course. DCA

Left: The first Dartmouth Winter Carnival in 1911 not only began a proud tradition in Hanover, but helped to popularize the little-known sport of skiing in the United States. Pictured are students who won prizes in the various competitions of that first year. In the center of the front row and wearing the Dartmouth sweater is Fred Harris, a founder of both the Winter Carnival and the Dartmouth Outing Club. From Fred Harris, Dartmouth Out O'Doors, *1913*

War II the overnight motel became ubiquitous.

By the end of the 20th century tourism was growing apace. Officially, 25 million visitor trips are counted per year by the Institute of New Hampshire Studies, which monitors tourism for the Department of Resources and Economic Development. The total impact of visitor spending on the state's economy runs in the billions and as recently as 1998 contributed 8.4 percent of the gross state product. For addi-

By the middle of the 19th century and for long thereafter granite quarrying at Concord was a major industry, employing at times more men (and more oxen) than any other Concord industry aside from the railroad. NHHS

It is midnight and the idyllic New Hampshire landscape and coastline are out of sight. This is Seabrook, when round-the-clock crews were building the nuclear power plant—the largest, most costly, and most controversial project ever undertaken in the Granite State. Photograph by Bob LaPree. Courtesy, New Hampshire Times

tional reasons, New Hampshire finds this convenient: a nine percent tax on rooms and meals has been thoughtfully arranged by the legislature for visitors, and the state liquor monopoly has placed its stores conveniently near all the state's entrances and exits. If there have been times, long ago, when New Hampshire wealth was systematically drained down into Massachusetts through the Boston and Maine Railroad, there are also times when New Hampshire ingenuity siphons Massachusetts cash up the turnpikes into Granite State coffers.

Tourism is seasonal, but it occupies most of the seasons. Summer or winter the White Mountains as well as the Lakes Region, meaning mainly Lake Winnipesaukee, are the main attractions. In autumn, as the foliage colors seep southward from Canada, streams of sightseers edge northward from Boston, and in early October they meet on schedule in the byways and notches of the White Mountains in some of the most scenically positioned traffic jams known to modern civilization.

Mid-Century and After

Different manufacturing industries have jostled each other for supremacy in the New Hampshire economy of the 20th century. In 1920 the manufacturing field was led by textiles, which employed 40,000 workers; the leather industries, shoemaking in particular, occupied second position. Many New Hampshire cities—Manchester, Nashua, Rochester, Dover—had developed major shoe factories in the late 19th century, and leather overtook textiles in the late 1930s. By 1955 the order was leather goods, textiles, and paper products, with the Brown Company, a timber and paper firm, the largest single employer in the state.

Very soon, however, beginning already in the 1950s, the growth areas of the state's economy went to metal products and electronics, and the areas of decline were in the traditional and indigenous industries. The woolen industry, lumber and wood products, food production, textiles generally, paper and allied products, leather goods—these all employed fewer New Hampshire people by 1980 than they had in 1960 and 1970, and fewer still at century's end. Minor indigenous industries, such as stone and clay products and fishing increased marginally. Granite quarrying, much reduced from former times, started a modest upswing again in the 1980s, the market for markers, building blocks, and curbstones remaining steady and sometimes growing. In the 1990s Swenson's Granite even opened a granite retail business in Concord. But all the while the high tech industries were growing at high speed in New Hampshire and becoming dominant. As the century drew to a close it was clear that word processing had superseded wool processing and that computer chips had superseded both wood chips and granite chips.

IV

MIND
AND SPIRIT

Mythic New England is packed with very definite images of place and order, of tradition and geography; and New Hampshire, with its close linkages of land and art, contributes more than its share to that composite. Embodied in these images of New Hampshire are various impulses created by the encounter of the Puritan heritage and the new land. Striking contrasts abound: not only of wilderness and garden and industry, but also of a yeomanry beleaguered by a stern and rocky nature and blistered by cold and toil who, whatever they themselves felt, were represented to themselves in theology and art and sometimes in education as laboring in a Promised Land—living lives somehow continuous with Biblical drama. This part looks at some of the data that support these images, that connect the facts of history with the artifacts of mind and spirit.

The smell of pine still strong on the stumps, the Reverend Eleazar Wheelock establishes Dartmouth College in the wilderness. This 1839 engraving shows the original log building that preceded the grander Dartmouth Hall of 1791. DCA

CHAPTER
TWELVE

EDUCATION AND
THE SCHOOLS

Since New Hampshire was part of Massachusetts from 1641 to 1680, its educational and religious climate was set by the laws of Puritan Massachusetts. Puritans knew their enemies: education would help to keep barbarism and irreligion at bay. The first education law affecting New Hampshire was a very general pronouncement of 1642 that obliged town selectmen to have "a vigilant eye over their neighbors" to see that "none of them shall suffer so much barbarism" as not to teach "their children . . . to read perfectly the English tongue."

Solid Puritan advice—but lacking in details. Those came five years later in a 1647 law that included both a religious and a secular imperative for schools. First, since it was a "chiefe project of ye ould deluder, Sathan, to keepe men from the knowledge of ye Scripture" and, secondly, in order that "learning may not be buried in ye grave of or fathers," the law provided that every town of 50 householders appoint someone to "teach all such children who shall resort to him to write and reade." Further, a town of 100 householders was to "set up a grammar school" to instruct youth "so far as they may be fitted for ye university."

The basic intent of this law was reenacted by New Hampshire after its separation from the Bay Colony. This New Hampshire law of 1693, which lasted through the next century, obliged towns to provide by taxation for a schoolhouse, and a schoolmaster's salary. Schools and schoolmasters were mandated, but attendance was not. The law was neutral as to the sex of the children, but a school was nearly always run by a master, perhaps a young man still in college, and his scholars were usually boys. The early law also included stiff fines on a town for noncompliance and, after 1721, even upon the selectmen themselves for their town's failure to provide a school. Nothing suggests that miracles were expected from the schools; there was merely a commitment that they were absolutely necessary. The statutes set forth an ideal more than they described a practice. Governor John Wentworth II, a Harvard-educated man, may have been unduly harsh when he told the Assembly in 1771:

The promoting of learning very obviously calls for Legislative Care. The Insufficiency of our present Laws for this purpose must be too evident, seeing nine tenths of your towns are wholly without Schools, or have such vagrant Masters as are much worse than none; being for the most part unknown in their principles & deplorably illiterate.

Constitutional Beginnings

As boys they attended the New Hampshire public schools; as men they drafted the state Constitution of 1784. New Hampshire's founding fathers had faith in education, and they wrote that faith into the document.

Knowledge and learning . . . being essential to the preservation of a free government . . . it shall be the duty of the legislators and magistrates . . . to cherish the interest of literature and the sciences . . . to encourage private and public institutions, rewards, and immunities for the promotion of agriculture, arts, sciences, commerce, trades, manufactures, and natural history of the country.

The U.S. Constitution contains no such sentiment, and only a few of the early state constitutions speak of education. These particular New Hampshire words echo a similar passage written into the Massachusetts Constitution a few years earlier by John Adams.

Hundreds of laws since then have shaped these ideas into policy. Concern for teacher quality emerged early, and a 1789 law obliged towns to have prospective teachers examined by an "able and reputable" person (normally a minister) to insure that they were qualified. In the midst of the rapid development of the New Hampshire countryside, an 1805 law authorized the individual towns to set up multiple school districts within their borders. Before this some towns had made similar decisions on their own: in 1801 the town of Hampton voted: "That the North

District shall have Jonathan Sanborn's Barn for a school house." In 1827 the legislature took school matters out of the hands of town selectmen, where they had been since 1647, and put them into the hands of a separate school committee. In 1846 the state created the office of Commissioner of Common Schools—a general supervisor with a special mandate to focus upon teacher education—and secured a Dartmouth professor to fill it. The result was a series of teachers' "institutes"—two-day to four-week sessions in various parts of the state for the recruitment and training of teachers. In 1847 the Commissioner reported:

Every Institute that has been held has sent a wave of elevating influence to every retreating cove and every shadowy eddy where mind lay sleeping and stagnant.

In 1854 there were 2,294 such coves and eddies—separate school districts in New Hampshire, every one of them an independent fiefdom.

It was the schools that opened the door to female suffrage. An 1877 law held that "female citizens of adult age may hold and discharge the duties of prudential or superintending committee." The next year women were even allowed to vote in district school meetings. In 1883 at the height of the temperance movement a new law said that "physiology and hygiene, including special reference to the effects of alcoholic stimulants and narcotics upon the human system, shall be prescribed in all schools sufficiently advanced." The last two words were a loophole that left the matter up to the teacher.

In 1885 a new law changed the scene drastically. By that time the school year in many a one-room district school had dwindled to 10 weeks of haphazard classes kept by an ill-prepared teacher for a half-dozen children in a collapsing building. The new law obliged the independent school districts within a town to consolidate into one town district. Separate district schools were permitted but only under a single town board—a major shift away from what was then called "local control." The state superintendent wrote that "as long as the idea prevails that every man must have a school-house within a few rods of his door, regardless of *what* that school may be, so long there will remain a great obstacle to the complete education of all the children of the state."

A by-product of the 1885 law was that New Hampshire women for the first time had a vote in a townwide meeting. Long since, of course, women teachers had come to far outnumber men, one reason being that it was cheaper to hire women: their salaries were invariably one-third to one-half lower than those of men. Thus during the 19th century the schoolmaster of folklore gave way to the schoolmistress of memory.

Teachers and Academies

For a long time public high schools—after Portsmouth's early beginning in 1830—were a rarity in New Hampshire. Private aspiration and enterprise, not state policy, led the way in secondary education. The 19th century witnessed the bright, brief flowering of classical academies all over the New England countryside. The first example had been set shortly after the Revolutionary War by Phillips Exeter (1783), and it was

SCHOOL EXHIBITION.

Laſt Thurſday Mr. Eaſtman cloſed his School in this town, and entertained the inhabitants with an exhibition, by his ſcholars, conſiſting of Orations, Dialogues, Poetry, &c. &c. The judicious manner in which the ſcenes were arranged—the diſplay of his whole School, upwards of 70 in number, on the ſtage,—and the ingenious performances of the ſcholars—did honour to the Tutor and his Pupils, and gave great pleaſure to the parents & ſpectators. A numerous audience manifeſted their approbation by repeated clapping of hands, and other tokens of applauſe.

Like most schoolmasters of his day, Edmund Eastman, Concord's schoolmaster in 1793, was little appreciated and poorly paid; his annual salary in 1793 was £18. Nevertheless, Mr. Eastman and his students had their day in the sun with a "School Exhibition" that was reported in the Concord Herald *of April 3, 1793. NHHS*

Phillips Exeter Academy is pictured here as it appeared in 1831. The academy opened in 1783, having been founded by John Phillips, an Exeter merchant and "worthy gentleman" who had done well in banking and finance. The main part of the building shown was constructed in 1794-1795, with wings added between 1821 and 1829. After the building burned in 1870, other Exeter Academy buildings in the neo-Georgian style were designed by New Hampshire native Ralph Adams Cram. NHHS

The arrival in New York of the "Vacation Special from St. Paul's School" brought crowds of anxious mamas, papas, and coachmen to Grand Central Station. The scenario was depicted with some humor in a December 1889 issue of Harper's. *NHHS*

followed soon thereafter by academies at New Ipswich, Chesterfield, Charlestown, Atkinson, and Amherst. By 1850 there were 46 incorporated academies in the state and at least as many unincorporated private secondary schools. Many offered both a classical course based on languages and literature and a teacher preparation program. By 1860 many of the elementary schools of the state were "kept" by young women, and occasionally by men, who had spent a part of one or two of their teenage years in such an academy. Some of these academies began under direct religious auspices. For example, New Hampton Academy (1826) and New London Academy (1853) were Baptist; Tilton School (1845) was Methodist; and St. Paul's School (1850) and Holderness School (1878) were Episcopal.

New Hampshire academies waned as fast as they had waxed, and their decline was a setback for female education. In 1877 an essayist for *The Granite Monthly* wrote: "The Academies have dwindled away like the mountain streams when the forests are cut down. A few have survived and have been specialized into expensive college preparatory schools. Boys alone are the students. . . . the tendency of the population toward the cities and the preference for machinery over individual labor . . . have killed the academy." Some survived and are thriving still a century later.

From a private academy a candidate often went to employment in a district school in a neighboring town, so much of what transpired in education was outside the sphere of state government. The New Hampshire legislature liked this arrangement, and it long resisted any further involvement in teacher preparation. From 1850 onward a State Teachers' Association and others tried to get a normal school, or teachers' college, bill through the legislature and even pledged money on a matching basis to pay for it. These efforts finally bore fruit after the academy movement crested. The first state normal school was established at Plymouth in 1870, and the legislature fastidiously stipulated that it was to be run without expense to the state. New Hampshire educators of the time found it hard to square the passive and reluctant legislative stance with the categorical statements of legislative duty toward education written into the state constitution by an earlier generation.

Official Views

The 20th-century habit, in New Hampshire and elsewhere, of looking to the public schools as either the cause or the remedy of all our social ills is rooted in the remarkable 19th-century faith in schooling as preventive medicine. The *Annual Report* for 1857 declared that had the teachers for the past 200 years "been in heart and head what they ought to have been, today we should have no need of an organized police in any city, a prison, an asylum, or a house of reformation in any State, or a standing army to guard domestic tranquility. Can anyone deny this?" (The founders of New Hampshire's school system 200 years earlier would have denied it.) The next year's *Report* bespeaks a better insight and a calmer eloquence: "A mind undeveloped by culture is a captive, and walks round its narrow cell of thought from childhood to the grave in unconscious servitude. But knowledge breaks the shackles from the soul and permits it to

Soon after its completion the Ash Street School in Manchester was nominated as an outstanding example of innovative school architecture at the 1876 Philadelphia Centennial Exposition. After more than a century the school—seen here in 1982—is still in regular use. Photograph by Gary Samson

Among the earliest of New England's boarding schools, St. Paul's—situated two miles outside downtown Concord—opened in 1856. Girls were first admitted to St. Paul's 114 years later. Members of a coed student body are pictured at morning chapel in 1971. Courtesy, New Hampshire Times

rise to a higher and better life." During the 19th century the annual state *Report* was often a well-written and well-documented analysis of New Hampshire's educational needs. However, by the turn of the century, the practical problems faced by a state undergoing urban immigrant population growth and rural decline were dominant: transportation, teacher quality, public apathy, dilapidated buildings, finances. The "abandoned farm" and the "rural school problem," two verses of the same song, echo down the decades well into the 20th century. The 1906 *Report* recapitulated the problem of teacher quality:

> *In earlier days the schools were kept . . . by college students, usually men of force and character and often of qualities destined to make them famous. They were succeeded first by women scarcely inferior to themselves in ability and forcefulness, but afterward by an increasing generation of girls without education, training, or maturity, and more often than not without ability.*

Perhaps the most persistently disconcerting problem addressed by these officials year after year was the inequality of education among the different towns and the lack of adequate state financial support. "New Hampshire is dependent upon direct local taxation for support of schools to an extent scarcely equalled in any other state," stated the *Report* in 1906. This sentiment has been voiced countless times thereafter, even to the present day.

The Twentieth Century

By 1901 there were laws on the books concerning compulsory school attendance up to age 14, forbidding the employment during school hours of anyone under 16 who could not read and write, and obliging towns to pay minimal high-school tuition costs for anyone attending high school out of town. Beyond that New Hampshire lacked a coherent education policy in the early decades of the 20th century. Standards were often haphazard, teacher quality varied greatly, and the school term differed among towns from a few to 30 weeks per year. No law prescribed a minimum school year. The best small schools, those in academy towns, were sometimes very good. But they were very few.

Something deeply ironic was at work in the educational system: it was precisely the schools that were draining the talent from the countryside. The better the school, the better the chance that it would awaken interest in life beyond the hillside communities and lure the more promising young people from the farm to the city. It was, of course, an ancient dilemma, poignantly reenacted from one end of New Hampshire to another for more than a generation before and after 1900. Even in the cities, school problems were complex: Manchester, for example, had to cope with large immigrant groups. And everywhere the lack of minimum standards enfeebled the schools. Good advice could not supply what laws had left undone.

The early Puritans, convinced that Satan himself had a vested interest in human ignorance, assumed that growth in Christian virtue required secular learning—an assumption later transmuted into the grand and bland educational optimism of the 19th century. Though these complex impulses had largely spent themselves in New Hampshire by the beginning of the 20th century, there remained the perennial, thoroughly American, idea that illiteracy is not only a regrettable waste but is politically dangerous as well.

Toward the end of World War I, all this high-toned ideology, coupled with the lowly practical facts about the state's schools, gave birth to a new doctrine in New Hampshire. Public opinion had been startled by the reports that hundreds of New Hampshire wartime draftees "were unable to read the orders they were expected to obey." On March 28, 1919, the General Court passed a comprehensive law that emphatically acknowledged the state's responsibility for promoting educational standards. Education officials had long pleaded for this, and Article 83 of the state constitution had long suggested it, but not until 1919 did the law embody it—this during an otherwise politically dry and infertile time. The new law created a five-person State Board of Education to oversee the state's public education, with a Commissioner of Education responsible to the Board. It mandated 36 weeks of school per year, reorganized the supervisory unions, tightened requirements for teacher certification, gave the state responsibility for approval of private elementary schools, and made the physical welfare of students a concern of the public schools. Historian J.D. Squires calls it: " an epochal law, reflecting the trends of the time, yet actually going further in some ways than had been anticipated. At one jump, New Hampshire went from a condition of relative backwardness in public educa-

tion to a status of being somewhat of a pioneer.

Thus New Hampshire education entered the 20th century. Though much amended, the 1919 law has for more than 80 years supplied the essential framework within which New Hampshire conducts its public education. Students in the public schools numbered over 200,000 by the end of the century. The school programs are unimaginably more complex than anything foreseen in 1919, the costs still continually outrun resources, and the lack of substantial statewide tax support for schools is still a sore spot diagnosed in almost the same terms, only more pessimistic, as were familiar generations ago. The isolated rural school is but a marginal issue now; the problem of teacher quality, no longer the disaster it once was, is dealt with by an educational bureaucracy that manages a thousand other matters and, just as the law intended, is responsible through a commissioner to a five-person State Board of Education.

A century before, the Toleration Act of 1819 had been both a revolutionary and a successful redrawing of the lines between church and state; similarly the State Board Act of 1919 was a

Above: New Hampshire's village schools often put several grade levels into one classroom. In 1948 Lavina Dole's Campton classroom contained grades 5 through 8—and one dog. Courtesy, New Hampshire Department of Fish and Game

Opposite page: Concord's Cogswell Elementary School was photographed in 1906. Just a few years earlier the schoolboy hero of The Real Diary of a Real Boy, *by Henry Shute, had confided to his diary: "tonite i had to studdy Colburn arithmatic. It is the wirst book i ever studded . . . . i had ruther be a merderer if nobuddy gnew it than be a feler whitch rote a arithmatic." NHHS*

This posthumous portrait of the Reverend Eleazar Wheelock, founder of Dartmouth College, was commissioned by the trustees of the college in 1793. It is the work of Joseph Steward, who had graduated from Dartmouth in 1780. DCA

Intercollegiate athletic rivalries were well established by the end of the 19th century. Here Dartmouth entertains the Amherst College baseball team in 1890. There are still those in New Hampshire who shake their heads and say that the decline of farming in New England coincided with the rise of baseball as a national pastime. At the turn of the century nearly every town in New Hampshire had its own uniformed baseball team. DCA

revolutionary and successful redrawing of the lines between school and state. If at the outset, early in the 17th century, church and school had been viewed by the law in almost the same way, 300 years of New Hampshire experience had steadily awarded the churches more independence and accorded the schools more supervision.

Dartmouth College

In the 1740s the Reverend Eleazar Wheelock, a Yale-educated Congregational minister serving in Lebanon, Connecticut, began tutoring nearby Indian children in the Christian religion with remarkable success. As more Indians came to him in the next decade, Wheelock began to contemplate an enlarged school, perhaps far off at the edge of the wilderness, where English and Indian boys could be educated together in a Christian community. Ironic backdrop for this noble dream was the French and Indian War, then raging in New Hampshire and elsewhere. In the 1760s Wheelock sent one of his early Indian converts, Samson Occum, to England to raise money for the project Occum and renowned New Hampshire Indian fighter Robert Rogers arrived in England at about the same time, and each was a spectacular public-relations success. Rogers spun embellished tales of exploits fighting Indians; Occum elaborated the Reverend Wheelock's dream to educate Indians and embodied in his own person the fruits of such a plan. Lord Dartmouth, Secretary of State for the Colonies, contributed money for the school, energetically organized dozens of others to do the same, and persuaded George III himself to put up £200. The college was Britain's last best gift to New Hampshire before independence.

Word of the planned school had filtered to New Hampshire. In 1762 the Congregational Convention of Ministers in New Hampshire endorsed Wheelock's plan, and shortly thereafter the citizens of Hanover, a young Connecticut River town, offered him a large tract of land. On December 13, 1769, Governor John Wentworth signed a college charter "for the education and instruction of Youth of the Indian tribes . . . and also of English youth and any others." Wentworth College was the preferred name, but the governor shrewdly deferred to his English friend and fund raiser, Lord Dartmouth. Wheelock journeyed to the frontier with several transfer students from Yale and began the college in 1770 in a log building, a voice in the wilderness. The next year, 1771, the first class of four was graduated, with Governor Wentworth in attendance. Subsequently the training of Indian scholars and missionaries was only sometimes successful, but the training of "English youth and any others" has been very successful for two centuries.

Early on, Dartmouth entered vigorously and contentiously into the political life of New Hampshire, and its graduates and faculty did much during the 19th century to energize the political and cultural tone of the state. Characteristically, New Hampshire's first statewide public-school administrator came from the Dartmouth faculty, and when New Hampshire came to revise its educational system in the early 20th century, the principal intellectual force behind the 1919 statute turned out to be President E.M. Hopkins of Dartmouth. During the recent half century Dartmouth has been rather less oriented toward the affairs of New Hampshire than it was formerly—in deference, perhaps, to the emergence of the University of New Hampshire during that same period. Today Dartmouth is a small "university" of some 4,300 undergraduates and about 1,300 graduate students in three professional schools and sixteen arts and sciences graduate programs.

A most valuable link that has emerged in the last quarter century between Dartmouth and the people of New Hampshire is the Dartmouth-Hitchcock Medical Center. The Medical Center trains students from the Dartmouth Medical School (founded 1797) and serves patients at the Dartmouth-Hitchcock Clinic, the Mary Hitchcock Memorial Hospital, the Veteran Affairs Hospital, and the outreach clinics in area communities.

The University of New Hampshire

Like many other state universities, the University of New Hampshire owes its origins to the 1862 Morrill Act of the U.S. Congress, which earmarked money derived from the sale of Western public lands for what became known as "land grant colleges." Each state was offered 30,000 acres per Congressman for maintaining "a college where the leading object shall be, . . . such branches of learning as are related to agriculture and the mechanic arts, . . . to promote the liberal and practical education of the industrial classes." Each state had five years to take it or leave it. The New Hampshire legislature hesitated. Was this a gift or an imposition? Where put such a college? Taking courage, the legislature incorporated the New Hampshire College of Agriculture and Mechanic Arts in 1866, and decided that it would be in Hanover, leaning on Dartmouth, now a vigorous enterprise.

The new trustees hired Ezekiel Dimond of Massachusetts as head of the new college; they gave him $3,000 for equipment and sent him to Hanover to set up the new institution with its practical course of study, alongside Dartmouth's classical curriculum. By nearly a century Professor Dimond was following the footsteps of Eleazar Wheelock to Hanover, to carry out an educational mandate that was, like Wheelock's, both a deep personal commitment and a broader mandate of his culture. Neither mandate bore bounteous fruit in quite the way intended—one did not rescue New Hampshire Indians, and the other did not rescue New Hampshire farming. They succeeded in other terms.

Professor Dimond distributed 2,000 circulars throughout the state, hired an associate, planned his courses, borrowed his classrooms, set up his gear, and waited curiously to see what would happen when he rang the bell in the fall. On September 4, 1868, ten young men came to register, and what was eventually to become the University of New Hampshire was on its way. In a few years the college had a building of its own, a faculty of two, the land grant endowment of $80,000—and still only a very few students. Professor Dimond, a versatile man and a strong leader, correctly insisted that the Morrill Act specifically encouraged "other sciences and classical subjects" as well, and from the first he regarded the institution as a state college. Dartmouth viewed its adoptee otherwise, mixing bemusement and disdain. During

Twenty-nine years after Dartmouth's first Winter Carnival, collegians in 1940 put the finishing touches on their impressive Winter Carnival ice sculpture, The Starshooter. *DCA*

Harvard president Charles Eliot once called the organized summer camp "the most important step in education that America has given the world." Throughout the late 19th and early 20th centuries, city youths flocked to New Hampshire's lakes each summer, where summer camps offered them a unique educational and recreational experience. Hebron's Camp Pasquaney, founded in 1895, featured a wide range of programs in its early years, from baseball (opposite page, top) to "backpacking"—finding this Civil War veteran and his wife was a bonus (above). Courtesy, Camp Pasquaney

its 25 years spent in Dartmouth's shadow, the college never ha more than 14 graduates in a year.

Once more fortune smiled. In a will drafted long before th Morrill Act, Benjamin Thompson, a prosperous farmer i Durham, New Hampshire, bequeathed his land to the state fo an "agricultural school, to be located on my . . . farm . . . in sai Durham, wherein shall be thoroughly taught . . . the theory an practice of that most useful and honorable calling." When th will was probated in 1890, there was again considerable hesitanc about accepting a gift with its implied faith that agriculture had bright future in New Hampshire. Journalists opposed starting u another such school. According to one voice: " . . .all th agricultural colleges between here and the setting sun will n convert the rocky hills of New Hampshire into gardens Eden."

At this point common sense intervened, disguised as geniu the Thompson tract in Durham and that struggling college Hanover, each a mixed and fragile blessing in itself, could b combined into one solution. A legislative act in 1891 lifted Ne Hampshire's state college from the shades at Dartmouth an sent it down to Thompson's farm in Durham. There, a fine re brick Gothic academic building was erected in the pasture, an duly dedicated as Thompson Hall in 1893. Nearly a century lat it still presides grandly over the academic landscape, and th university property, once within a farm, now has a farm within

In May 1917, with the nation going to war, the faculty of UNH decided to launch a patriotic potato patch under the supervision of Frederick W. "Pa" Taylor, seated at left in the wagon. While the launching may have been fun, the work was to follow. The faculty harvested 260 bushels of potatoes in 1917 and 324 bushels the following year. UC, UNH

Early growth at Durham, though moderate, was much more rapid than it had ever been in Hanover, and by the turn of the century there were nearly 200 students at the college.

Slowly, inexorably, like many another land grant college in many another state, New Hampshire College developed an inner logic which, propelled by outer circumstances, headed it in the direction of a university. Founded in Hanover and refounded in Durham in terms of explicit service to the state, the college had new demands laid on it—in teaching, research, and dissemination—by the New Hampshire citizenry. By the 1920s it had become clear that while Dartmouth might continue to dwell in the luster of its ivy, New Hampshire College would stick closer to its grass roots; it had become clear, too, that a liberal-arts impulse, frail at first, was coming alive in the center of the college, earnestly poking a taproot toward the veins of traditional academic culture. Eventually, like the other New England land grant colleges that were planted in the shadows of powerful private colleges, this one became a modern university. The transition came in stages.

In 1923 the General Court redefined the college as the University of New Hampshire, composed of three colleges Agriculture, Technology, and Liberal Arts; a graduate schoo was formally added in 1928. In 1939 the standard two-yea agricultural program became the Thompson School of Applied Science. A new burst of expansion and reorganization came in the 1960s. The Whittemore School of Business and Economic was founded in 1962; in 1969 the Agricultural College becam the College of Life Sciences and Agriculture, and a new Schoo of Health Studies was added; in 1975 the College of Technolog became the College of Engineering and Physical Sciences; and a the end of the decade the School for Lifelong Learning wa created.

One of the most significant changes during this time was th 1963 creation of the University System of New Hampshire which officially brought the Plymouth and Keene state colleges née normal schools, into one system with the University of Nev Hampshire under a single board of trustees. By the early 1980 enrollment at Durham was over 10,000; at Keene, well ove 3,500; and at Plymouth, just under 3,500. Approximately two thirds of these students are from New Hampshire.

Above: This is how the University of New Hampshire looked as it began its second century in 1968. Thompson Hall is near the center of the picture, Dimond Library to its left. UC, UNH

Left: The circa 1893 view of New Hampshire College of Agriculture and Mechanic Arts was photographed shortly after Thompson Hall (upper left) was completed. At the time Thompson Hall housed all of the college's non-agricultural academic disciplines. Today it is the central administrative building at the University of New Hampshire. UC, UNH

Wallace Nutting may have loved the New England countryside, but he had little love for the region's road signs, complaining in his 1923 book, New Hampshire Beautiful, *that it "would require a year's course at a university to become thoroughly posted on the signs in New England. . . ." Fortunately this very readable 1921 Durham road sign was near a center of higher learning. UC, UNH*

CHAPTER
THIRTEEN

RELIGION
AND
THE CHURCHES

In colonial New Hampshire there was no such thing as separation of church and state: worship service was town meeting at prayer.

Unlike the Puritans and the Pilgrims farther south, the early settlers in the Piscataqua region were not seekers of religious freedom. Most of them were Anglicans like their sponsor, John Mason, who had taken care to send over a pulpit Bible, copies of the *Book of Common Prayer,* and communion silver. An Anglican parish was established at Strawbery Banke (Portsmouth) in 1640, but Anglicanism virtually died out there during the next decades as New Hampshire towns united with Puritan Massachusetts Bay Colony. The remaining Anglicans were taxed in support of the Congregational Church, which was to become virtually the established church of New Hampshire.

Nearly a century later, in 1732, the Anglican communion was reconstituted in New Hampshire (an attempt in the 1680s had failed) with the beginning of Queen's Chapel (now St. John's) in Portsmouth. Since the Anglicans were a minority in Portsmouth, their church taxes went routinely (until they got exemptions in 1740) to the Congregationalists, and they paid their own minister's salary. Prior to the Revolutionary War many important Portsmouth merchants and politicians were Anglicans, including the last two Wentworth governors. As was to be expected, a number of prominent Loyalists, or Tories, during the Revolutionary period came from among the Anglicans. Samuel Livermore of Holderness, an ardent Anglican and an ardent Patriot, was a notable exception. Later, in 1791, Livermore became president of the New Hampshire Constitutional Convention.

Quakers also appeared early in New Hampshire, fleeing persecution in Massachusetts Bay. After one bizarre incident in 1662 in which, in accordance with the law and under the orders of Magistrate Richard Waldron, three Quaker women were publicly whipped in Dover, simply for being there, one hears no more of persecution of Quakers in New Hampshire. A Quaker Society was formally established in Dover before 1700, and tolerance, offically expressed in a Royal decree as "liberty of conscience," was then the norm. Laws requiring oaths made exception for Quakers, who conscientiously objected to oath-taking, which they viewed as an act of worship not to be forced upon anyone. Despite the early persecution, Quakers prospered in Dover during the 18th century.

But the vast majority of New Hampshire churches were Congregational. By the time of the Revolutionary War, there were nearly 120 organized churches in New Hampshire. Eighty-four were Congregational; two were Anglican; 15 were Presbyterian; 11 were Baptist; and 5 were Quaker. Other denominations appeared soon after the Revolutionary War: Freewill Baptists, 1780; Universalists, 1781; Shakers, 1790s; Methodists, 1790s; Christian Church, 1803. Until well into the 19th century there were no Catholics or Jews in New Hampshire to disturb the comfortable Protestant bias of the laws and the state constitution. Each new denomination, however, was one more tug away from the center of the Congregational "establishment."

Church and State

From the start religion and education in New Hampshire were undergirded by a common assumption: school and church are social necessities to be supported by public taxation. There were also further assumptions: schools should be required; churches should be encouraged. Accordingly, the New Hampshire laws that required a schoolmaster for a town did not mandate hiring a minister (as they did in Massachusetts), but they did require that the meetinghouse be public property and that the minister, if any, be paid through town taxes in exactly the same way as a schoolmaster. Moreover, most township grants and most town charters given by the governor included—as a condition of

Top left: The Shaker Village at Enfield, one of two in the state, lasted from 1793 to 1923. The brothers and sisters pictured here are standing on the steps of the office of the South Family around 1870. The family's ruling Eldress and Elder stand in front. From the Leavitt Collection, NHHS

Top right: The interior of the minister's dwelling at Enfield's Church Family was plain, but by no means uncomfortable. Elder Abraham Perkins, photographed circa 1870, had ministerial duties in several Shaker communities, which might explain the map of New England on his study wall. From the Leavitt Collection, NHHS

Above: Canterbury Shaker Village, founded in 1792, may have had as many as 300 residents at its largest. Pictured in this H.A. Kimball photograph are the buildings of the Church Family circa 1870. The meetinghouse is the gambrel-roofed building on the right. NHHS

Above: The Washington meetinghouse, of classic lines and proportions and once one of hundreds like it, is now a very rare specimen. It was erected in 1787, in the style of the Sandown meetinghouse on the opposite page, but with a two-story enclosed entrance, called a "porch," at each end. In 1825 the bell tower replaced one porch, and the side and transom windows were added to the front door; later in the 19th century the interior was altered to accommodate new uses. Town meetings were held here for over two hundred years, until the space available was too small, but the building has always been, and is now, in daily use. This picture was taken late in the 19th century by Gustine Hurd, since which time no major changes have been made in the building. Courtesy, Ronald and Grace Jager

Opposite page: Both inside and out, the Sandown Meetinghouse remains a superb example of 18th century architecture and craftsmanship. It was built between the summer of 1773 and October 1774; construction was briefly interrupted at one point when the workmen ran out of rum and walked off the job. Between 1778 and 1929 Sandown held its town meeting here, although regular church services stopped in 1834. NHHS

ownership, not as a matter of law—requirements that a minister be secured within a certain period of time. It was simply taken for granted that the minister was a civil officer of the town.

Thus, until well into the 19th century a New Hampshire town decided by majority vote which religious denomination it would support; the minister was called, his salary set, and the church expenses decided at town meeting. Unless they secured exemptions—rare during New Hampshire's first hundred years (granted only to Quakers), difficult to obtain during the next 50 years, and widespread during the following 50 years—all taxpayers supported the church, whether they went to it or not, whether they liked it or not. The 1693 New Hampshire law that set the general pattern for well over a century was careful about loopholes, intending that no one

under pretence of being of a different perswassion be Excused from paying toward the support of the settled Minister . . . but only such as are Conscientiously So; and Constantly attend the publick worship of God on the Lords day according to their owne P'rswassion; And they only Shall be Excused from paying toward the Support of the Ministrey of the Towne.

New Hampshire had followed the example of Massachusetts, and Massachusetts had followed England. The American innovation lay in allowing each town to decide *which* church to support. The New Hampshire innovations in 1693 lay in allowing individual exemptions and in not mandating a town minister. At the time these provisions were the most liberal of their kind in New England. Indeed, to a thoughtful person of open mind the New Hampshire colonial church/state system seemed like a good idea. Yet the system crumbled slowly over the course of two centuries; the fact that it became unworkable and therefore unwise probably did as much to break it down as did the conviction that it was unjust. In a more general sense, however, the system fell victim to its own virtues—one of which was liberty of conscience.

"Liberty of Conscience"

Shipped over from England, "liberty of conscience" embodied a noble sentiment of uncertain meaning. It was affirmed for New Hampshire citizens, "Papists" excepted, in the Royal charter of the province in 1679; it was repeated in laws and was regularly reaffirmed in the commissions of the Royal governors. It meant at least this: no one, not even a Quaker, is to be persecuted for religious beliefs. (The implications for Catholics were not worked out, for there were then no Catholics in New Hampshire.) "Liberty of conscience" in this sense was valued and practiced, thus inoculating New Hampshire against the witchcraft hysteria that swept through the less tolerant Bay Colony. No one then would have suggested that paying taxes to support a religion not one's own was a violation of conscience any more than one would have suggested that paying taxes to educate children not one's own was a violation of conscience.

Liberty of conscience helped to undermine the established system. For example, tax exemptions encouraged non-Congregationalists. Encouraged, they multiplied; discouraged

they complained to the Selectmen, to the Assembly, and to the courts. The more denominations that were recognized, the more complicated became the system, and the more burdened became town and state governments with religious and church affairs. In Newton, in 1769, Baptists and Quakers ganged up, took control of the town meeting, and voted themselves the tax exemptions they had been denied. In a more characteristic case, in 1801 the New Hampshire Supreme Court had to decide whether the Universalists qualified as a "sect" within the meaning of the law that authorized the exemptions. They didn't. So Universalists continued to pay taxes to the support of Congregational or Presbyterian ministers. Sometimes the unchurched simply joined together, as they did in Durham in 1805, and voted to inform Mr. Coe, the town's Congregational minister, "that his preaching is no longer beneficial to the Inhabitants of Durham." A way to ax the tax.

The opportunities for quibbling about tax exemptions were endless, forever new and forever the same: Was last Sunday's gathering at the Jones farm a "publick worship" or just a murmuring of malcontents? And does the MacGregor family go "constantly" to the Presbyterian Church, 30 miles away in Londonderry? Deny them exemptions and they may enlist others and incorporate a Presbyterian parish right here in

Chester and then petition the Assembly and the Selectmen for their share of the town taxes. In Bedford and Londonderry it was easy: the Presbyterians were in a majority and "established" their church and let the Congregationalists off free; in Goffstown and Pembroke it was hard: Presbyterians were only a large minority and so the legislature eventually created special parishes for them. The system was a frequent headache for the towns, for the legislature, and for the courts, where grievances piled up, and for the churches, when squabbles about where to locate a church or whether to call a pastor or change his salary, and disputes about doctrine or morals easily became townwide issues. After 1800 many towns voted somewhat evasively, as did Durham in 1814, "that each Religious Denomination in this Town raise their ministerial money in their own way and manner." This peace-keeping maneuver was probably illegal and probably wise.

Slowly, inexorably, the venerable "liberty of conscience" idea began—especially in the latter days of colonial New Hampshire—to assume a profounder meaning: not only "no persecution" but also "right to worship as one chooses."

The Constitution and the Law

The New Hampshire Constitution of 1784 was not designed to change any of the basic assumptions and practices of "established" town churches. Yet it did—almost imperceptibly at first, but permanently.

Liberty of conscience, the "constitutional" principle of colonial days (affirmed in the Bill of Rights of the Constitution), had begun the subtle subversion of the established system. However, a new principle present in the 1784 Constitution worked quietly and efficiently to subvert the system further. The new principle was that all churches should be treated equally by the law. "No subordination of any one sect or denomination to another shall ever be established by law," says the Constitution. It was difficult to reconcile this ideal with many of the town practices or with the fact that the same Constitution, until changed in 1877, restricted state offices to Protestants.

The surprising thing is that the *theory* of state/church relations, despite strife in practice, was not really controversial at the time. The topic was scarcely debated in the several conventions that led to the final text of the 1784 New Hampshire Constitution, which declared that "the best and greatest security to government" lay in "morality and piety," to be achieved by "the institution of the public worship of the Deity." Since a *state* church was unthinkable, there seemed to be no genuine alternative to the publicly supported town church.

The 1784 New Hampshire Constitution also empowered the *legislature* "to authorize from time to time the several towns . . . to make adequate provision . . . for . . . Protestant teachers of piety, religion, and morality." Thus the legislature could change the practice without changing the Constitution, and they did so by the Toleration Act of 1819. The new act resulted from a growing consensus that the town-church idea was outdated, and it resulted too from years of journalistic and political agitation against tax support of churches by Democratic-Republicans William Plumer and Isaac Hill. A town's right, granted by the legislature, to hire and dismiss its own ministers, initially the greatest privilege, had become the greatest burden.

The 1819 Act repealed the towns' authorization to support ministers and churches; it left existing contracts between towns and ministers in place; and it provided that "no person shall be compelled to . . . support or be classed with . . . any congregation, church or religious society without his express consent." In addition, anyone resigning from a religious society and so notifying the town clerk "shall thereupon be no longer liable for any further expense" of that society.

The 1819 Toleration Act was *the* watershed law in the history of New Hampshire church/state relations. Many problems remained—disposal of church property, use of meetinghouses, and the like—but the major intent of the act was soon absorbed into the everyday assumptions of the people: towns were now out of the church business. Suddenly it was quite obvious that the way for the government to treat the churches equally and subordinate none of them was not by financing them equally but by financing them not at all. So complete was the change of mind during the period from 1791, when church/state matters were first seriously debated at the Constitutional Convention, to the time of the new law in 1819 that it seemed superfluous to change the Constitution. Nearly 150 years later, in 1968, a badly muddled constitutional amendment finally withdrew from the legislature the power to authorize towns to support ministers.

The Great Awakening

The arrangements of religion are one thing; the religious life another. For a time New Hampshire people organized religious practice with a few laws, a few central ideas. Then the arrangements wore out, their breakdown contaminated religious life itself, and the local dramas that ensued are left as the principal stuff of record. Easily lost to memory and to history, or drowned in the melancholy din of neighborhood clashes, is the texture of religious life itself: the flow of feeling and passion and the faith, piety, and pride that the churches labored to refine into the living worship and service of God. Something of the force of this spirituality may be suggested by two other dimensions of New Hampshire church history: the Great Awakening, a representative and revealing 18th-century episode; and the rise and fall of theological seminaries, obscure but revealing episodes of the 19th century.

In the early 1740s intense religious revivals swept through the American colonies, especially throughout New England. Religious life had become cold, formalistic, complacent—according to the critics of the day. Moreover, in the frontier communities of New Hampshire many people were out of touch with an established church: it might be hard to get to, without a settled pastor, not worth the trouble, or not yet established in a town. The Puritan zeal for righteousness that had burned so fiercely in the 17th century was often submerged in the strenuous secular business of wresting a living from the wilderness. In many places active church members were a minority of the townspeople. Though religion died almost nowhere, it often moved to the margins and slept.

A critical instrument of awakening was the "itinerant," a traveling evangelist, usually gifted in direct and dramatic Biblical oratory aimed at the emotions. An itinerant's success in a community was marked by numerous conversions, by a great intensification of religious interest, Bible study, prayer, and, frequently, by extended, emotional, sometimes disorderly religious meetings lasting late into the night, sometimes night after night. Most itinerants active in the New Hampshire of the 1740s—perhaps a dozen at different times—pale beside the eloquent George Whitefield, an English evangelist who preached up and down the American coast with enormous effect, and the incomparable Jonathan Edwards, a central American figure of the Awakening, whose powerful preaching in his own church in Northampton, Massachusetts, was indirectly felt in all the towns of New Hampshire.

Supporters of the Awakening, called "New Lights" (they would be called the "born again" today), focused on the slumbering and unfeeling orthodoxy of the churches and on the forthright faith and vigor of the awakened. Critics, or "Old Lights," focused upon the excesses of religious commotion, often deliberately cultivated, in the souls of the New Lights and deplored the "enthusiasm" (18th-century word for fanaticism) that boiled and bubbled in the wake of the fiery preaching of the itinerants.

The Great Awakening of 1740 began in New Hampshire

dozen years early. It started with an earthquake at 10 p.m., Sunday evening, October 29, 1727. The next Sunday and periodically for years thereafter hardly a preacher failed to remind his congregation regularly that this dramatic sign from the Lord should prompt repentance and rededication. And it did. Contemporaries and statistics tell the same story: every congregation for which records are available shows an upsurge of membership in 1727 and 1728. Fifteen years later William Shurtleff of Portsmouth expressed the common opinion, declaring that the "Earthquake in the Year 1727, that put the whole Country in such a Surprise, was a Means of Awakening a great many here: and . . . the Impressions have remain'd."

Two of New Hampshire's most prominent clergymen remained Old Lights. It was no surprise that Governor Benning Wentworth's pastor, Anglican Arthur Browne of Queen's Chapel, Portsmouth, was not amused by the goings on. He wrote to a friend in London that

> Impressions, Impulses, Experiences are altogether in vogue & become the Test of Regenerate men; whilst the true Scripture works are quite out of request . . . . He is the best and most edifying Preacher who is most presumptuous and unintelligible.

The Reverend Timothy Walker, a Congregationalist of Concord who preached and published two anti-Awakening sermons in 1743, was concerned after seeing "one Vain Boaster after another start up," that the "Form of Godliness would be destroyed, under Pretence of farther advancing the Power of it." Nevertheless, most New Hampshire ministers supported the revivals and attempted to redirect the excesses. A number of hell-fire itinerants, like Daniel Rogers of Exeter, eventually settled into regular pastorates and became solid churchmen. Some of the New Lights became Old Lights as they aged.

The Awakened infused the churches with valuable spiritual energies; new openings for other denominations, Baptists especially, were created, as perhaps was a keener sensitivity to certain democratic attitudes. Intense piety before a Biblical God, almighty and forgiving, who is "no respecter of persons," is an effective social leveler. Though the fine links from religious revival through social attitude to democratic revolution are tenuous, complicated, and hard to track, they are essential threads in the tapestry of the New England experience.

In the Wilderness

Some itinerant preachers of the Great Awakening were notable, occasionally notorious, for being essentially self-educated—supplying with zeal what they lacked in knowledge. Leaders of New England churches, themselves usually alumni of Harvard, Yale, or, occasionally, Oxford or Cambridge, were perennially concerned about the supply of educated pastors in remoter regions such as New Hampshire. They were haunted and inspired by the idealism voiced as far back as 1636 in the founding rationale of Harvard College: "dreading to leave an illiterate Ministry to the Churches, when our present Ministers shall lie in the Dust." The 1812 ecclesiastical convention acknowledged that more trained pastors were needed lest "new settlements, where they

This posthumous portrait of Mary Baker Eddy was painted by J.N. Marble in 1916. A native of Bow, Mrs. Eddy formed the Christian Scientist's Association in 1876; the church of Christ Scientist was chartered in 1879. In 1889 Mrs. Eddy returned to New Hampshire from Massachusetts, living in Concord until 1908. NHHS

The Baptist churches in New Hampshire originate from the Great Awakening and the successive visits to the state by the evangelist George Whitefield. The first of these churches was organized in Newton in the 1750s, and by 1800 there were 16 others. During the Revolutionary War a Free Will Baptist Church—inspired indirectly by Whitefield's 1770 visit to New Hampshire—was founded in New Durham. Pictured is the community's church building, erected in 1818-1819. NHHS

have not faithful ministers, will be left a prey to sectarian preachers, who disseminate errors... who create divisions, which weaken society."

By the 1830s, with the state's population rising rapidly, there were 50 New Hampshire Congregational churches without full-time pastors. In those days of unsettled church/state relations, it was difficult to know how to go about supplying church needs. Should the state government do something for ministerial education? Who should develop a seminary and by what authority? Should it be denominational? How should it be financed?

The New Hampshire response, reiterated in different ways and places, came directly from Biblical impulse, not from organizational theory. The brick and mortar that emerged was firmly laid upon a unique pillar of New England theology, namely the Biblical concept of the "wilderness," or "desert": a place of testing as well as the providential setting for the eventual strengthening of the true church. Millenialist theology—the belief that Christ would soon return and usher in the end of the age—was frequently a part of the concept. New England, including New Hampshire, though an alien and unpromising wilderness, was to be God's instrument for working out his kingdom in America, a promised land destined to be a blessing to all nations. The planting of a seminary in the desert, a seed plot of teachers and preachers awaiting "showers of divine blessings" of which the revivals were an emblem, was not only a practical necessity but a reenactment of Biblical history, trial, and blessing. It was to be God's way of building up "the waste places of Zion," that is, the unpastored towns of New Hampshire.

The rich ambiguity and inspirational power of these Biblical metaphors lie behind a good deal of the spiritual history of 19th-century New Hampshire, spilling over into education and eventually into art as well. The motto of Dartmouth College, plucked from the Bible by founder Wheelock, was fitting: *Vox clamantis in Deserto.* But the hope that Dartmouth would strongly supplement the small trickle of trained clergymen from Harvard, Yale, and Andover, had faded unfulfilled. Something more was needed.

A cold summary of the main institutions that emerged from all the warm theology looks like this. *Baptists:* Calvinist Baptists set up an Academical and Theological Institute at New Hampton in 1825, with a three-year academy and theological course. When that school moved to Vermont in 1853, the building was taken over by the Free Will Baptists as New Hampton Biblical and Literary Institute; in 1870 it joined Bates College in Maine, where it was renamed and where it eventually died. *Methodists:* A Vermont-based seminary moved to Concord, New Hampshire, in 1847 and became the Methodist General Biblical Institute. For 21 years it was housed in the old North Congregational Church, and 211 young men graduated from its three-year seminary course. In 1868 the Institute moved to Boston to become the Boston University School of Theology. *Congregationalists:* Kimball Union Academy was established in Meriden in 1813 to prepare young men to enter college with advanced standing so as to enter the ministry more quickly. In 1835 the Academy of Plymouth (founded in 1804) added a theological department, renamed itself Plymouth Literary and Theological Seminary, but, partly because of competition from a more carefully planned seminary effort at Gilmanton, it soon petered out.

The Gilmanton Seminary was academically the most formidable of the New Hampshire seminaries. Founded in 1835 and attached first to the academy that had existed there from 1794, the Seminary soon erected a fine three-story brick building, assembled a good library, admitted students from any orthodox denomination, and graduated its largest class of 10 in 1841. "The wilderness has become as the garden of God," exulted the Reverend David Lancaster, longtime Gilmanton pastor, leading promoter of the Seminary, and short-term Hebrew teacher there. The faculty was distinguished and the course of study solid, largely post-collegiate, with Dartmouth and Harvard graduates among the students. On the faculty prolific scholars such as Herman Rood, Isaac Bird, and William Cogswell stood out. Cogswell left his Dartmouth history professorship to head the Seminary in 1844, and while there he founded a quarterly, which eventually became the *New England Historical and Genealogical Register.* He later edited several volumes of the New Hampshire Historical Society's *Collections.* A half-dozen different journals were started at Gilmanton during its Seminary days. In 1846 activities were suddenly suspended for lack of funds. The Congregational churches, clutching their independence, had never formally and financially backed the project. David Lancaster left Gilmanton for Concord to become chaplain of the legislature and of the insane asylum. The Biblical metaphors had finally failed.

Yet, for a time these various theological institutions had supplied New Hampshire with educated clergymen, and to many they visibly embodied the striking vision of *Isaiah:* "the wilderness and the solitary place shall be glad—and the desert shall rejoice and blossom like a rose." Like many of the classical academies in whose image they were created, the seminaries faded or failed financially or moved away as transportation and communication problems eased. Moreover, the distinctive theological outlook that prompted the seminaries became permanently blurred in New Hampshire as an utterly different kind of moral wilderness, that of an industrial economy, came to prominence on the landscape.

With the influx of immigrants in the beginning of the 20th century, several Eastern Orthodox congregations were formed in New Hampshire. Today the state has a dozen Greek Orthodox and three Russian Orthodox congregations. Pictured is the Holy Resurrection Orthodox Church in Claremont. NHHS

The Seventh-Day Adventist faith, which now sponsors a worldwide missionary service, was born in the New Hampshire hill town of Washington in the 1840s, when several Adventist members of the Christian denomination in that town elected to worship on Saturday. The original Seventh-Day Adventist Church was subsequently organized there in 1862. The 1842 meetinghouse which served the first congregation, shown at left, is now a church of pilgrimage for Adventists from all over the world. Courtesy, Ronald and Grace Jager

CHAPTER
FOURTEEN

AESTHETIC AND LITERARY HAUNTS

New Hampshire has nourished the aesthetic life in dozens of ways, not just in paint and print and photograph and sculpture and architecture but also in crafts and arts innumerable—from Dunlap chests to Prescott violas to Stoddard glass to Graves clarinets.

In the 20th century three very different vehicles have stimulated artistic creativity. The most recent is the publicly funded New Hampshire Commission on the Arts, which supports individual and group projects in music, dance, theater, and related arts. Another is the League of New Hampshire Craftsmen, which, since its founding in 1932, has variously supported its members' work through exhibitions, access to markets, support of the educational aspects of crafts, and by sustaining high standards of craftsmanship. A very different vehicle, whose influence on artistic effort has spread far beyond Granite State borders, is the MacDowell Colony in Peterborough. Created in 1907 by the musicians Marian and Edward MacDowell, its cluster of woodsy workshops and cottages provides short-term retreats for artists, composers, writers, and others. From this colony have come more than two dozen Pulitzer Prize-winning works. Some colony residents have settled in Peterborough and nearby Dublin—the latter town being associated especially with Abbot Thayer and other distinguished painters. Together these two towns may have sheltered more notable musicians, writers, and artists than any similar small communities in America.

In three centuries New Hampshire has produced aesthetic riches too many and too varied to survey. One way to sense the aesthetic impulse within the state is to observe the creativity inspired at just three quite dissimilar locations: the White Mountains, the Isles of Shoals, and the rolling hills of Cornish and Plainfield along the Connecticut River. Each was at one time (and, in a sense, the White Mountains continues to be) a special kind of aesthetic haunt—like the MacDowell Colony, but more spontaneous, and each formed a unique response to the allure of the hills or the sea or the land.

Somewhat apart from these colonies of artists, a counterpoint to them, is the solitary figure of New Hampshire's greatest poet, Robert Frost. Others were caught up in the spell of the landscape, but his was "a road less traveled by," an attachment directly to the land itself, to its people, and to the particular places where their dreams had been.

White Mountain Images

Jeremy Belknap was the first writer in America to give expression to the romantic view of mountains, which had originated in Europe in the late 18th century. He had not yet read Wordsworth on the Alps when he wrote of the White Mountains: "A poetic fancy may find full gratification amidst these wild and rugged scenes. . . . Almost every thing in nature, which can be supposed capable of inspiring ideas of the sublime and beautiful, is here realized. Aged mountains, stupendous elevations, rolling clouds, impending rocks, verdant woods, crystal streams, the gentle rill, and the roaring torrent, all conspire to amaze, to soothe and to enrapture."

That was the view of the White Mountains that lured the first artists there in the early decades of the 19th century, and among them Thomas Cole is preeminent. Both a painter and a writer, Cole saw in mountains the place where "the savage is tempered by the magnificent." Many of his paintings after his first trip to the White Mountains in 1827 explore this view of nature raw, extravagant, fearful, where intimations of morality and religion lurk. Mountains, he wrote, are "a fitting place to speak of God." Towering cliffs, gnarled trees, and stormy skies dominate his best White Mountain canvasses, while analogies dominate his essays: "the broad sheets of untrodden snow that capped the mountains above us were like emblems of nature's purity."

Many other writers and painters picked up these dramatic perspectives on the wilderness. Travel books, such as those of Theodore and Timothy Dwight, highlighted the romance of the White Mountains, as did even such London books as Nathaniel Willis' *American Scenery* published in 1840. Among painters the work of Alvan Fisher, Jasper Cropsey, and Orford's Henry Cheever Pratt supply outstanding expressions of the same themes. Thomas Cole and these others were attracted to the most intimidating aspects of the mountains: to the Crawford and Franconia notches, to cataracts and avalanches, to the peaks and shadows of the Presidentials—to what was called the "sublime" in nature.

Artists who came later in the century often sought out another view, the softer aspect of the slopes, the velvet hills, and cultivated valleys and pastured uplands—the pastoral side of romanticism. Here the mountain peaks provided a distant and stately setting for meadows, cultivated and tame, beside quiet rivers—nature more beneficent than overpowering. If this art suggests an idealization of rural America, it is no wonder: after the Civil War rural New Hampshire was heading for the city faster than at any time in history. It thus also hints of wilderness not merely as a savage thing to be dominated, but as a resource to be

In the mid-19th century, Concord was a center of musical instrument making. Much of the activity was spurred by Abraham Prescott, who had been born in Deerfield but moved to Concord in 1831 to expand his manufacture of bass viols, double bass viols, cellos, and violins. Praised as "the Stradivarius of their type," Prescott viols (such as the bass viol shown here) were sold worldwide and, along with Abbot-Downing's overland coach, made Concord famous around the globe. NHHS

Opposite page: By the 1840s Abraham Prescott was manufacturing melodeons and reed organs as well as his famous stringed instruments, as seen here in this Concord City Directory advertisement from 1856. The business stayed in the family until 1917. NHHS

John S. Blunt was a Portsmouth artist and sign painter in the 1820s. Breaking out of the restrictions of sign work, Blunt advertised this exhibit of paintings in 1828. NHHS

Below and below right: Various exhibitors demonstrate their crafts at a League of New Hampshire Craftsmen's fair around 1940. For many decades the League has held its annual fair in August at Mt. Sunapee State Park in Newbury. Courtesy, League of New Hampshire Craftsmen

cherished—an intimation just breaking into the industrial consciousness of the Granite State in the last quarter of the 19th century.

At about the time of the Civil War, Benjamin Champney settled in North Conway and there gathered around him a group of artists often called the White Mountain School. Among them are the familiar names of Ashur B. Durand, Aaron D. Shattuck, John F. Kensett, Thomas Hill, Albert Bierstadt, Winslow Homer, and many others. The last half of the 19th century also saw the publication of many distinguished illustrated books for the White Mountains fancier—paintings, drawings, engravings, and finally photographs, often accompanied by rather florid texts. "The Switzerland of America" was the phrase that was supposed to make hearts flutter. Moses Sweetser's *Views of the White Mountains* (1879) is a classic example of these books. In prose, nothing excels the loftiness of rhetoric and feeling that was poured into Thomas Starr King's *The White Hills* (1859), wherein piety toward God and nature are remarkably combined but not confused. His special talent, or compulsion, was to describe in exact detail the scene from the best viewing spots and then to quote a bit of verse to heighten the experience.

These artists and others gave form to different and competing conceptions of New Hampshire wilds. One extols wilderness *as wilderness*—provided that it is distilled in painting or prose or even framed by the window of an excursion train crossing the Frankenstein trestle or climbing Jacob's Ladder. The other is a more contemplative view, wilderness itself is domesticated, some order has been imposed, and the central landscape is at peace with itself.

Such contrasting images are also summaries of historical realities. For it is plainly true that the White Mountains as first found were ragged and raw, that Mt. Washington undeniably has a certain stolid and durable majesty, and that the region as a whole has a climate Arctic enough to keep the treeline at 4,000 feet (compared with 10,000 feet in the Rockies), just as it is also true that by mid-century this region was partially subdued—roads and railroads had brought in people, farms had crept to the base of the slopes, and villages had sprouted in the valleys.

In the wake of the stock market crash of October 1929, Manchester put the finishing touches on the State Theatre, billed as the largest theater north of Boston (with 2,187 seats) and extolled for its "futuristic design." Workmen (left) put the finishing touches on the theater's figurehead. On Wednesday evening, November 27, 1929, the theater opened to an overflow audience (above), including Governor Charles Tobey. For those lucky enough to get in, an orchestra seat cost 40 cents and a balcony seat cost 30 cents. MVHC

The Sea and the Shoals

Here is a very different sort of landscape-hardly a *land*scape at all. These isles are piles of irregular green-crowned and treeless granite off the coast of Rye: nine small islands, nine miles out, together only a few hundred acres. "A stern and lovely scene," wrote Nathaniel Hawthorne. Bleak in appearance, rich in historical association, their record goes back to 1614 when Captain John Smith noticed "the remarkablest isles . . . a heap together . . . a many of barren rocks." Their destiny has turned with tides and time: in the 17th century a major fishing station with hundreds of residents; in the 18th century intermittent fishing and a washed-out maritime community; in the 19th century a tourist retreat and a haven for artists and writers; and in the 20th century a center for marine biology and religious conferences.

During the middle of the 19th century two large hotels on the Isles were often filled the summer long. Visitors sought island seclusion, sought stern and lovely scenery, and they also sought each other. For a chosen few the center of attraction was Celia Laighton Thaxter, who had grown up on the Isles, married there, and became a much-published poet. For 30 years, from the Civil War onward, she spent most summers on Appledore

Island, gardening, writing, painting, and playing host to a coterie of "beauties and geniuses" (as a contemporary called them) from all over New England, who were captivated by her talents, her friends, her gardens, her island setting, and her hospitality. A salon of latter-day transcendentalists thrived at her cottage, including artists who came to paint her flowers, the seascapes, the rocks, and to illustrate her books, musicians who came to play, and writers who came to talk. Many returned year after year. Among the writers were John Greenleaf Whittier, Oliver Wendell Holmes, Ralph Waldo Emerson, James Russell Lowell, James Whitcomb Riley, Harriet Beecher Stowe, Sarah Orne Jewett, and Thomas Bailey Aldrich.

One visitor, John Albee, later reminisced: "She could make the musician play his best, the poets and scholars say their best—even Mr. Whittier could be vivacious and communicative. . . . To see Celia Thaxter so surrounded by her flowers, lovers, pictures, books, and souvenirs, to listen to the speech and music of her gifted friends, was the most picturesque and exciting spectacle afforded in this part of the country." "Picturesque"—it had become a favorite term of approval by the latter part of the 19th century.

Celia Thaxter's own verses were well known at the time and much admired. If today they appear to be somewhat dewy with sunsets and dawnings, the sweet voice of 19th-century femininity, her other work is of more universal appeal. John Greenleaf Whittier coaxed, cajoled, and flattered her into writing a small volume on the Isles themselves. Her book, *Among the Isles of Shoals*, first published in 1873 and much reprinted, is a graceful prose poem that catches and blends the austerity and romance of the Isles. No one has captured more feelingly than she the sublime aftermath of a dark storm over the Isles: "this solemn gray lid was lifted at its western edge, and an insufferable splendor streamed across the world from the sinking sun. The whole heaven was in a blaze of scarlet, across which sprang a rainbow unbroken to the topmost clouds, 'with its seven perfect colors chorded in a triumph,' against the flaming background; the sea answered the sky's rich blue, and the gray rocks lay drowned in melancholy purple. I hid my face from the glory,—it was too much to bear."

Above: The Isles of Shoals had been a center of fishing and commercial activity throughout the 17th and early 18th centuries, but by the time this picture was taken, circa 1875, the tiny church at Gosport was serving the needs of very few. Built in 1800, the church stood up to many Atlantic storms, although its wooden tower pictured was blown down in 1890, to be replaced by another of stone. NHHS

Opposite page: "Swept by every wind that blows, and beaten by the bitter brine for unknown ages, well may the Isles of Shoals be barren, bleak, and bare." Nineteenth-century poetess Celia Thaxter knew the islands about which she wrote and understood why the stranger might be "struck only by the sadness of the place,—the vast loneliness; for there are not even trees to whisper with familiar voices,—nothing but sky and sea and rocks." From the Historic Photograph Collection of Strawbery Banke, Inc.

The Flowering of Cornish

As the Thaxter circle at the Shoals faded and the White Mountain School of artists dispersed, another New Hampshire flowering, not connected with the others, opened at another place.

A New York lawyer bought up several thousand acres of cheap, abandoned farmland near the Connecticut River in Cornish in 1884. One tract featured a bleak old brick structure, and this property he sold to a fellow New Yorker, the sculptor Augustus Saint-Gaudens. Other New Yorkers came to visit and some stayed to paint the scenery, whereupon the countryside itself began to work its spell upon a whole train of voluntary exiles from New York. Something oddly wonderful was going on: farmers' sons were seeking the city for a new lease on life; city artists were seeking out the abandoned farms for a new inspiration.

Some of the earliest to come to Cornish were assistants of Saint-Gaudens, sculptors on their way to important careers of their own. Among the early painters were George de Forest Brush and Thomas Dewing, and after them were others, including Charles Platt and Stephen Parrish, both distinguished etchers with other talents, too. The latter's son, Maxfield Parrish, came to Cornish in 1898 and found there a perfect setting for his extraordinary talent as illustrator and artist. From his studio (just over the Cornish line in Plainfield) flowed a stream of illustrations for everything from chocolate boxes to children's books, to magazines and calendars, all in a wonderfully personal style, colorful, droll, and dramatic. There came too a stream of paintings, stunning portrayals unlike anything seen hitherto, at once accurate and romantic: beige hillsides and exquisite blue skies and haunting purple dusks. Fortunately it was work more than good enough to survive the indignity of having been immediately and highly appreciated: not for Parrish the doleful legends of the struggling artist starving in a garret; most of his life he was rich and famous. Parrish's landscape work—his favorite subject—is largely untouched by the traditions of White Mountain painting and constitutes today the major 20th-century New Hampshire answer to that great tradition of the 19th century.

Writers migrated to the Cornish hills as well—the poets William Vaughn Moody and Percy MacKaye, and the novelist Winston Churchill, who later went on to a bright brief political career in New Hampshire, were joined—sometimes for just a summer or two—by a dozen other critics, authors, playwrights, and editors. Arthur Whitney, the composer and musician, came and went as did others. Charles Platt, who was first an etcher and a painter and then a landscape artist and architect, designed houses for his Cornish friends, many with hillside terraces or Italian gardens. By the turn of the century there was a "little New York" on the banks of the Connecticut, and Augustus Saint-Gaudens was its most distinguished citizen. Indeed, right from the time he came he was perhaps the best-known sculptor in the nation—with such memorable achievements as *The Puritan, The Standing Lincoln, Sherman,* and others which, like Parrish's landscapes, are now a permanent part of the American artistic canon.

The other eminent national sculptor of the time was Daniel Chester French of Exeter, and he, too, spent several summers of the 1890s in Cornish. Dublin, New Hampshire, was the base of

Beginning in 1900, Augustus Saint-Gaudens made Cornish his home and around him developed a colony of artists, writers, and summer guests— attracted as much by the ambience he evoked at "Aspet" as by the "further vales and big irregular hills" along the Connecticut. This portrait by Kenyon Cox, a summer colonist, shows the sculptor at work in 1908. Courtesy, The Metropolitan Museum of Art, gift of friends of the sculptor, 1908

an older and, by some accounts, a somewhat stuffier artistic colony. George de Forest Brush did leave Cornish for Dublin when he joined the painter Abbot Thayer. Barry Faulkner of Keene bridged the two colonies, being a student of both Saint-Gaudens and Thayer. A Dublin friend wrote to Mrs. Churchill, wife of the novelist, asking what clothes to bring on her proposed visit to Cornish, and Mrs. Churchill replied in a private letter: "In Cornish we wear our oldest clothes, and when we go to Windsor, the little Vermont village across the river, we wear nothing at all." In 1879 the Windsor paper had written: "We continue to absorb all the noted artists and sculptors in America."

The Cornish colony lasted little more than a quarter-century. Homer Saint-Gaudens, a writer and son of the sculptor, observed that the colony as a separate entity had already peaked by 1907, the year Saint-Gaudens died; a new generation of artists went elsewhere, sought other inspirations. But for a time something had "called strongly to these artists," he wrote; perhaps it

was the "peace and dreamlike ripeness of the hills . . . their dark clumps of trees . . . their river winding south" before Mt. Ascutney. The grip of the place was strong: Maxfield Parrish declined an invitation in 1913 to head Yale's art department and continued to live and work productively at his Cornish home and studio for many decades after the colony had dispersed. In a sense he outlived his early fame and carried on, still painting, into his "rediscovery" in the 1960s. He died at his home, The Oaks, in 1966 at age 95.

The Italian gardens have been abandoned. Some of the houses have burned. The pastured fields have turned to trees. The old beloved scenes are mostly gone. Some of the houses and a few of the studios remain, hidden now behind the new-grown forests. A Maxfield Parrish museum and studio still stands near where his home, which burned, has been rebuilt. And the old brick tavern that Saint-Gaudens turned into a magnificent house, "Aspet," stands regally amid mowed fields surrounded by his yard and studios, open to visitors. Well preserved and well cared for, it is now a National Historic Site.

Frost Country

While the Cornish colony flourished in western New Hampshire there lived on the opposite edge of the state an awkward and shy young farmer, who had a great gift within him but no very cer-

tain sense of direction. He was Robert Frost of Derry. He had probably never heard of the Cornish colony, wouldn't have been in the slightest interested anyway, and would have found such company and setting no inspiration at all. Unlike the young Frost, the artists of Cornish knew who they were and what they were about. They were nourished by the scenes of Cornish—which might have been anywhere but happened to be in western New Hampshire. Frost was not moved by scenes, but by things he saw.

Robert Frost was born in California from an old New Hampshire family and came to New England at the age of nine. He had little talent for conventional study; he tried two colleges, Dartmouth and Harvard, and left them both. He took up farming at a time when New Hampshire farming was going downhill. On the Derry farm, which he had inherited from his grandfather, he was, by 1906, working harder at his poetry than at his farming; neither was producing a decent living, so he sought employment at Pinkerton Academy. Part of his application was "The Tuft of Flowers," read aloud by a friend, and someone glimpsed there a spirit that could be turned to advantage in a classroom. Weak as a student, Frost proved strong as a teacher, and best of all as a teacher of teachers. His stint at Pinkerton and later at the State Normal School at Plymouth, where he went in 1911, were only stopping places, stages on the way to his liberation as a country poet.

Having sold the farm in 1912, Frost gathered his courage, his unpublished pieces, and his family, and went to London to make a stab at a literary career. To a New Hampshire friend he wrote "My dream would be to get the thing started in London and then do the rest of it from a farm in New England where I could live

Left: Birches line an unpaved road in New Hampshire's "Frost country." SPNHF

Opposite page, left: In 1827 Sarah Josepha Hale of Newport published the novel Northwood, *which became a bestseller. Subsequently she became editor of the* Ladies' Magazine, *a new Boston periodical, and later of the original* Godey's Lady's Book *where she worked for close to 40 years. She was involved with a number of social causes, including raising money to complete the Bunker Hill Monument, persuading President Lincoln to declare a national Thanksgiving Day, and promoting higher education for women. NHHS*

Opposite page, right: Boxed in by the attitudes and cultural constraints of the 1950s, Grace Metalious (who was born in Manchester and lived subsequently in Belmont and Gilmanton) wrote of futility, alienation and hypocrisy in her 1956 novel Peyton Place. *The book sold more copies than had any previous American novel; even among those who did not read it, "Peyton Place" came to stand for all the dark undercurrents of small-town life. Photograph by Larry Smith*

In the title poem of his 1923 Pulitzer Prize winning book New Hampshire, *Robert Frost wrote:*

> I choose to be a plain New Hampshire farmer . . .
> It's restful to arrive at a decision,
> And restful just to think about New Hampshire.
> At present I am living in Vermont.

Lotte Jacobi, the well-known photographer who made her home in Deering for many years, took this picture of Robert Frost in Ripton, Vermont, in 1959. Photograph by Lotte Jacobi.

cheap and get Yankier and Yankier.'' He did just that. His first two books of poetry were published in England, and he returned to New Hampshire in 1915 to find his reputation established. He settled in Franconia, lived cheap, and got Yankier. In a 1916 interview he said: ''You can't be universal without being provincial, can you? It's like trying to embrace the wind.''

Perhaps no province of the country has ever been more carefully or more profoundly rendered into poetry than New Hampshire has been in the poetry of Robert Frost. He captured the cadence and diction of his neighbors and the actual ingredients of their lives—moving rocks and cutting trees and mowing hay and feeding chickens—using the furniture of land to let us in on the meaning of life. He wrote of loneliness and tragedy and of the simple silent satisfaction of doing a small job well, and he wrote the tang of the New England weather and the seasons into his poetry. He constantly caught country people being human—sad, elated, perplexed—and he caught them speaking poetry unawares, and slyly told on them. ''Poetry is simply made of metaphor,'' he declared, ''saying one thing and meaning another, saying one thing in terms of another.'' He almost made his New England, his New Hampshire, America's metaphor. In the course of a very long career that lasted into the 1960s, there fell to Frost a vast responsibility he had never sought and which no one conferred: he formed and handed over to the American public an image of New England that is now inescapable. ''The land is always in my bones,'' he said. Fortunately, even natives acknowledge that he was on pitch: a singular but accurate voice, halting at first in those Derry years, but soon flowing clear and strong as if arising directly from the New Hampshire soil, limpid and natural as a sidehill spring, speaking the land's own language.

Wilderness and Village

Landscape is what catches the eye of the New Hampshire artist: landscape, robust, sublime, and irresistible, like an avalanche in a howling wilderness, or landscape pastoral and reposed like a village in a rolling countryside.

''Wilderness theology,'' that blend of faith and hope, was sowing seminaries and academies into small towns just when the actual wilderness of New Hampshire, driven to a corner in the northern part of the state, was being redeemed in another way— by being reaffirmed in art. Nathaniel Hawthorne and others came to Crawford Notch, picked up bits of mountain history and legend and turned them into story. Throughout New Hampshire, wilderness as a fact of life became also an artifact of imagination, a mixture of record and myth. For a generation artists produced canvasses and reproduced engravings of the scene of the Willey slide, the avalanche of 1826 that destroyed a family and left their home intact. From 1830 onward, painters, poets, and writers came north to revel in mountain gloom and mountain glory.

As for the wilderness, so too for the countryside: record merged with myth. The self-sufficient farm of the early 19th century was extracted from the forest and hillside, framed with stone walls, presented to the village by a winding road, made a pillar of a rural economy, and promptly entered into history and fable at

one stroke. The family farm became a tenet of American theology; town government, the political emblem of the village community, became the touchstone of New Hampshire politics, giving to everything a sense of place. Jeremy Belknap, New Hampshire historian, praised the simplicities of a "happy society" of rural villagers. And so on and on. All this sentiment poured out upon the soil seeped into New England's self-image, there to work its wonders and then to spill out eloquently in many places, including such oddly contrasting crossroad towns as Northwood, Coniston, Grovers Corners, and Peyton Place.

That at least was the general shape of things as delivered to the mid-20th century.

It was not quite the same in the last quarter of the century. For one thing, the wilderness of New Hampshire as summed up in the White Mountains seldom evokes that old rapture and awe—the majestic, the terrible, and the sublime are ideas we now associate with the mountains more through art and literature and history than through direct experience. In our day the main experience linked with the mountains is recreation—a social commodity in which New Hampshire specializes and a valid mode in its own right. But recreation does not reenact the original confrontation with "nature red in tooth and claw," nor is it the old 19th-century encounter with gloom and glory. We have changed at least as much as the mountains. For a thousand related reasons the New Hampshire small town too, beloved and beleaguered as it is, is also now an ambiguous locus of value. Half of those shapely colonial homes in the village are owned by the folks from Connecticut.

But the aesthetic eye in New Hampshire—especially of the writer and the painter—is artfully selective, and when it wanders over the images that simplify and distill the state's historical drama it settles again and again on the associations of wilderness and village. They embrace New Hampshire's earliest and longest experiences. As images these survive partly through the effective way in which they mix and contrast with other facts and other images: for here, there, and everywhere the machine crept into the village garden and the red-brick factory rose up on the riverbank beneath the elms and willows; tourists trouped in and reminded natives of what is all about them; technologies and their economies swept into the southern regions of the state and prevailed, and by prevailing reminded everyone of what had once been.

And Robert Frost—who had lived in villages and near mountain wilds—came and blithely took for granted this whole century-long dance of general truisms about the landscape, and started gazing hard at the land itself to see what particularly was true of it: bent birches and ax handles and broken paths to cellar holes and hayfields and mud season, and also poetry lived and spoken inadvertently by people as real as the neighbors.

Nevertheless, village and wilderness, and the intricate web of experiences that radiates over the centuries from them, have supplied New Hampshire artists and writers—custodians of our imagination and thus of our history—with their most durable raw material. Even were wilderness and village themselves to pass away entirely, as they emphatically have not, their place in New Hampshire landscape and memory is intact.

The Robert Frost Farm as it appears today. This was home to the Frost family from 1900 (with brief stints in Derry Village and in Plymouth, New Hampshire) until he sold the farm in 1911 and moved to England. The poetry he wrote here and published in England established his reputation. During the 1960s this farmstead was a junk yard for autos, and was known as Frosty Acres. Eventually, public embarrassment at the spectacle prodded the State of New Hampshire to purchase the property and restore it. It is now open to the public, as is Frost's later New Hampshire home, in Franconia. Courtesy, R. & G. Jager

Pinkerton Academy in Derry was an early and well-endowed New Hampshire academy. It opened in 1815 and this elaborate Romanesque Revival brick and brownstone building was erected in 1886-7. Robert Frost taught here from 1906 to 1911, the approximate date of this photo. Courtesy, R. & G. Jager

Amy Cheney Beach (1867-1944), born in Henniker, was a child musical prodigy, playing piano by ear at 4, and performing with the Boston Symphony Orchestra at 17. Married at 18 (to a husband who didn't wish her to perform) she turned to composition, and at 25 was the first woman to have her work performed by the Handel and Haydn Society in Boston. Her Gaelic Symphony (1896) was the first published symphonic work composed by an American woman. She was on her way to becoming the country's foremost woman composer and (especially after her husband's death) also a virtuoso pianist who performed her compositions with many orchestras in this country and in Europe. Her lush romantic style fell from favor after her death, but a half century later is again much appreciated. Her name was recently inscribed on the Hatch Shell on the Esplanade in Boston—the first woman to be thus honored. Concord Monitor

Right: Daniel Chester French (1850-1931), born in Exeter and educated in Concord, New Hampshire, first showed his talent as a sculptor in The Minutemen statue now in Concord, Massachusetts. Later he created the sculpture over the entrance of the New Hampshire Historical Society's Tuck Library, also the John Harvard now in Harvard Yard and many others, culminating in his masterpiece, the seated Lincoln of the Lincoln Memorial in Washington, DC. NHIFIS

Not until 1914 was President Franklin Pierce honored with a statue on the State House Plaza. The pedestal of the bronze statue carries a resume of the former president, chiseled in granite, including these words: "A lawyer who loved his profession and was a great leader in it. Member New Hampshire Legislature at 25 and Speaker at 27, Congressman at 29, United States Senator at 32. President of the United States." There is also this tribute from Ulysses S. Grant: "He was a gentleman and a man of courage." Photo by Andrea Bruce, Concord Monitor

The Pierce Homestead, two views. The home of Revolutionary War officer and popular New Hampshire Governor (elected to two one-year terms, 1827 and 1829) Benjamin Pierce. Also the boyhood home of his son, later President, Franklin Pierce. The family first occupied this house in 1804, shortly after Franklin was born in a small house nearby. The porch was added and several windows lowered to accommodate it in the 1870s, the beginning of the era when long piazzas became the latest statement in architectural assertiveness. In 1925 the house was sold to the State of New Hampshire for one dollar. Afterwards, the porch was removed and various preservation efforts undertaken. Serious restoration dates from the 1980s when the Hillsborough Historical Society assumed full responsibility for the Homestead. Under their leadership the house is being authentically restored, down to the last detail of 1830s color and style, and furnished with period pieces. The picture with the porch dates from about 1900, the other from 2000. Courtesy, R. & G. Jager

The Pierce Manse. This is the 1830s Greek Revival home purchased in 1842 by Franklin Pierce when he resigned from the United States Senate and returned to Concord to resume his law career. The Pierce's son Franky died here, and from here he left for the Mexican War, but sold the house soon after his return. Threatened with demolition by an urban renewal project in the 1960s, it was saved by a voluntary group, The Pierce Brigade, which bought the house and had it moved to the present site in Concord's Historic District in 1971. It is kept as a memorial to the nation's 14th President. Courtesy, R. & G. Jager

When Concord schoolteacher Benjamin Thompson was chased from New Hampshire for his "Tory" sympathies in 1774, he apologized to his family, saying, "I thought it absolutely necessary to abscond for a while and seek a friendly Asylum in some distant part." His quest for a "friendly Asylum" led him throughout Europe, where he gained a reputation as one of the great scientific minds of the 18th century. In Bavaria he was knighted "Count Rumford" in 1791, in honor of the New Hampshire town that forced him to leave 17 years before. This William Lane chalk drawing of Rumford was considered by Rumford's daughter Sarah to be "the best likeness to my fancy, that was ever taken of him." NHHS

Above right: Ezra Woolson of Fitz-william painted this portrait of Jesse Kittredge Smith, "a skilful surgeon and physician" in Mont Vernon. The pink, blue, and green potions identify Smith's profession, and the scene out the window is probably of his dwelling. Woolson's career as a painter was brief. Born in 1824, he died suddenly in 1845 at age 21. Courtesy, Old Sturbridge Village

Right: Franklin Pierce was only 27 years old when he became speaker of the New Hampshire House of Representatives. By the time he became the 14th President of the United States, he had served in the United States House of Representatives and Senate, and the U.S. Army—as a brigadier general in the Mexican War. As President, he tried valiantly to hold North and South together, yet his belief in the limited constitutional role of the federal government doomed his efforts. At least he was a good-looking President. This circa 1852 portrait is attributed to the artist George P.A. Healy. NHHS

Left: This circa 1825 watercolor shows a parlor in the home of Moses Morse, a cabinetmaker in Loudon. The floor is painted in a checkered pattern, and the walls are decorated with stenciling, popular because it approximated the color and motifs of more expensive wallpaper and provided charms of its own. The desk to the right is typical of late Federal inlaid furniture, which was fashionable in New Hampshire until the 1830s. Privately owned

Above: Although discovered in New Hampshire and titled Piano Recital at Count Rumford's, Concord, N.H., this stylish circa 1800 watercolor may well depict an English setting. Nevertheless it presents a charming picture of the fashions of the day. Courtesy, National Gallery of Art, Washington; gift of Edgar William and Bernice Chrysler Garbisch

Above: It is appropriate that English native and Concord resident John Burgum painted this circa 1868 picture, Shipment of Thirty Coaches to Wells Fargo. *He also painted the coaches—all 30 of them. Burgum, and later his son Edwin, made their living (or at least much of it) painting the world-famous Concord Coach. Burgum based this painting on a photograph of the train leaving Concord and heading down the Merrimack River Valley. NHHS*

Top: Artist Enoch Wood Perry, Jr., painted The Pemigewasset Coach *probably around 1899. Unlike Crawford Notch, Franconia Notch was never violated by the railroad. Hence, tourists wishing to get to the Profile House or the hotels in Bethlehem often took the coach north from Plymouth or North Woodstock, much to the delight of children living along the route. Courtesy, Shelburne Museum, Shelburne, Vermont*

Above: The Concord Coach, a product of Concord's Abbot-Downing Company, gave 19th-century travelers around the world the best ride one could expect on 19th-century roads. This circa 1852 coach was used for many years in Massachusetts, until it appeared in the New York World's Fair of 1941-1942. After second-generation coach painter Edwin G. Burgum (son of John Burgum) redecorated the vehicle in 1942, it was "retired" to the Boston & Maine Railroad Station in Concord before coming to the New Hampshire Historical Society. Photograph by Bill Finney

Cutting wood—saw wood and cord wood—provided income in the wintertime for many New Hampshire farmers, occupying their days from mid-November even until early April if spring thaws held off. Edward Hill's Lumbering Camp in Winter *is dated 1882; Hill and his better-known brother Thomas were among the most prolific of the White Mountain artists. NHHS*

This circa 1860 lithograph shows activity at Amoskeag Falls with the new city of Manchester on the horizon. NHHS

Top left: At a time when skill in needlework was an important social grace, the making of a sampler was as much a part of a young women's education as learning to read and write. This florid show of silk embroidery on linen was worked by Hannah Foster of Canterbury when she was 12 years old. NHHS

Top right: The founding of the League of New Hampshire Craftsmen in 1932 prompted a renaissance of traditional crafts and their increased populartiy. this poster, celebrating the League's 50th anniversary, was designed by Lance Hidy. Courtesy, League of New Hampshire Craftsmen

Above: Maxfield Parrish came to the Cornish colony in the 1890s, and in 1898 he built his home and studio nearby in Plainfield where he painted for almost 70 years. Afterglow, *painted in 1947, effectively explains the attraction New Hampshire had for Parrish. Privately owned. Photograph courtesy, Vose Galleries*

Left: Since it was built in 1902, the Mt. Washington Hotel in Bretton Woods has carried on the tradition of the "grand hotel" in the White Mountains. In July 1944 the 44-nation Bretton Woods Conference that framed monetary policy after World War II was held there.   Photo by Peter Randall.

Opposite page, top: Amusement parks were often built outside city limits to increase the use of car lines. Burgett Park in Somersworth, an attractive example located between Dover and Great Falls, was developed in 1890 by H. W. Burgett. NHHS

Opposite page, bottom: Although the Amoskeag Manufacturing Company went on to become the world's largest manufacturer of textiles, this circa 1856 John H. Bufford lithograph extols one of Amoskeag's other interests, the manufacture of locomotives. Prior to the Civil War Amoskeag machine shops turned out over 200 locomotives. NHHS

BURGETT PARK

On line of
Union Street Railroad
between DOVER and GREAT FALLS, N.H.

In 1826 Thomas Cole was the first major American artist to visit the White Mountains. The scenery, he wrote, furnished "a rich profusion of the sublime and beautiful." Through the remainder of the 19th century artists in great numbers followed. Pictured, clockwise from above, are The Notch of the White Mountains, *painted in 1839 by Thomas Cole (courtesy, National Gallery of Art),* Albert Bierstadt's circa 1862 Moat Mountain, Intervale, New Hampshire *and Jasper Cropsey's 1857* Indian Summer Morning in the White Mountains *(both courtesy, Currier Gallery of Art), and* Autumnal Snow on Mt. Washington, *painted in 1856 by Aaron D. Shattuck (courtesy, Vassar College Art Gallery).*

The Winchester-Ashuelot Covered Bridge is in the southwest corner of New Hampshire. Photo by Peter E. Randall

The Wentworth-Coolidge Mansion in Little Harbor, Portsmouth was the home of Benning Wentworth, a conspicuous and powerful colonial governor of New Hampshire for 27 years (1740-1767). Lilacs were first mentioned in New Hampshire documents in 1750 when the Governor had this house and its plantings enlarged. Accordingly, these lilacs are celebrated as having been here since that time. In 1919, after much confusing but benign controversy in the Legislature, the purple lilac, Syringa vulgaris was selected as the New Hampshire state flower—beating back strong advocacy for the apple blossom, goldenrod, and purple aster. Photo by Peter E. Randall

Each July Concord declares a short week of Market Days, closing Main Street to traffic and opening it to pedestrians and marketing, while stores move merchandise out of doors and the public has a cheerful spendthrift time. In a tribute to its architectural distinction, this region of Concord has recently been placed on the National Register of Historic Places. Concord Monitor

Preceding page: In Richard Whitney's award-winning Edges of April Sky, painted between 1976 and 1978, New Hampshire's landscape is seen as a blend of urban and rural. Thriving town and city centers, which mix the old and the new, are surrounded by forested hillsides. The artist is a 1968 graduate of the University of New Hampshire and a resident of Keene. Courtesy, Richard Whitney.

V
INTO THE 21ST CENTURY

CHAPTER
FIFTEEN

THE CENTURY TURNS

In the earlier chapters of this book the Granite State's long and meandering history is channeled for review into four streams—natural, social, economic, and cultural history. As the state closed out the last decades of the 20th century these four ideas again provide a convenient way to survey the most recent high points and changes in the state's historical landscape.

Natural History

New Hampshire frets a great deal over the care and keeping of its oft-praised rural character—an issue that has engaged and vexed the state for a very long time and may be there until the White Mountains themselves are leveled and paved over. It is a recurring challenge because New Hampshire is again the fastest growing state in the Northeast, and it is really much more industrialized, urbanized, and commercialized than is Vermont, its neighbor and twin. Vermont truly is rural, it knows that and says so; New Hampshire remembers that it was, pretends, hopes, and boasts of its high tech economy, and is generally ambivalent on the matter.

Reports from New Hampshire's Department of Agriculture firmly state that "agriculture is a major component of the New Hampshire economy and a major influence on the state's character and quality of life." Yes, true since colonial days, and true today: agriculture adds nearly half a billion dollars to the state's yearly economy. Yet, one senses that traditional farming as a way of life may now be more praised than appreciated, and is probably more appreciated than understood. The dairy farms of the state, about 200 of them, are fewer and larger than they were 20 years ago, and the cows are fewer too, but total milk production is up while the profit margin is down. That, in brief compass, is the commodity farm story: fewer, larger, more efficient, narrower profits, and an encircling network of global markets. The latter is especially pertinent to the state's apple farmers, for example, who produce over a million bushels of apples a year, a bushel for every resident, though many of those apples are in fact exported. Meanwhile, New Hampshirites today (unlike 20 years ago) eat tons of apples from New Zealand, South Africa, China, Israel and a dozen other countries. Now we live in a global village and munch from a global orchard.

Agriculture today also has a direct influence on the scenic quality of the state, as it always has, for farming provides the rolling pastures and meadows that buffer commercial and residential areas, and farm fields afford the long views of valleys and mountains. How, then, to repay the farmer for this inestimable service? And will it continue into the indefinite future? Well may we fret. Today there are fewer fields than before, and far fewer of the state's milk cows now graze on grassy hillsides: unfortunately, cows produce more, and do it more efficiently, when their dinner is brought to them. We notice the absence of cows on the distant slopes because our preferred memories are, indeed, rural memories.

While New Hampshire still produces bulk commodity crops in abundance, such as milk and maple syrup and apples, there remain only a few major egg producers and no longer any major growers of potatoes, both farm staples of earlier times. On the other hand, greenhouse and ornamental horticulture is a fast-growing sector of the state's agriculture, as are speciality and processed food products. In fact, the number of New Hampshire farms is presently increasing and now totals nearly 3,000, slightly above the number of 20 years ago (though less than a quarter of what it was 50 years ago), suggesting that by one measure the long slide from an earlier farming high point has been arrested. However, a farm is still defined, as it has been for many decades, as a place that sells $1,000 or more in grown products per year, so the definition and hence the number of farms is subject to inflation. Variety has become the hallmark of New Hampshire farms, and the list of different farm products raised and sold for profit gets longer each year. Speaking of alternative animal agri-

New Hampshire apple growers harvest about a million bushels each year, and they produce rivers of cider; some growers have up to 75 different apple varieties. Planting apple trees involves a long-term commitment, and growers today survive on ever narrower margins and an insecure market. Concentrate (for apple juice) from foreign apples now floods the American market, wholesalers are increasingly fussy about unpasteurized cider, and apple competition itself is now worldwide. Nevertheless, New Hampshire trees will produce another million bushels this year. Photo by Lara Solt, Concord Monitor

culture, Agricultural Commissioner Stephen Taylor recently wrote: " I'm now convinced it's here to stay. Across New Hampshire we've got elk, deer, bison, llama, alpaca, emu, and ostrich farms and plenty of enthusiastic owners."

For decades the state's landscape has been nearly 90 percent forested, and to many that seems about right, though forested does not necessarily mean rural. Whatever rural character does mean, exactly—certainly different things to different people—it is pretty clear that in New Hampshire it is still regarded as a good thing, deserving of appreciation and requiring preservation. In fact, the state's unspoken social assumptions still lean toward the ancient and romantic: rural character is good, urban is not good, developments are bad, farming is good, forest land is good, wilderness is excellent, strip malls are bad, country is good, sprawl is very bad, and to "save" land from development is a noble social virtue. Anyway, that's the widespread bias—even as we know our world is not quite that simple, and even as our economists and politicians boast about our growth rate and many citizens deplore the regulations that are necessary to accommodate it. The truth is that our natural and rural environment, which we both cherish and misuse, is awash with messy details. Here is a pair of details: in 1999 Adopt-a-Highway volunteers filled 24,283 litter bags from state roadsides, but the state legislature has yet to pass a "bottle bill."

Proper use of open land is a perennial issue, and every rural town now wrestles with it, a microcosm of the larger struggles which tell the larger story. One such struggle, unique in the state's history but typical of its character, was nicknamed "The Great Nuclear

New Hampshire maple trees still sprout buckets in early spring when the snow still lies against the stonewalls. For hundreds of years, the making of maple sugar and syrup—in a season when not much else is going on—has supplemented New Hampshire farm income. Technology is transforming the practice: plastic tubing, sometimes with a vacuum pump, is now often used to gather the sap and, for the larger sugar orchards, reverse osmosis machines are used to extract some of the water from the sap. In a typical year New Hampshire produces about 75,000 gallons of syrup. Photo by Kim Brent, Concord Monitor

In January 1998 much of Western New Hampshire suffered the most severe ice storm in memory. Many higher elevations were transformed into surreal landscapes, at once beautiful and terrible, where lines were down and trees were stripped or flattened as if in a war zone. The National Guard was activated and in many communities Guardsmen went door-to-door to check on residents' supplies of water, fuel, and food. Here two Guardsmen walk through an eerily beautiful and stricken New London neighborhood. Photo by Andrea Bruce, Concord Monitor

Dump Fight." In January 1986 New Hampshire learned that the United States Department of Energy (DOE) had identified a dozen sites in seven states from Maine to Georgia, including one in New Hampshire, as having potential for a permanent nuclear waste repository—all in accord with a 1982 federal law laying out a 16-year timetable for creating a permanent repository in the eastern United States. The idea was to study these dozen sites systematically, narrow the list slowly, and choose just one eventually. At the chosen site engineers would hollow out enormous caverns and a series of narrower tunnels, deep within the solid granite; the tunnels would be miles wide and miles long, and more than a half mile underground. And there, surrounded with solid granite, they would store the nuclear waste, most of it lethally radioactive for half a million years. (Such a cavern for nuclear waste was completed in the year 2000 deep within the salt beds of southeast New Mexico. The Eastern repository was to be its granite counterpart.)

The designated spot in New Hampshire was 78 square miles of granite centered under the town of Hillsboro and spilling into eight neighboring towns. Initially, to many New Hampshire people the whole idea seemed utterly fantastic, lunatic even, and to some it seemed almost sacrilege even to contemplate such a treatment of the granite of the Granite State. Within a fortnight the idea had triggered genuine waves of alarm and disbelief. "They simply can't do that; this is our state, our land!" But there lay the official DOE report, four volumes of heroically-bland, bureaucratic prose; and there lay the geological map of the site where about 13,000 people lived, most of it idyllic postcard New Hampshire landscape, parts of it also somewhat billboarded and bedraggled. New Hampshire was given 90 days to comment and the clock, they said, was running. Like an impending hanging, this concentrated the mind of the people. The comment? A spontaneous grassroots explosion of frustration, anger, and resolve as hard as granite, "Never!"

Two citizen groups ignited in Hillsboro, first "The Citizen Task Force," and then "The People of New Hampshire Against the Nuclear Dump." Protests, rallies, action groups, and research sub-committees sprouted and spread and then flowered throughout the spring of 1986. The strategy of the Task Force was to assemble

Electric power companies maintain about 2,000 miles of transmission lines in New Hampshire, requiring 30,000 acres of land— terrain that is rough and rocky, requiring expensive cutting every few years to control brush and trees. Public Service Company of New Hampshire has contracted with Dick Henry of Bellwether Solutions to employ sheep to do some of the mowing, and eventually kill the undesirable plants. Of the three flocks at work in New Hampshire, this one of about 350 Rambouillets, is managed by Christopher Smart and his team of border collies, all from Scotland. Photo by Ben Garvin, Concord Monitor

mountains of hard evidence and prove beyond all doubt that a New Hampshire nuclear dump was a hopelessly stupid plan. The strategy of The People was to create political and media events and dramatize public and personal outrage. One media event was a five-mile long parade of cars and pickups, flags and banners aloft, from Hillsboro to a press conference in Concord, the capital city—which, as intended, received the attention of the Boston and national press. The state's congressmen, its senators and Governor Sununu were early into the battle, predictably denouncing the siting plan (as did everyone within earshot), but the grassroots protesters were wary of them: they were government, and government was the adversary. Besides, Governor Sununu was a strong supporter of nuclear energy and in particular of the Seabrook nuclear power plant, which was even then being built and suffering huge cost overruns. Moreover, he was generally disliked by many of the nuclear waste protesters. Inevitably, opposition to the Seabrook nuclear plant, brewing in New Hampshire for years, merged with opposition to the nuclear dump plans. In effect, it was King George and the Boston Tea Party all over again. Indeed, the Tea Party, Lexington and Concord, and Yankee Minutemen were the favored political symbols of the hour. As citizen protests go, this was New Hampshire's most rebellious, and perhaps its finest, hour.

The Department of Energy had badly miscalculated, supposing there was nothing alarming about pinpointing a dozen potential sites in seven states. Wouldn't each blithely assume some other one would be finally chosen, a choice years away in any case? In fact, each assumed that it was already targeted and reacted with instant vigilance, as if dump trucks with spent nuclear fuel were already throbbing at the door. A dozen brush fires in seven states fanned each other's flames. In the midst of this very angry spring it was duly noted that 1986 was an election year. Accordingly, Washington officials, including Congressional leaders, thought very hard and then solemnly concluded that the elaborate engineering plan (on which hundreds of millions of dollars had been spent) for a nuclear waste repository in east coast granite—judged strictly from the point of view of science and technology, it was said—was not really a good idea after all. At the end of May the entire scheme, its enabling legislation, and all its high-powered research was summarily suspended, never to be revived. Everyone jubilantly declared victory. In five months the earthquake and the fire and storm had come and gone.

Since the Great Nuclear Dump Fight, other preservation initiatives have sprung up in New Hampshire, some involving public-private collaboration. The New Hampshire Preservation Alliance (founded as Inherit New Hampshire), for example, is a statewide organization focused on historic buildings and landscapes, including

Although it appears to be a blackfly on the Old Man's brow, in fact it is Dave Nielsen, making the annual facial inspection of the old gentleman. Back in 1916, E. H. Geddes, a quarryman authorized by the state, discovered that the 25-ton forehead was but a few inches from slipping off balance. With an assistant team Geddes fastened the boulder to the parent head rock with chains and turnbuckles. Thereafter, Niels Nielsen monitored the Old Man for 38 years, and since 1991 his son David has been designated by state law as "official caretaker." Photo by Andrea Bruce, Concord Monitor

A small piece of the White Mountains, as the birds view it. Photo by Andrea Bruce, Concord Monitor

By the end of 2000 this newly-constructed $30 million medium security prison in Berlin will house 500 men. Here construction workers install coiled razor wire along the perimeter of the new facility. Photo by Ben Garvin, Concord Monitor

agricultural buildings, such as barns. Another is the Great Bay Resource Protection Partnership, formed in 1994, and representing 10 state and environmental organizations plus four local towns, which labors to protect the Great Bay's estuaries and tributaries.

In the year 2000, the legislature created a far-reaching conservation initiative, the Land and Community Heritage Investment Program, promptly nicknamed LCHIP. It provides 50/50 matching funds to preserve choice land and buildings, as nominated by local communities. Precedent for such a long-range conservation project was set back in 1987 when the Society for the Protection of New Hampshire Forests, in particular its president Paul Bofinger, developed and pushed through the legislature a temporary Land Conservation Investment Program (LCIP). That project, shrewdly designed to be administered with private funds, was eventually appropriated over $40 million by the legislature to purchase threatened lands, and in a few years it had protected over a 100,000 acres. In a similar but bolder spirit, the new LCHIP is designed to make public preservation a permanent feature of state policy—although it is still dependent upon future legislative appropriations. In this particular case New Hampshire, notoriously frugal in such matters, surprised itself by making this far-reaching enabling legislation easier to accomplish, and less partisan, than anyone had expected. It helped that the Society for the Protection of New Hampshire Forests disclosed that as of the year 2000, each day 55 acres of New Hampshire open land goes into development. That's 20,000 acres a year, and that's about the size of a typical New Hampshire town. A town a year?

Sometimes different perspectives on preservation of land and water and rural character reflect an unavoidable north/south New Hampshire difference, for the state lives with certain givens of landscape and location, and recent economic history tends to sharpen them. South is Boston's doorstep and and more than ever alive to the buzz and purr of high tech and steeped in startups and sub-divisions; there the city constantly invades the new woodlands that invaded the old farmland. North is lovely lakes and forests and the White Mountains and the vastness beyond, steeped in timber and tourists, a rural kingdom, with a third of the state's land mass and a tenth of its economy, a place where villages are still villages. In these matters it is now widely recognized that the state requires sophisticated balance, as well as community and economic formulas that foster it.

In 1992 the New Hampshire Historical Society and the Society for the Protection of New Hampshire Forests joined forces in a unique multi-media educational effort, to embed New Hampshire land use challenges within a sensitive historical context. Included in that project were a Historical Society exhibit, a series of public educational programs, and a book of essays and

It is the first day in the major leagues for Carlton "Pudge" Fisk of Charlestown, on September 25, 1969, and he is joined in the Boston Red Sox dugout by his high school coach, Ralph Silva. In 1972 Fisk was voted the American League's Rookie of the Year, and in July 2000, again wearing a Red Sox cap, he was inducted into the Baseball Hall of Fame, having caught more games and hit more home runs (376) than any other catcher in major league history. Says Pudge: "My core was always anchored in New Hampshire. Being stubborn and unwavering, never giving in, never giving up, keep going no matter what the obstacles, dig in, knuckle down, work harder, all that stuff." Courtesy, Ralph Silva

photographs abrim with data and insights and vignettes concerning New Hampshire's long and loving, and sometimes callous, engagement of mindscape and landscape. Edited by the Forest Society's Richard Ober, *At What Cost? Shaping the Land We Call New Hampshire*, stands as a vivid permanent record of the kind of effort that seems ever to be timely and never to be finished.

Society and Politics

Marilla Ricker, born in Dover, New Hampshire, is a heroic and largely forgotten woman who spent 50 years (1870-1920), mostly within the Granite State, agitating for women's voting rights. In 1902 she saw female suffrage accepted by the state's Constitutional Convention, then rejected by the state's voters; but she continued her campaign, even attempting to run for governor. In 1920, at age 80, two months before her death, Marilla Ricker was finally allowed to vote—after the passage of the 19th Amendment to the United States Constitution. She lived to see (by a few weeks) the first two women elected to the New Hampshire Legislature, who won by write-in votes at the September primary, 12 days after the 19th Amendment was adopted.

That was then. Could Marilla Ricker now see the Granite State 80 years after her first vote and last battle, she would be amazed and gratified. By 1999, New Hampshire had a woman Governor, Jeanne Shaheen, a woman Senate President, Beverly Hollingworth, and a woman Speaker of the House, Donna Sytek, and nearly

Left: During the campaign prior to the 2000 Presidential primary, New Hampshire Republicans and Independents felt that Candidate George W. Bush never really allowed them to become acquainted with him, and in any case they were not impressed with what they did see. In the voting in February they handed a huge victory to Senator John McCain. Bush dismissed his loss as a mere "bump in the road"—which it turned out to be. Dan Habib, Concord Monitor

While testing the political waters in the Granite State in 1999, Vice President Al Gore joined Governor Jeanne Shaheen in a scenic canoe ride on the Connecticut River. Photo by Andrea Bruce, Concord Monitor

a third of the state's legislators were women. Since 1920 New Hampshire has developed a distinguished tradition of women leaders, especially women legislators, and many citizens felt that the tradition reached its natural fruition when the state filled these three high offices with women.

It would appear that politics is the Granite State's number one participatory sport. For a half century the New Hampshire Presidential primary has regularly been the first in the nation, a position achieved by accident and retained by design. As a result, campaigning is now chronic in the state, becoming acute every four years. Moreover, it is a tradition cherished here, not least because it directs rivers of publicity and patronage this way; and the citizens themselves take it very seriously indeed, setting records in voter turnout. A recent study found that 20 percent of New Hampshire citizens actually shake hands with a presidential candidate. Inadvertently, the media have devised two ways for candidates to win: by getting most votes, and by exceeding expectations. In recent decades, the more urgently New Hampshire's priority in the primaries is challenged (there are always challenges from other states before the respective party committees), the more eagerly it is defended. The defense has been successful for decades because it seems impossible to devise, and agree upon, an alternative system notably better than this curious one, which was bequeathed to us not by deep or lofty thought but by the irony of history.

Frequently something happens in the New Hampshire primary to get the nation's attention. In 1964 write-in votes for Henry Cabot Lodge, who was in Vietnam, overran both Nelson Rockefeller and Barry Goldwater. Ronald Reagan nearly upset President Ford in 1976; Gary Hart seemed to glide in from nowhere to snatch victory from the favored Walter Mondale in 1984; Bill Clinton came in behind Paul Tsongas in 1992 but surprised many and claimed "victory" as the "Comeback Kid"; Bob Dole was briskly pushed aside by the force of the "Buchanan Brigades" in 1996; John McCain, in a recent insurgency, overwhelmed George W. Bush in 2000. Also, the tradition that a candidate must win his party's New Hampshire primary to win the presidency, though broken by candidate Clinton in 1992, adds spice to the drama. In a political world now saturated with media and money, the New Hampshire primary, which starts in neighborhoods and schools and remains largely local, more than ever provides a cogent and relatively inexpensive retail-politics vehicle for the country as a whole to do its early winnowing in the race. No one would have invented this system and there is little good to be said for it—except that it works.

Older by far than the Presidential primary is another New Hampshire institution, also somewhat beleaguered, namely, the venerable town meeting. For many centuries it has been the political centerpiece for small and

This photo was taken at an April 1997 rally to protest, once more, the Seabrook nuclear power plant (now operating smoothly, if not profitably) but mainly to remember the 20th anniversary of the massive protests and arrests that attended the birth of the plant.

In April 1977, shortly after Seabrook received a construction permit, about 2,500 anti-nuclear activists (led by the Clamshell Alliance, the longtime Seabrook nemesis founded by Guy Chichester) marched on the site. Governor Meldrim Thompson flew over the scene in a helicopter and ordered the arrest of the activists. In the largest mass arrest in New Hampshire history, 1,414 people were removed to National Guard armories and held. The courts were tied up for months. In long retrospect a newspaper editorialized: "That weekend...changed the lives of many of the people involved. It helped stop the momentum of nuclear energy in the United States and bent the course of New Hampshire history." Photo by A. J. Wolfe, Concord Monitor

medium-sized New Hampshire communities, where it has served them noisily, picturesquely, inefficiently, and generally well. No wonder it is often dismissed as outdated—or revered as a priceless tradition. Or both. But a drastic alteration of it took place in the early 1990s with the passage of the law known familiarly as SB2.

Under the traditional system the town meeting is the annual forum where all spending and policy matters are thrashed out and settled; similarly for the annual school meeting, a mirror image of town meeting, where the school budget and policies are set. The standard critique of this system is that the turnout is often too small to be truly representative, that people no longer take time or have patience to sit through long debates. The rejoinder has always been that citizens who are really interested do come, even to day-long meetings, and that the debates, whether colorful, tedious or brief, serve an indispensable educational function.

Under SB2, the new law, towns may choose to conduct their affairs under a system which divides the traditional town (or school) meeting into two. First comes a deliberative session, where the warrant (agenda) articles are discussed and amended, but not voted on; second, and a few weeks later, comes the voting by ballot: no discussion, just a yes/no vote on each warrant item, several dozen of them. By adopting this system, for school or town business or for both, a town allows its citizens to bypass the informing discussion and still vote.

In the early 1990s a few dozen towns rushed in immediately to embrace the new SB2 system for their school or for their town meeting. Thereupon, the most common predictions all came true: more people did come to vote; but attendance at the first non-voting deliberative sessions was drastically lower; and it proved very easy to kill projects and budgets (skip the rationale, just come and vote No). In particular, school bond issues were too easily killed, so the state legislature tinkered and lowered the required bond issue vote (only for SB2 towns) from 2/3 to 3/5; but that promptly led to several lawsuits, and that led to suspension of already approved school building projects—which was a mess. The law of unintended consequences has not been repealed. Also, it proved hard for a town that had adopted the new system to muster the votes to undo it. New Hampshire citizens began to wonder: Was there really a problem for this solution? Have we embarked on the path of suicide for town-meeting government? As of 2000, the SB2 law still had defenders, but no new towns adopted that system.

"It's that stupid Pledge." Those were the words of Governor Hugh Gallen when he was defeated for reelection by John Sununu in 1982. The Pledge—an unqualified promise by gubernatorial candidates to veto any broad-based tax—has been a local hot button for over three decades. (New Hampshire relies more heavily than any other state on local property taxes, especially

Above; New Hampshire twice gave its electoral votes to President Clinton, and the President sometimes makes a quick stop in the state. Here, in February 1999, he joins Governor Shaheen in a forum in Dover. Photo by Franka Bruns, Concord Monitor

Below: John Sununu was an often combative presence during his six years (1982-88) as New Hampshire's governor, later named as chief of staff to President George Bush. Sununu's son, John E. Sununu, was elected to the United States Congress in 1996 (reelected 1998), and here father and son are shown at the 1996 victory party. Photo by Denise Sanchez, Concord Monitor

Before he was impeached by the New Hampshire House of Representatives in July 2000, David A. Brock had served effectively as the Chief Justice of the New Hampshire Supreme Court for 14 years. There he had authored many important decisions, including the landmark "Claremont" decision, which disoriented the governor and legislature. Photo by Ken Williams, Concord Monitor

for education.) In the last 16 elections no one has been elected to the governor's office in the Granite State without having taken the Pledge, a kind of weird oath of office in this state. Governor Walter Peterson, a Republican, refused to take the Pledge in 1972 and was defeated in the primary by Meldrim Thomson; similarly Governor Hugh Gallen, a Democrat, was defeated in the 1982 general election. The Pledge, which harks back to old anti-tax campaigns of the 1920s, and has been exceedingly explicit every year since its revival by Meldrim Thomson in 1968, has always been bitterly divisive: clarifying and valuable to some, helping to keep taxes low; pernicious and obtuse to others, making serious discussion of tax issues impossible. Democrat Jeanne Shaheen dutifully took the Pledge before she was elected governor in 1996 and took it again in 1998, despite protests from within her own party. However, in ultimately accepting a temporary statewide property tax she retrospectively narrowed the meaning of the Pledge to opposing an income tax. Thus, at the beginning of the 21st century an income tax had moved to the center of the political spotlight.

In the burgeoning economy of the late 1990s many states are awash in new revenues, but not New Hampshire. In 2000, New Hampshire was cutting budgets, squeezing its university, postponing work on its infrastructure, and running a large deficit. Moreover, as New Hampshire enters the 21st century almost everything in government—including the Pledge—is colored by the "Claremont decision." In December 1997 the New Hampshire Supreme Court, responding to a suit brought by Claremont and several other school districts, pronounced the state's near-complete reliance on local property taxes to fund its schools "inherently unfair" and unconstitutional, and the Court gave the legislature 16 months (two legislative seasons) to devise an equitable, statewide school funding system. Such a decision was not unpredicted, for something similar had happened in other states. But it shook the earth in New Hampshire.

Consequently, the next sessions of the General Court (as the legislature is formally known) were consumed with trying to find new revenue, and failing to agree: the governor wanted to extend gambling and the legislature didn't; the legislature seemed willing to accept an income tax, but the votes in the separate chambers were ambiguous and unreconciled; and, moreover, the governor was both opposed and Pledged. Ultimately, a temporary statewide property tax for school funding was passed, but as the 2000 elections approached it seemed clear that the Claremont decision had not only shaken, but actually reshaped, the political landscape. Early in the year Governor Shaheen, having twice taken the Pledge, appointed a committee to propose the best way to finance education, and shrewdly used this fact to sidestep the Pledge when announcing for reelection. Meanwhile, she was challenged in her own party's primary by State Senator Mark Fernald, who openly advocated an income tax; also, among Republicans, State Senator James Squires ran in the gubernatorial primary on an income tax platform. For the first time within memory both a Democrat and a Republican were running seriously for governor without "that stupid Pledge."

The year 2000 was headline-making in a still more dramatic way, as the New Hampshire Supreme Court itself suddenly came under unprecedented fire and scrutiny, and suffered by far the worse crisis in its history. New Hampshire's Attorney General, Philip McLaughlin, dramatically reported ethical and legal violations by members of the Supreme Court, involving participation of justices in discussions of cases from which they were officially recused. When the attorney general convened a grand jury, Justice Stephen Thayer (who had recently been involved in a very public divorce) resigned rather than face more negative publicity or prosecution.

The crisis atmosphere in the spring of 2000 was heavily, not to say lethally, charged with strong and lingering resentments (carefully denied or declared irrelevant) concerning several judicial matters, but in particular two recent cases. One was the "Fairbanks Case" in which a conspicuous and felonious Probate Court judge had fled the state and evaded justice (for which the "old boy" judicial network was blamed); the other was the school funding issue, namely, the vexing Claremont decision, which had been authored by Chief Justice Brock, and which was repugnant to the legislature as well as to the governor. "Payback time!" said some. More generally, it was the latest and hottest version of a very ancient dispute in New Hampshire—the legislature seldom satisfied with judicial independence, the judiciary often exasperated with legislative interference. A never-resolved New Hampshire problem is: how to reconcile judicial independence and accountability? In the spring of 2000, the state government itself seemed poised for a courtly war between the General Court and the Supreme Court. In April the volleys began. The House of Representatives authorized its Judiciary Committee to investigate and determine whether impeachment of Chief Justice David Brock, or of other justices, was warranted. The Supreme Court suspended operations. The House Committee hired legal counsel, and the public waited for another shoe, or justice, to drop.

Meanwhile, many citizens and eventually a strong minority of the House Judiciary Committee, regarded the alleged offenses of the Justices—when put under the microscope of extended public scrutiny—as unintentional human failings, entirely unworthy of such a massive inquisition, and to these observers there was something weirdly hysterical about making it into an impeachment case. But the investigation had its own legislative animus and its own historical momentum, and in July, after hundreds of hours of depositions and public hearings and thousands of pages of testimony, the full House of Representatives, in special session, acceded to the majority report of its Judiciary Committee and voted, 253 to 95, to impeach Chief Justice David

Above: Winter sports are an important element of the New Hampshire economy, and skiing is a major part of it. Long ago the state government itself got into the skiing business (a matter of frequent controversy), and it owned and operated two ski resorts: Cannon Mountain in the White Mountains and, farther south, Mt. Sunapee in Newbury. The latter, shown here, was leased in 1998 to Mt. Sunapee Resort (affiliated with Okemo Mt. Resort in Vermont) which made major improvements. The state used lease money to upgrade Cannon Mountain. Photo by Dan Habib, Concord Monitor

Brock; and only by relatively small margins did they decline to impeach two other Justices. It was a stunning outcome, such as had not occurred in New Hampshire since 1790. On July 13, 2000, the House delivered four Articles of Impeachment to the New Hampshire Senate for the trial of the Chief Justice. The Senate, acting as judge and jury, conducted a highly-publicized trial, lasting over three weeks, and on October 10 by large majorities, acquitted Chief Justice David Brock of all charges.

Economy

A hundred years ago the New Hampshire economy, though heavily invested in textiles, was symbolized by such revolutionary technologies as the railroad and the telegraph. Today, the stimulus and symbol of what some call the state's New Economy is the computer industry—a seismic shift, much of it very recent.

When New Hampshire began, and for centuries thereafter, its energy supply was cheap and comparatively easy to come by, for the state's rolling and mountainous terrain yielded abundant water power. The shift to electricity changed all the rules, of course, and by the end of the 20th century, New Hampshire had the highest electricity rates in the nation. That fact is largely traceable to the controversial and ultimately ill-fated decision by Public Service Company of New Hampshire (PSNH) to build a nuclear power plant in the town of Seabrook. Ironically, the idea of local nuclear power was sold to the public in the early 1970s as a way to produce cheap electricity for the state. The Seabrook plant was begun (amid massive public protests) as a two-generator project, but one of these was abandoned in the 1980s as unnecessary and too costly, and the expense of the second generator, which came online a decade behind schedule, sank the company in a sea of red ink. Led by then-governor Judd Gregg, the legislature refloated the company and bailed it out with a long-term rate agreement (5.5 percent rate increase for seven consecutive years) that some thought of as legalized extortion.

By the late 1990s, after a larger company, Northeast Utilities, had bought out PSNH, "competition" and "deregulation" were the new buzzwords. An agreement designed to lower rates and encourage competition was reached in 1997, and then promptly went to a U.S. District Court where it slumbered for three years, while rates continued to rise. In 2000 a new long-term rate agreement promised to keep the utility company solvent, lower rates slightly and briefly, and open the door to competition. Not that serious competitors were in sight. The agreement committed rate payers to a 12-year timetable for repaying the huge costs of the Seabrook nuclear power plant, thus ensuring that paying for the "cheap" nuclear electricity promised in the 1970s would continue after 2010. High energy costs and spirited controversy about it appear to have a secure future in New Hampshire.

Despite such background noise the New Hampshire economy dances to other rhythms, too. While the 1970s were not exciting economic times in the Granite State, those days were quickly forgotten, for throughout most of the 1980s the New Hampshire economy rocked along at a rapid clip. Defense and other high tech industries systematically superseded the traditional New Hampshire textile, leather, and wood products industries. "Growth" soon became the buzzword and managing it became an issue. New Hampshire grew faster for several years in the mid-1980s than any state in the Northeast, and real estate prices sailed cheerfully out of sight. But the end of that decade saw an utterly different story. Just as New Hampshire's economy of the 1980s exceeded the national pace, so its recession at decade's end sank deeper than in much of the rest of the country. Pease Air Force Base in Portsmouth closed, defense-industry contracts shrank, banks tightened credit in the wake of the national savings and loan scandals, and the second home real estate business collapsed. Then bankruptcies multiplied six-fold, and among them was the state's main energy supplier, Public Service Company of New Hampshire. For two years even the heavens declined to drop snow enough to cover the embarrassed ski slopes. New Hampshire fell to last place in the nation's job growth in 1991 (it had been first in 1987), and unemployment rose to 7.5 percent.

In 1992, the Granite State, with its conservative ethos, should have been captive territory for President Bush, but the state repudiated him and chose candidates Bill Clinton and Al Gore, who campaigned effectively throughout New England on domestic economic issues. Before the mid-1990s the New Hampshire economy revived, like that of the country as a whole, only more swiftly and intensely, due to a massive infusion of high tech businesses and service industries and the rapid expansion of global markets. By the end of the 1990s boom times had returned to the Granite State. This vivid recent cycle of boom-bust-boom prompts a small crop of prophets to warn of the black bear that might lie around the corner, but at century's end it was hard to find an audience for caution, and many numbers suggested that New Hampshire luxuriates in the New Economy.

But ironies abound. Recall, as noted earlier, that 55 acres of New Hampshire open land enter the maw of the New Economy every day—20,000 acres a year. The land of one New Hampshire town is needed each year to feed the beast and store its sprawl. And such a vigorous, growing beast! According to *Business NH* magazine, high tech industries—software, defense electronics, telecommunications, and internet-related businesses—now make up the fastest-growing segment of the state's economy, and most of the state's exports (which go to 165 countries, led by Canada and Ireland) today come from there. The internet is globalizing New Hampshire markets and resources. Moreover, New

Above: During the 1990s a new racetrack, the New Hampshire International Speedway, with seating for 91,000, appeared in the countryside northeast of Concord in Loudon. In 1999 over 500,000 attended events at the track, and fans in 90 countries watched events on television. Courtesy, International Speedway

Below: These white pine logs, which are resting in Hooksett, are on their way to the Charlestown (Mass.) Navy Yard where they are destined to become new masts for the USS Constitution. Long ago, New Hampshire's colonial economy was very heavily dependent on the mast trade, and for generations the province was a principal source of British naval stores. Then the pines came mainly from the vicinity of the Piscataqua River and its tributaries. It happens that these pines came from, well, Vermont. Photo by Lara Solt, Concord Monitor

The middle of June in New Hampshire means motorcycles, and more of them every year. In 2000, New Hampshire's 77th Annual Motorcycle Week brought in an estimated 350,000 motorcycle enthusiasts. If bikin's your thing, this week's your ritual. From all over the country they come and congregate— in dozens, hundreds, thousands—at Weirs Beach, in Meredith, Guilford, and Laconia, at Gunstock races, and at the International Speedway in Loudon. The state has learned to roll with it; businesses hang out "bikers welcome" signs. Shown here is the 1997 Freedom Ride, on behalf of POW/MIAs. Photo by A.J. Wolfe, Concord Monitor

Opposite page, bottom: Christa McAuliffe was a much admired Concord High School teacher who was invited to join the NASA space program. One of her goals was to teach a class while orbiting the earth, but it was not to be. She was tragically killed along with her companion astronauts in the explosion of the space shuttle Challenger in January 1986. After her death a planetarium was erected and named in her honor in Concord.
Mel Bolden, well-known African American artist who worked in Concord from 1954 until his death in 2000, created this famous portrait of Christa, making sure that there was a racial mix in her classroom. The portrait hangs in the National Air and Space Museum. Photo by Ken Williams, Concord Monitor

Hampshire is second among the states in the most recent percentage increase in gross state product. Even small and medium-sized technology firms increased in number by 50 percent in the last five years and now approach 4,000 (for comparison, New Hampshire farms number about 3,000). According to the same source, New Hampshire (at 8.2 percent) is second in the nation (at 4.5 percent) in high tech employment concentration. More than 40,000 residents are employed in high tech industries, about the number employed in textile mills 80 years ago. Since wages in the high tech world are better than those in textiles, farming, fishing, lumbering, and other traditional industries, it is not surprising that in the last quarter of the 20th century New Hampshire moved from 25th among the 50 states in per capita income to seventh.

A large portion of the New Hampshire population in the year 2000 (about 11 percent, highest in the Northeast) moved into the state since 1980, and this is bound to have a long-term effect on the general ethos of the place. Some newcomers were retirees, certainly, but many were attracted by a bright vision of the best of two worlds: high technology in a bucolic setting. Many are drawn by an economy that seeks out and rewards certain skills—for risk-taking, agility, entrepreneurship, competitiveness—and by an environment where networking and alliances are crucial and old-fashioned self-reliance much less so, where independence is not as important as collaboration, and where companies are ready on short notice to reinvent themselves, reposition products, merge, alter services...or perish.

This is no longer the old Yankee business climate of the yeoman and the water wheel, nor yet of the telegraph, the steam engine, and the railroad.

And yet. Periodically, against the 21st-century hymn and hum of high tech can be heard...rumors of the railroad's return! New Hampshire is a tourist and commuter state, after all: Boston and the Atlantic coastal megalopolis is not far from the state's famed scenery, its rural living environment, or the seductions of its lake and mountain retreats. (The New York to Montreal Amtrak now makes one New Hampshire stop in Claremont.) The latest railroad promise is a plan for a commuter run from Portland, Maine, through southeastern New Hampshire to Boston; and there is exciting talk of a regular run from Burlington, Vermont, through the White Mountains and Concord and Manchester to Boston. Partly it is dread of sprawl and congested highways that stimulate such talk, and revive it again when it falls silent. It seems agreed that while passenger trains would do little for the New Hampshire economy, they could do much for its quality of life.

Culture

The edge has worn off New Hampshire speech, and the distinct and regional accent is disappearing. Time was when you would pick it up routinely at the grocery, but in the new century it is largely exiled to certain rural areas, and to fall fairs, and there especially to the horse-pulling contests (hoss pullin') and to the oxen shed. Animals understand it well, but some Midwesterners struggle. To those with an ear for such things, the New Hampshire accent is distinct from that of Vermont, Maine, or even of Boston—distinctions destined to vanish within a generation. Many New Hampshire people are fond of the accent, especially if they don't have it, but ambivalent about celebrating it.

"Celebrate New Hampshire" was the name of a New Hampshire exhibition mounted and enacted in Washington D.C. in the summer of 1999, as part of the Smithsonian Folklife Festival on the Mall. The Festival idea is to give each state a chance to celebrate itself on the nation's Mall; and, according to the press reports, New Hampshire's exhibition won nearly universal praise. After the successful road experience it seemed right to bring the festival home and lay it on for the people of New Hampshire. So it was done. For five days in June 2000, "Celebrate New Hampshire" ran full-throttle at the Hopkinton Fair Grounds. This was a fitting setting, for such it was: a big tub-thumping State Fair, "a celebration of New Hampshire's culture and traditions," according to Governor Shaheen.

Almost inevitably, such things will be celebrations of the New Hampshire the citizens love and remember and fantasize about, as much as the New Hampshire they live in. At least it was fun and it had a lofty goal. According to Van McLeod, Commissioner of Cultural Resources, "the educational legacy of this project is to ensure the transfer of traditional New Hampshire culture from generation to generation." Maybe it did that. To someone who might have arrived at the Fair Grounds fresh and innocent from, say, Mars, the emergent portrait of New Hampshire would be a place of apple cider, folk singers, sheep dogs, stone walls, covered bridges, bagpipes, barn dancing, quilting, ox pulling, maple syrup, gospel singing, draft horses, French-Canadians, baklava, and basket weaving. It may be a rather crafty definition of culture, and of New Hampshire, but it is hard to fault such a world; of course Granite Staters love it and celebrate it. Many think they might like to go and live there for a time.

Throughout the 1990s cultural life in the real New Hampshire flourished in many directions. Music thrived, old opera houses were refurbished and some turned to arts centers, theater prospered, and town libraries expanded. Public Television and Public Radio now seem like New Hampshire fixtures, and we almost forget that they, too, were new within the last couple of decades. The New Hampshire Humanities Council, created in 1974 as a state/federal project and long a healthy symbol of the states's cultural vigor, reached farther into the corners of the state's life with poetry readings,

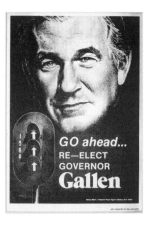

Mel Bolden in 1997 at work in his Concord studio. Photo by Ken Williams, Concord Monitor

This poster for Governor Hugh Gallen's re-election campaign was another Mel Bolden creation. Concord Monitor

In 1966 James Bolle founded Monadnock Music, and shortly thereafter it was incorporated as a not-for-profit organization. Monadnock Music is dedicated to bringing the highest quality professional musical performances to local audiences of the region—chamber music, choral, orchestral—and to creating an atmosphere (often in churches and meetinghouses) conducive to a close audience-performer relationship. Musicians who spend a summer with Monadnock Music, playing together and recording, come from all over the world and bring impressive professional resumes. Communities which host the local concerts raise money for Monadnock Music, but many concerts are free to the general public. Bolle also started the New Hampshire Symphony Orchestra in 1974, now an affiliated organization, and has since then served as its music director. In this photo James Bolle and musicians are shown at a typical Monadnock Music summer concert. Photo by Jane Billings. Courtesy, Monadnock Music

lectures, writers' workshops, book discussions, library displays, teachers' institutes, private research, public lectures. The old New England Lyceum-idea now seems alive and well. The Council's theme, "Connecting People With Ideas," was enacted daily, drawing people by its programs to libraries, parish houses, town halls, theaters, auditoriums. Recently Council programs began including extended initiatives, such as literacy programs for adult new readers, memoir reading and writing workshops for seniors, and summer institutes for high school teachers. In 1996 the Council started a project called "What is New Hampshire Reading this Month?" a series of library discussions of a particular book chosen on a statewide basis, and about the same time initiated a summer "Chautauqua," called "New England Voices," which trains amateurs in reenacting for public performance significant moments and words from memorable figures of the past.

Meanwhile, the New Hampshire Historical Society, energetically led by John Frisbee, purchased new downtown property in the early 1990s and quintupled its floor space. New areas in this former "stone warehouse" soon included vastly enlarged exhibition halls and bookstore, also office and storage and classroom space and, most importantly, in 1995, a new Museum of New Hampshire History. The granite edifice is now known as the Hamel Center. The original Historical Society building, the elegant "marble palace" near the State House constructed (granite outside, marble inside) in 1912, was refurbished and dedicated to library and archival materials, and is now known as the Tuck Library. In the summer of 2000 the National Park Service named a 25-acre area of downtown Concord, a comfortable and intact region of classic brick and granite structures which includes the Hamel Center, to its Register of Historic Places.

Steve Schuch, on the left, is a successful author and story teller, and also a champion fiddler. Derek Owen is an organic farmer, State Representative, and also a distinguished master builder of stonewalls. They are here rehearsing for a recording session, wherein they will blend the strains of the fiddle with the soothing sounds of seven maids a-milking. Photo by Ken Williams, Concord Monitor

Brick and granite did we say? In the center of the capital city of the Granite State? Phillip Carrigain, born in Concord in 1772, at one time New Hampshire Secretary of State, had surely watched the oxen hauling granite blocks out of Rattlesnake Hill to build the State House; and surely he had seen them draw granite building slabs down to the loading dock on the Merrimack, had watched the laborers load the granite on barges, and push off to a Boston building site. Composing a song to herald the 1825 visit of General Lafayette, Carrigain caught an image that encapsulated his New Hampshire: the granite state. And the nickname stuck.

The Granite State. Here in New Hampshire granite is all around us and beneath us, it is common as water, it is the infrastructure of the state. It juts out of our hills, it lines our valleys, beds our rivers, and crowns all our highest, proudest mountains. The skin of our soil is fragile and thin but the granite beneath is thick and tough and durable. Granite, miles deep, gathers and stores our drinking water deep in its cracks and faults, and in wintertime, where we have cut it open for our roadways, granite bleeds its scenic ice sculptures. Granite is in our roadbeds, our curbstones and hearthstones and gravestones, and in the foundations of our homes; and our forefathers etched their farms and fields and outlined their roadways with stonewalls of granite. From granite New Hampshire people first constructed State House and prison, library and warehouse, train station and church, and half of downtown Concord. For hundreds of years we have been quarrying it and splitting it up and sawing it out and polishing it smooth and putting it to use in our buildings: barging it to Boston and shipping it to New York and training it to Washington D.C. We won't run out of granite soon. Of course, the Old Man of the Mountain, the Great Stone Face of Nathaniel Hawthorne, natural symbol of the Granite State, is also composed of natural granite—great gray slabs of it, seamy and craggy and cracked, and homely and handsome beyond words. Granite, the ultimate symbol of the Granite State.

Above top: Ken Burns has created a unique filmmaking style, which he employs with a master's touch. From his home base in Walpole, New Hampshire, far from the film centers in New York or California, he has created extended historical films—using diaries, journals, letters, historians, photographs, sound tracks, clips, and interviews—which have won awards, had Oscar nominations, and become major popular successes: The Civil War, Baseball, *the* Lewis and Clark Journey *of the* Corps of Discovery, *and a string of others. Photo by Ken Williams,* Concord Monitor

Above bottom: In 1975 Donald Hall moved with his wife Jane Kenyon to his ancestral farm (Eagle Pond Farm) in Wilmot, New Hampshire. The former professor wanted to find out if he could make it as a New Hampshire writer (poet, critic, reviewer, essayist) and she wanted to find out if she really was a poet. It turned out that both answers were Yes. The farm was where Hall had spent his summers as a boy, so they had returned to a landscape still full of the past and of poetry and memories—and indeed to the world of Robert Frost. In 1995 Jane Kenyon died, a successful poet, and Donald Hall continues to live and write from Eagle Pond Farm. Photo by Ken Williams, Concord Monitor

Left: Tomie dePaola has written and illustrated so many children's books that his name is almost synonymous with "good reading experience" for children. Working from his studio in New London he has written nearly 100, illustrated over 200, and sold over five million copies of his books. "Children look at my art style and feel comfortable," he says. Photo by Ken Williams, Concord Monitor

SYMBOLS OF NEW HAMPSHIRE

New Hampshire sees itself in symbols. When the New Hampshire Historical Society thought about celebrating the 21st century, they hit upon a novel device: why not poll New Hampshire citizens for their favorite symbols of the Granite State, then feature the results in a full exhibition of 21 state symbols? And so, they did. The public voted, online and on paper, from among more than 50 familiar New Hampshire icons—places, objects, events, institutions. Some teachers took the project into their classrooms and some newspapers bantered (none too seriously) about what belonged on the master list. (Didn't the New Hampshire accent deserve a place?) Contest rules were relaxed—nothing scientific here and write-ins were welcome—and after the votes were counted the 21 emergent symbols were graphically highlighted in a special exhibit of relevant photos, displays, and historical objects at the Museum of New Hampshire History. Creating this unique "people's exhibit" meant, among other things, that several tons of New Hampshire granite field stones had to be lugged up to the second floor of the Museum to construct a genuine stone-wall—since stonewalls, appropriately, were high among the chosen. At the top of the list of symbols, and not a surprise to anyone, was more granite, namely, The Old Man of the Mountain. He was not himself brought to the exhibit, but he sent a curriculum vitae and photographs instead, as did others, such as Lake Winnipesaukee and the Cog Railway.

It was preordained that the final list and exhibit would tell Granite Staters what they already know: that many symbols resonate warmly with the state's much-textured history and character, and that altogether they are an index of what may come to mind when New Hampshire people think of home. For visitors the symbols may evoke the New Hampshire history they have visited and found distilled, as it were, on a postcard. One wonders what would a list of, say, 20 such symbols have been like if compiled a century ago? (Or be like, when compiled a century hence? What picture postcards will our great-grandchildren send?) About half, perhaps, would have made the list 100 years ago—Mount Washington, The Old Man, covered bridges, maple sugaring; but many others did not exist at the beginning of the 20th century. Some, which are now resonant historical ideas and relics (Amoskeag Mills, Canterbury Shaker Village) would have been seen very differently when they were living, sweating institutions, and not yet symbols, 100 years ago.

Thus state symbols are formed over time, and change slowly gathering accent and meaning like green moss growing. If someone today proposed to snake a railway up our favorite mountain, we might shout him down; but the Cog Railway on Mount Washington has been in place for 130 years, and we love it. It's one of our state symbols. Our covered bridges were once just functional, but now they are much more than that. And stone walls, born of the unyielding granite of the Granite State, were themselves in slow transition a century ago, shifting from utility to aesthetics, fashioning an enduring symbol out of base raw material. More generally, it is time...time and lived historical experience and memory, that turns brute realities into living symbols. In alphabetical order, here are the Granite State symbols the citizens chose (a tie included) at the beginning of the 21st century.

Amoskeag Mills: *Beginning in the early 1830s and lasting for just over a century, the Amoskeag Mills in Manchester grew to be the largest textile mills in the world.*

The Balsams Resort Hotel: *One of the two remaining White Mountain Grand Hotels,*

Canterbury Shaker Village: *Shaker religious communities formed in Canterbury and Enfield in 1792.*

Country Fairs: *Agriculture fairs, which go back to the Middle Ages as a celebration of rural and farm life, were revived in early 19th century New Hampshire.*

Covered Bridges: *For hundreds of years, craftsmen have built wooden bridges over New Hampshire streams and rivers, using various lattice truss designs.*

Daniel Webster Birthplace: *Webster was born in 1782 in Salisbury, New Hampshire, in a modest farmhouse.*

Dartmouth College: *It was founded in 1769 by Eleazar Wheelock, chiefly as a school for Native Americans.*

Isles of Shoals: *Nine miles off the New Hampshire coast, austere, beautiful, and nearly bare, these nine small isles were long a fishing center, later a tourist attraction and aesthetic haunt.*

Kancamagus Highway: *This curvy, scenic 36 mile road, especially famous during the color season, joins Lincoln and Conway through the southern White Mountain National Forest.*

Lake Winnipesaukee: *A major resort attraction, this is the largest of the state's 2,000 lakes and ponds.*

Maple Sugaring: *Native Americans first taught Europeans how to extract sweet sap from maple trees in the Spring and boil it down.*

Old Man of the Mountain: *(Silhouetted above). (1920s)*

Mount Washington: *The highest mountain in the Northeast, Mount Washington is famous for the extreme weather at its 6,200 foot summit.*

Mount Washington Cog Railway: *In 1869 it began taking tourists two and one-half miles to the top of Mount Washington. The railway has operated ever since.*

Mount Washington Hotel: *Constructed in 1902 in Bretton Woods, near Mount Washington, this magnificent resort structure has nearly 200 rooms in its seven stories.*

New Hampshire State House: *The State House, built of Concord granite, was completed in 1819, and extensively remodeled twice since.*

Old Man of the Mountain: *This stern and craggy profile is a natural and miraculous formation of massive granite ledges high over Franconia Notch.*

Phillips Exeter Academy: John Phillips of Exeter opened the state's first private academy for boys in 1783, emphasizing classical languages, rhetoric, and mathematics.

Robert Frost Farm: Frost's poetry career began on the Derry homestead his grandfather financed in 1900.

Stonewalls: The granite of the Granite State was subdivided by nature into myriad forms, and farmers early put it to use: stone walls marked boundaries, separated fields, fenced livestock, and cleared crop fields of rubble.

Strawbery Banke: In the 1630s strawberries on the banks of the Piscataqua gave a name to the settlement. Since 1965 it has been a much-admired, outdoor museum.

The Presidential Primary: New Hampshire has held presidential primary elections since 1916. Since 1952 voting has been for presidential candidates.

The White Mountains: Occupying more than 1,000 square miles, the White Mountains have been part of a National Forest since 1911.

Amoskeag Mills (1911)

Daniel Webster Birthplace (1948)

Dartmouth College (1914)

Isles of Shoals (1915)

Mount Washington Cog Railway (1930s)

Mount Washington Hotel (1920s)

New Hampshire State House (1910)

Stonewalls (1920s)

The White Mountains (1906)

These postcards from the Granite State's past, with all their dated details, may suggest the maturing of state symbols through time, and they invite reading on many levels. They date from 1906 to 1948. Courtesy, R. & G. Jager. Stonewalls, Courtesy, Phelps Photo

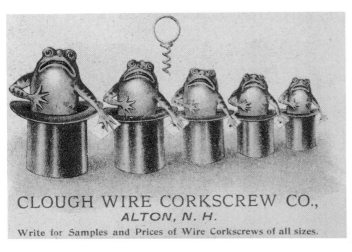

CLOUGH WIRE CORKSCREW CO.,
ALTON, N. H.
Write for Samples and Prices of Wire Corkscrews of all sizes.

E. B. CRAPO'S
TRIMMING STORE,
70 NO. MAIN ST.
CONCORD, N. H.

NEVER MIND JOHNNIE I'LL SEW IT UP WITH
CLARK'S O.N.T. SPOOL COTTON. IT WILL
BE AS GOOD AS NEW AND MA WON'T KNOW!

With the Best Wishes

Of Lothrops, Farnham & Co.
THE OUTFITTERS,

FOR BARGAINS IN
MILLINERY AND FANCY GOODS
VISIT J. E. ESTEY & CO'S
BEE-HIVE.

Above: A craze for colored tradecards dominated American advertising during the second half of the 19th century. The lithographed cards were cheap and effective, sporting pictures that ranged from sentimental, to comical, to plainly descriptive. NHHS

VI
CHRONICLES
OF LEADERSHIP

In 1827, only a few years after the first great textile mills began to operate on the power of New Hampshire's rivers, a group of farmers in the state petitioned the United States Congress for protection against less-expensive imported cloth.

"Of our climate and the fertility of our soil, we have little to boast," they wrote. "But, unkindly as our soil is, we are blessed with streams, which afford a water power inferior to that of no State in the Union. . . . Our hills, too, may be covered with flocks to their summits."

That was no exaggeration in the days when forests were plentiful and the farms seemed promising. New Hampshire's small factories making cotton and woolen cloth, shoes and boots, lumber, and paper went hand in hand with forestry and husbandry. Flax was grown to make linen, paper, and oil; sheep were pastured for their wool. Timber was cut for masts and lumber (and later for pulp), and it was burned on the farmer's cleared land for potash to make soap, glass, and fertilizer.

Yet in the years after the Civil War, the failed and abandoned farm became a sad fact of life in a state that had betrayed its true industrialism early in the 19th century. "The state lives by manufacturing, and by manufacturing only can there be any advance," one Charles C. Coffin wrote in *The Future of New Hampshire* in 1881. "There must be something besides rocks and trees to make a state."

Industries have grown up in New Hampshire and have been part of a consistent record of industrial innovation: The medical X-ray, the paper towel, and the video game were all, for example, invented here. But alongside them are industries that have managed to thrive on what some think of as the state's eternal liabilities. The rocks made its remarkable granite industry; the trees are the stuff of numerous New Hampshire wood products and of its recreational charm. The soil that disappointed farmers created the largest silver polish manufacturer in the country; precipitous slopes in two of the state's smallest towns are home to its largest ski area and one of New England's two four-star resorts.

Even in the late 1930s, when the widespread failure of textile mills might have seemed like the state's last gasp, New Hampshire was far more industrialized than the average of all 47 other states. And within two decades, new businesses came to fill the empty mills and shoe shops and employ people whose work ethic seems uniformly to have impressed out-of-staters. New Hampshire historian Jeremy Belknap described their traits as early as 1797—"firmness of nerve, patience in fatigue, intrepidity in danger, and alertness in action."

And for many companies, it is not so much the able population, the historically favorable attitude toward business, or the tax structure as much as it is simply New Hampshire that draws them and keeps them here. Some of the principals of these companies summered here as children, honeymooned here, went to college here, supervised campers here, hiked and skied here. They have come to live in what Robert Frost called "a most restful state," a place that remains quite rural despite the impressive statistics about New Hampshire's industry.

ARCOM, INC.

Arcom, Inc. was incorporated by Lamberto Raffaelli in Massachusetts on the Epiphany (January 6) of 1995. Its name originated from the idea that it was "Our Company," and the name Arcom sounds like those words, "our company." In addition, after playing with several names, Lamberto's wife discovered that by moving the "M" to the front of the name ARCOM it became MARCO, their son's name.

They started by borrowing some space from a gentleman and scientist named Dr. T.B. Ramachandran, president of MDT, a corporation located in Westford, MA. They had very little money from few friends, and obtained a line of credit from a second mortgage on their home. Lamberto had been working at Alpha Industries for 12 years and at Elettronica in Italy for seven years prior. Lamberto was from Italy and had received his electronics engineering degree there. "When I came to this country, probably like most emigrants, it was supposed to be for only two months," Lamberto muses. "The reason we started the company was because Alpha was not interested in our product. Their focus became the huge cellular phone, low-frequency

Arcom initial team.

chip market, and our high frequency transceivers for point-to-point radios and other communication applications didn't look large enough."

So, during a summer vacation in Italy, tired of complaining about his employer's direction, Lamberto decided to take some action and wrote a business plan for a new company focused on the Millimeter-wave communication market. "When I started," says Lamberto, "I was not sure about the opportunity, but I thought, 'If you don't try, you will never know,' and started to type."

The more he wrote the more he was convinced that the plan had something to it, and by the end of the summer he felt good about the overall idea. He then called a few friends and asked them to read it. The feedback was positive. Finally, the ultimate test would be if the same people who liked the idea were also interested in investing some money. The answer was yes, and after the legal paperwork was ready, Arcom's adventure began.

"When you start a company," Lamberto reflects, "you need a lot of good ingredients to succeed, but probably the most important one is luck, and good timing. You also need a market, customers that want to buy from you, cash to implement your plan and a great team to make it happen."

The Arcom team had been working together for many years and had, and still has, a great expertise in its field. However, this is not enough. "The team has to be ready to work really hard," says Lamberto, "and to do that you need strong, motivated individuals...and

Arcom employees in 1996.

Arcom engineers.

In one year they reached profitability and in four years they reached $13 million in sales. Several companies began looking at Arcom as a good acquisition and in September 1999, when the offer looked appealing, the investors, the team and the wives decided to sell to Dover Corporation, a $4 billion company.

In just a few years what looked like a dream had become a beautiful reality. "When I go back to the initial phase," says Lamberto, "I always thought that our main problems were going to be cash, customers and products. In reality, we never really had major problems in these areas. The real issue is always people. When you have a great goal, you need a "dream team" very united and very committed to make it happen. We had that, and we also had the luck to start at the right time. That's why we succeeded."

Lamberto also thought that the same ambitious project would have been more difficult in Italy. "Everything included, this country still offers the best business scenario to individuals who want to try and risk. And, that's why so many people from other countries still believe in the American dream."

spouses." Thus, before starting, Lamberto organized several dinners with "the wives" to make sure that they agreed to having their husbands spend long hours to do something different. "If we succeed, we guarantee a good future for you and your children," he told them. "But it will not be easy...and it will require real hard work." What if they didn't succeed? "If we don't, at least we will tell ourselves that we were not afraid to try." And so, Lamberto convinced the investors to give very good equities to the team, and started with a terrific desire to win.

They knew what they were doing, and so did the customers. Therefore, the orders arrived suprisingly soon. At the beginning, the money was terribly scarce, and their facility looked so poor that Lamberto, "...was ashamed to invite our customers to visit us. But, the market exploded quickly and so did we."

After 12 months, Arcom moved to a new facility. "We decided to go to New Hampshire and I'm still convinced it was a great decision," remarks Lamberto. "In southern New Hampshire there are many people that work in Massachusetts and spend too many hours to commute. So we felt that, by placing the facility in Salem, NH we would have access to a skilled workforce eager to commute less and save state taxes to Massachusetts."

Arcom employees in 1997.

BARETT & GOULD, INC.

The year 2000 marks the 50th anniversary of Barett & Gould, Inc., a contract manufacturing company located in Hillsborough, New Hampshire. The history and success of Barett & Gould can be traced to Lynn, Massachusetts, in the 1930s. Louis Barett, who immigrated to the U.S. from Russia after the turn of the century, manufactured metal shoe buckles on the first floor of his Lynn home. Hard to believe now, but a large pot belly stove was the center of the early business.

Barett, his wife Sonia, and their two daughters lived upstairs. They had one telephone in the shop with a very long cord so they could pull the phone upstairs in the evening. Their oldest daughter, Ethel, learned to operate a kick press for assembling buckles in the kitchen.

Although the family escaped a house fire in 1934, the business did not survive. Not to be deterred, Barett established Superior Products, a metal stamping and manufacturing company. The company thrived, moving twice to larger locations in Lynn. Ethel was assigned the job of head accountant after completing a

A series of aluminum parts produced by B&G today on a computer controlled press.

bookkeeping course in the eighth grade. Her involvement in the business would encompass her entire life, particularly after her marriage to Howard Gould in 1944.

In 1945, Gould went to work for Superior Products. After several years, Gould approached his father-in-law about purchasing a few machines to start up his own business. Barett wasn't ready to retire and suggested a partnership. In 1951, Barett & Gould was incorporated and began its long and successful history as a New Hampshire business.

Barett & Gould's beginnings in New Hampshire were in a converted, water-powered grist mill in Windham. Initially, the company manufactured umbrella frames, cake pans and jingle bells. The quality of the work—even for such diverse products—was soon recognized by Western Electric's engineers. B&G's capabilities expanded to the production of components for telephone switching and transmission equipment

Punch press operators in the B&G Nashua millyard building in the early 1960s.

for Western Electric, a relationship that would span several decades.

B&G outgrew the grist mill in three years and moved into larger quarters in Nashua. As the customer base expanded, components were produced for the audio and electronic industries. Parts were manufactured for audio speakers, record players and the first projection television on the market. Continued growth of the business necessitated yet another move, and in 1960 the company relocated to a larger space in the Nashua Millyard, where it thrived for 37 years.

In the early 1960s, Barett retired to pursue various political, charitable and civic endeavors. Howard and Ethel remained to run and expand the business. They were very active in the growing Nashua community and raised a family of three children: Sunny, Susan and Bob.

The daughters explored other pursuits, but Bob began full-time

A variety of metal components manufactured by Barett & Gould, Inc.

at the company in 1976 after being a part-time employee in the summers and during college breaks. He bought the business from his father, who retired in 1985. In his 15 years as president, Bob took the business beyond metal stamping to a complete contract manufacturing service.

Barett & Gould is unique as a "one stop shop" for precision metal fabrications and stampings, powder coating and silk screening, assembly, packaging and other value added services. The company's strength lies in its ability to collaborate, in partnership with its customers, from concept through design and manufacturing.

Over the years, new processes have been implemented to meet customers' needs and keep pace with automated technology. The diversity of work continues expanding to include the automotive, computer, appliance, hardware and machine tool industries. Jobs that were once manually designed and hand set on the machines are now "digitized" by the customers, sent to B&G via the internet and computer programmed into the machinery. B&G engineers track the sta-

tus of each job through integrated manufacturing software.

The fabrication department offers quick turnaround for prototypes, pilot and volume production requirements. The stamping facility operates 20 punch presses, with both short run and high volume automated capability, supported by a complete in-house tool and die shop. Parts are finished on an automated powder coating line.

Due to plans for a new road to bypass downtown Nashua, in 1997 the company was notified by the state that it would have to relocate the business. Barett & Gould moved from the historic mill building in Nashua to a modern, 45,000-square foot building in Hillsborough. B&G is one of the largest employers in the area and many of its employees relocated from Nashua to work and become active in the community.

From the manufacture of belt buckles in the 1930s to the production of precision metal components, customer satisfaction is the number one priority. B&G retains many long-term clients, including Lucent Technologies, a successor of Western Electric, its first major client some 50 years ago.

B&G has maintained a successful relationship of more than 25 years with Vermont Castings, Inc., an international manufacturer of gas and wood stoves and related metal products. B&G has also produced metal stampings for over 25 years for Felton Brush, Inc. of Londonderry, an innovative supplier of automotive products.

Barett & Gould truly remains a "family business." Bob has been involved with the company for 25 years. His sisters Sunny Macmillan and Susan Aliah Sage have also contributed to the business. In fact, Sunny's daughter Kate, the great-granddaughter of Louis Barett, wrote the first draft of this story!

Over the years, Sunny directed various administrative, personnel and marketing projects for B&G. Aliah is an artist in Taos, New Mexico, whose work in tile and metal has been internationally recognized. In his spirit of adventure, Bob collaborated with his sister Aliah on the design, manufacture and installation of a metal sculpture at the entrance to the Pillsbury Building at the Concord Hospital.

In 2000, B&G continues to evolve from working "the manual way" to using state-of-the-art, automated machinery. Quality remains central to the business: in 1999, B&G attained ISO 9002 certification, an industry standard for quality in all aspects of operations. Barett and Gould, Inc. is proud to maintain its role in the state and national manufacturing economies of the 21st century.

The company's prosperity can be attributed to the foundation established by Louis Barett and Ethel and Howard Gould: customer satisfaction, extremely hard work and a little luck. Although the Goulds have been retired since the mid-1980s, their contributions are appreciated by many and their experience considered a vast resource to the company and to the state of New Hampshire.

Howard and Ethel Gould with their son Bob at the Barett & Gould, Inc., Hillsborough facility in 2000.

BRITA CORPORATION

Heinz Hankammer founded the BRITA company in 1966, as a one-man operation. It has rapidly developed into a modern, medium-sized company, and increasingly expanded into many international markets. Today, BRITA is the worldwide market leader of portable household water filters. In addition, BRITA customers on all continents worldwide are absolutely convinced of the quality of filtered water.

The product category "water filter pitcher" did not exist until BRITA founder Heinz Hankammer introduced the BRITA filter. Today, BRITA GmbH is one of the rare global players of German provenance, a hidden champion located in the center of Germany in Taunusstein, close to Frankfurt and Wiesbaden.

In addition to household water filters (pitchers and online systems), BRITA also manufactures products for commercial use. Special filters condition water for requirements in the vending and catering industries, e.g. coffee machines, dishwashers, or steam cookers.

"Our specialization was, and still is, our great advantage," says Marcus Hankammer, who recently became chief executive officer. "For other companies, this market segment is only one of many—but for us, everything rotates around the BRITA filter."

The BRITA water filter pitcher is the standard in many markets including the U.S. and Germany. The filters use an ion exchanger to reduce the chalk in water, as well as lead and copper which may originate from the pipes in a building. Significantly better taste is the result. Furthermore, the BRITA water filter pitcher can also reduce aluminum, chlorine, and pesticides in tap water. Featured below is the "Family" model of the BRITA water filter pitcher.

The operative business division and the internal support departments have been recently separated

Left: The BRITA Cartridge "in action."

Right: The "Family" pitcher, Brita's best selling filter system.

from one another within the company group by subsidiaries and joint ventures in the USA, Canada, England, Ireland, the Benelux countries, Switzerland, Australia, Poland, and India. In the other markets, BRITA operates in cooperation with distributors.

The target of CEO Markus Hankammer is very ambitious: "A BRITA product in every household worldwide" is what he wishes to see in the near future.

It is necessary to keep an eye on competitors and to ensure that BRITA remains in the lead. Markus Hankammer says, "BRITA is the trade name which is to become the number one for water optimization at the point of use."

During the '90s, North America became the largest market for BRITA products. This new development prompted BRITA GmbH to build a raw material processing plant in the United States, in order to gain a foothold in this new market.

In 1995, the search for the location of the plant began. There were

The Brita Coporation facility located at the Manchester Airport.

many points to consider, such as a state with a reasonable tax structure, good standards of education, and a possible foreign trade zone. Of particular concern were the time differences between Germany and the United States, and for this reason the search was focused on the East Coast.

BRITA GmbH made the decision to build the new plant in Londonderry, New Hampshire, a location that met all of their standards. In September 1996, construction on the new plant commenced. By June of the next year, the Brita Corporation began production of raw materials for use in BRITA filters that are manufactured in Canada.

By the end of 1998, the Brita Corporation made an additional investment to add a resin treatment facility to the plant in order to process a technical resin into food grade resin for use in the BRITA cartridge.

Since then, the Brita Corporation has also started production of OEM filter cartridges. There are now 24 full-time employees working at the plant, a large jump from the original one employee when construction began. The Brita Corporation is located very close to the Manchester Airport, on the Londonderry/Manchester line.

The BRITA filter cartridge.

COMMUNITY COUNCIL OF NASHUA, N.H.

The Community Council of Nashua's efforts center on the mentally ill, working to eliminate the stigma associated with mental illness. This was not always, however, the focus of the 80-year-old social service organization. Nor is it the only element in its efforts to improve the lot of residents of So. Hillsborough County.

The organization has served the towns of Amherst, Brookline, Hollis, Hudson, Litchfield, Mason, Merrimack, Mount Vernon and Nashua since it was chartered, but its focus has shifted as needs changed. Led over the years by a virtual "who's who" of Hillsborough County's citizenry, it has adapted using the latest techniques and scientific discoveries. Its mission is to provide services when and where people need them, and in their chosen environment.

"Ever since its incorporation more than eighty years ago, this organization has been willing and able to respond to changing human needs in an efficient and effective manner," says Zlatko M. Kuftinec, M.D., Executive Director. He has devoted more than 30 years to the organization.

The citizens who founded the Council in April 1920, wanted to apply the community pride and enthusiasm of the war years to handling problems during peacetime. Then known as "The Community Welfare Council," they set out with the blessings of City Hall.

Initially, the group monitored streetcars for sanitation and proper language, chaperoned at dance halls, and pressed for observation of traffic laws. It supported daylight savings time and lobbied for the widening of Main Street. More in line with what the Council would become, it became an advocate for crippled children, arranged week-long fresh-air summer vacations on farms for underprivileged youngsters, and implemented a clearinghouse for

The Council House at 7 Prospect Street.

social agencies, a forerunner of its current Information and Referral Service.

The Council incorporated in 1924 as the Community Council of Nashua, NH, Inc. Its focus evolved from social and environmental concerns. It opened a mental hygiene clinic that year, a clinic for the blind in 1930 and a polio clinic in 1940.

In the late 1960s and early '70s, attention nationwide turned to the plight of patients in mental health institutions. This led to the closing of state hospitals in favor of mainstreaming. The Council became a leader in building support systems for patients moving into the Greater Nashua community to access care they needed. More and more, mental health took center stage in the Council's activities.

To change public perceptions, the Council showcased the talent and creativity of mentally ill individuals by including their art and writings in its 1991 annual report. Among other programs, it developed The Bargain Hunter, a downtown discount store that introduces individuals with psychiatric disabilities to work. Volunteers work with students in the School of Health,

Awareness, Rehabilitation and Employment (SHARE) to help them acquire the skills, behavior, and supports they need to live where they choose. SHARE concentrates on wellness rather than illness.

In 1995, Community Council expanded into behavioral services, establishing The Batterers' Intervention Program for domestic violence offenders and the Academy Case Management Program for first-time felons. Both are intensive, year-long rehabilitation programs the courts can order to supplement or replace imprisonment.

In 1998, it opened The Crisis Center, a 16-bed facility for adults with acute psychiatric needs, and a new home for its mental health services for children and adolescents, and their families. Other community support services include Deaf and Elder Services Programs.

Accredited under the strict standards of the Joint Commission on the Accreditation of Health Care Organizations, the Community Council continues to adapt to the changing needs of residents of Greater Nashua.

JACKSON JACKSON & WAGNER

When most Americans were villagers or farmers, decisions of self-governance were made in town meetings. Today, with 273 million people living in a highly organized social structure, new communication strategies and technologies have emerged to ensure democracy's survival.

Public relations plays a key role. It *keeps people informed, solicits their opinions, fosters public participation* in all types of organizations, and *helps organizations thrive* in the environment within which they operate.

A leader within this profession is Jackson Jackson & Wagner (JJ&W), an international behavioral public relations and management counseling firm with headquarters in the historic town of Exeter, NH.

JJ&W's work illustrates how public relations—merged with psychology, sociology and anthropology in a behavior-oriented application—has influenced New Hampshire.

JJ&W has counseled clients facing a variety of challenges, including: corporate restructuring, culture change, mergers, acquisitions & downsizing, message strategy & media relations during volatile crisis situations, union strikes & boycotts, SEC violations. JJ&W also deals with emotionally charged issues such as perceived waste disposal violations and discriminatory practices.

Since its founding in 1956, JJ&W has worked with every sort of organization. Starting in the '60s, the firm assisted many public interest groups in organizing and building coalitions.

The firm's first client in New Hampshire was a Portsmouth theater group in need of help with its fund raising and the organization of its management and marketing. The Society for the Protection of New Hampshire Forests was also an early client. As a board member, Patrick Jackson continues to be closely involved in its work.

JJ&W helped establish New Hampshire Civil Liberties Union. It helped found SPACE (Statewide Program of Action to Conserve our Environment) and the Environmental Coalition—an idea copied in many other states. Isobel Parke, senior counsel of JJ&W, actively supports New Hampshire Timberland Owners Association and, because of her outstanding involvement, received its highest award in 2000.

JJ&W works with many nationwide organizations including; public interest groups, universities, independent schools, health care, financial institutions, associations, utilities and Fortune 100 corporations.

One of JJ&W's specialties is strategic planning with the focus on action steps that tie the plan directly to overall organizational goals. Evaluation is an integral component of the plan.

Constituency relations, another specialty, identifies stakeholder groups and their opinion leaders; monitors their interests and perceptions; permits quicker, more educated responses to problems or opportunities; and strengthens relationships because it demonstrates the organization listens and is responsive.

JJ&W's subsidiary, Dudley Research, performs formal and informal perception, behavior and marketing studies. A variety of research techniques are used. For example, *focus groups* gave a utility client insights into customer receptivity to new services, a chance to communicate and test complicated information, and an opportunity to build relationships with its customers. A paper industry client found through *gap research* (in this case, how an organization views itself vs. the public's external view) that opinion leaders rated it higher as a community citizen than it rated itself.

The firm and its principals help

Jackson Jackson & Wagner is located in Exeter's historic Dudley House.

make New Hampshire known nationally for professional leadership in public relations. Patrick Jackson, one of the founders, conducts seminars and gives speeches across the country. In 1980, he served as national president of the Public Relations Society of America. In 1986, he received PRSA's highest honor, the Gold Anvil Award. Isobel Parke has also been a national officer of PRSA. Other JJ&W counselors currently hold both national and local positions in PRSA, as well as serving on boards for museums and other regional organizations.

Jackson edits *pr reporter*, an international newsletter now in its 42nd year, published in Exeter-another New Hampshire contribution to the public relations profession.

The counsel of Jackson Jackson & Wagner, with its unique blend of social science theories, provides insight and understanding to help organizations

- build relationships
- earn trust
- motivate mutually supportive behaviors.

These are the human interactions that build resilient organizations.

THE KELLER GROUP

As a teenager, Robert Keller was fascinated with bonding dissimilar materials; he experimented with wood and fabric to make his own gliders as well as pressboard to create a surfboard. "Make it, test it, and break it" described his research. Some years later, with business training from Dartmouth College, this "hands on" approach helped Keller convert a store fixture company into a World War II defense plant making molded plywood airplane parts and panels. By the time the war ended, Keller was ready to launch his own business in Manchester, New Hampshire. Plywood paneling was a booming industry, as Keller found his niche manufacturing an extruded aluminum molding faced with wood veneer to match the popular interior panels of the day.

His business experience was that of a generalist, always open to new ideas. It also made him a pragmatist. "If I can't get through a problem," said the young Keller, "I get around it."

Recipient of numerous lifetime achievement awards and recognition, Robert Keller was recently named a "Fellow of the American Solar Energy Society." For the first time in its history, the Society created a new class of recognition. He was previously awarded their Passive Pioneer Solar Award.

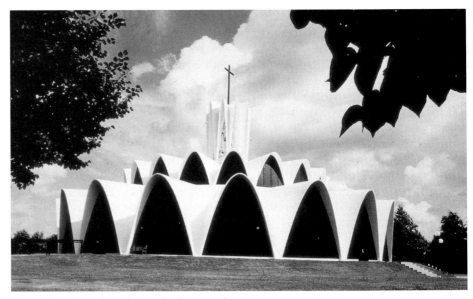

In 1958, the St. Louis Abby Church combined innovation of design and engineering with revolutionary building materials and technology to achieve its milestone status as one of the most highly acclaimed buildings of the era. Kalwall® translucent panels were used in both the original construction and renovation, nearly 40 years later.

Armed with this knowledge and experience—and no small amount of luck—his intuition made one thing clear: "I knew I had a profitable idea."

Keller sold "miles and miles" of wood-faced, aluminum molding. But for the next three years, while he managed a plywood company in Maine, he also experimented with acrylics and polyesters reinforced with glass and other so-called "filling cloths." He researched high-pressure laminates and the new experimental resins for plywood.

Soon, guided by his intuition and careful observation, Keller's shop manufactured various custom "bonded" products including aircraft glider parts; molded plywood furniture and cabinets; floor panels for the Stinson Stationwagon plane; honeycombed aluminum panels for the early Sikorsky helicopters; boat cabin rooftops; shoe heels; parts for government contracts; and custom work for architects. "We got more and more into the building technology of sandwich panels," says Keller. By the early 1950s, Keller "had as much experience in bonding panel construction as anyone in the world."

Keller's wartime contacts with architects and his postwar construction experience fed his fascination with panel construction. By now,

the liability concerns and short-term needs of the aviation industry were proving too demanding for his fledgling technology. By contrast, the building industry moved more slowly, involved less risk, and allowed time to perfect new ideas. He set a new goal: a finished, sandwich building panel like no one had ever made before, that would transmit natural daylight.

After consulting with over a dozen local architects, he developed a lightweight, inexpensive insulating panel that would last as long as the building in which it was located. Composed of thin, fiberglass sheets over an aluminum framework, it could also harness the sun's energy by transmitting daylight. The result was called Kalwall®: *K* for Keller, *AL* for aluminum, and *WALL* for the panel's intended use.

Next, he needed a way to attach the panels to a building, so he designed a "clamp-type fastener" which allowed for construction error and varying thermal expansion inherent to buildings. The system also guarded against delamination. However, just as the Kalwall® panels began to sell, he ran into building complaints and installation problems. The construction trade was unfamiliar with his technology; clearly, he needed to start his own installation company, which eventually included transporting the product to the building site.

Volume production was underway by the late 1950s. World-renowned architect Edward Durell Stone used the material on his pavilion for the 1959 Brussels World's Fair. Philip Johnson built a Kalwall® roof for his New York State Pavilion, and Hellmuth, Obata and Kassabaum employed it on the St. Louis Priory Church. These architectural milestones received international acclaim. The Kalwall® panel technology never constrained architects to a fixed design. Each building and application could be unique.

As the values of society have changed, the fiberglass used in the product has varied substantially over the years, reflecting concerns for vandalism, fire protection, quality and quantity of light and energy conservation. Research initiated by Keller was powered by his active imagination of what *could* be, and *ought* to be, achievable. Over time, his inventions have led to more than 30 patents and worldwide recognition for his pioneering work in composites, daylighting and solar energy control.

Keller's experience with meeting the myriad needs of developing products and technologies exposes an uncommon curiosity about the man and his companies. He explains, "I like to get into fields where the other fellow isn't. My kicks come from tomorrow's products." This thinking led to a failed venture into lobster farming, but resulted in the creation of fiberglass water storage tubes. When "water walls" came into use in the early 1970s, the water tubes were converted from containers for cold seawater to storage of energy-laden solar-heated water. Today, they are used in major aquariums as well as the fish farming and aquaculture industry worldwide.

More recent projects center on nanotechnologies related to solar shading, aerogel super insulation and "non-combustible" plastics. Even so, the ability of architects to deliver "museum quality" daylighting into buildings with Kalwall® translucent building enclosure systems is by far Keller's most recognizable commercial success. Today, it is almost impossible to find a city or town that does not feature Kalwall® in one of its shopping malls, airports, schools, or municipal buildings.

Keller has always relied on a dedicated team of people, including his four sons and two of his grandchildren, to partner in the fulfillment of his dreams. A philanthropist, especially in support of new ideas to improve the quality of life of mankind, Keller remains bullish on the future. He stays ahead of the pack, seeking new ways to harness natural daylight by exploring the use of space age materials like aerogels (used in the Mars Pathfinder probe), nano-size particles smaller than the wavelength of light and exotic chemical variants of the components of his commercial products.

His "Keller Group of Companies" employs over 700 people and provides unique products worldwide, from drumshells (used to manufacture percussion musical instruments) to tension structures, all to positively affect the quality of life for millions of people.

Keller's value as director of all of this activity transcends the technology involved. "I make progress through communications with people." He continues, "First I get the big picture, then I go step by step." He usually goes from the practical reality to the theory behind it and encourages as many multiple uses for his products as possible. He does not see himself as a good salesman. He adds, "Most of the time we have been very far ahead of the market. The innovator has to know when to either back off plans or stick with them when others bail out. Ideas are a dime a dozen; the value is to make something of them."

Another benefit of Keller's translucent panel system is seen here. At night, the exterior of a building seems to glow as the interior lighting is transmitted back through the panels to illuminate the night sky.

THE KEENE SENTINEL

In the particularly frigid winter of 1799, 20-year old John Prentiss boarded a stagecoach in Fitchburg, Massachusetts and headed up the frozen dirt road to Keene. The small New Hampshire village had no newspaper at the time, and the young printer saw an opportunity for one. A frontier town, the community was ready to grow, and its people needed a newspaper to keep track of current events.

He borrowed paper, ink and money, and on a second-hand press produced a four-page weekly that he sold to a modest 70 readers. His subsequent success represented a triumph of hope over experience; the small town, distracted by the rigors of 18th century rural life, had seen three previous papers wither and die.

Prentiss beat the odds. Indeed, the community did grow. And his printing company, which found customers for schoolbooks as far south as Philadelphia, generated funds to feed his newspaper enterprise as it expanded its reach beyond the village to surrounding towns.

Under his and his successors' hands, the newspaper chronicled the political, economic and cultural unification of the region and state, and over the centuries it reported on the advancement of science and technology, from the invention of the phosphorous matchstick to the introduction of the Internet.

The Sentinel experienced its own evolutions and revolutions. It launched its daily edition in 1890. Its distribution system shifted from stagecoach to bicycle and car to vehicles of the digital age; its production evolved from hand presses to machinery powered by steam, water, gasoline and, ultimately, electricity.

But for a short spell in the late 1800s, *The Sentinel* remained in Prentiss' control until 1954, when James and Ruth Ewing, who had previously owned a daily in Bangor, ME, acquired the enterprise with a partner. Nearly 40 years later, they sold *The Sentinel* to a nephew, Thomas Ewing, who runs what is an anomaly in American journalism today—an independent paper, locally-owned and unconnected to any chain. In 1999, *The Sentinel* marked its bicentennial year of operation as the oldest newspaper in New Hampshire and the fifth-oldest newspaper name in the nation.

In the tradition of founder Prentiss, the Ewings have sought a mix of local, national and international news coverage; philosophically they've favored a politically moderate line.

Over the years *The Sentinel* has played a progressive role in its expanding market, which now includes 31 communities in southwestern New Hampshire and southeastern Vermont. It's been an outspoken force for land use planning and open government. It has argued for advancements in education and in fields ranging from basic literacy to high technology. It has advocated the recruitment of clean industry, and supported the arts in many ways.

It's stationed very much as it was at its start: on a frontier. The scenery has changed, but *The Sentinel* today, with its 120 employees, still stands as a watchman, serving the information needs of a region that honors its past and strives to define its future.

Sentinel staff member Harry Ahern, in the get-up of an 18th century sentinel, with the modern version of the fifth- oldest newspaper in the nation.

MONADNOCK PAPER MILLS, INC.

When the Scotch-Irish left Ulster to settle in Londonderry, New Hampshire in 1719, they brought with them a thriving native industry—raising flax and weaving it into linen.

A century later a man named Moody Butler took flax left over from making cloth and thread, boiled and beat the fibers in a vat, and made paper from them. Butler's handmade paper was the first ever made from flax in this country. It was the beginning of one of the oldest continuously operating paper mills in the United States—Monadnock Paper Mills, Inc., of Bennington.

The "Great Falls" of the Contoocook River had been put to use since 1782, supporting a variety of local industries—lumber and grist milling, blacksmithing, tanning, carding and clothmaking, and fowling-piece manufacture. The papermaking enterprise Butler started there was one of the three earliest paper mills in a state known for its paper mills, and Monadnock is the only one of those three still in operation.

By the time Monadnock Paper Mills (not so known until 1880) had turned from handmade paper to machine-made paper; flax had also ceased to be used in favor of linen rags, and, later, wood pulp. After passing through a number of hands

An aerial view of Monadnock Paper Mills, Inc., situated on the banks of the Contoocook River. The main section of the mill was built in 1905.

in its early history, the mill was bought in 1870 by William T. Barker, who vastly widened its markets. He also took as an apprentice, Arthur J. Pierce in 1900, the man who would succeed him as owner of Monadnock Paper Mills upon his death in 1903.

Under "Colonel" Pierce, as he was known locally, the old wooden mill building was replaced in 1905 with a brick structure still in use today. Pierce died in 1948, at which time Gilbert Verney, a native Englishman with a history of success in textile manufacturing, bought the mill from the Pierce estate. Gilbert Verney's son Richard is now chairman of Monadnock, which remains privately owned.

Monadnock Paper departed commodity markets in the late 1950s in favor of specialty printing and converting grades of paper.

The rag room at Putnam's Mills, now Monadnock Paper Mills, Inc. In the background (center) is a rag boiler used to bleach colored rags; women are shown sorting rags at the tables. Though the rags were commonly used for papermaking in the 19th century, wood pulp today provides a more economical papermaking material.

Now known as one of the finest, small, specialty paper mills in the country, it manufactures premium text and cover papers and technical specialty papers.

Its technical papers include abrasive-backing papers, medical-packaging papers, chart papers, latex-treated stocks, and filter media. Its graphic arts papers are designed for limited-edition books, annual reports, and other markets that use high-quality, uncoated paper.

In 1998 Monadnock established Monadnock Non-Wovens LLC in Pennsylvania to produce synthetic fiber webs for filtration and a variety of other specialty applications. In 2000 Monadnock purchased Surface Tech LLC in Binghamton, New York, which has been renamed Monadnock Specialty Coatings LLC and significantly adds to Monadnock's off-machine coating capacity.

The consistent quality and performance of Monadnock's products and people have allowed it to succeed in a very competitive industry.

NASHUA CORPORATION

Nashua Corporation in Nashua, New Hampshire specializes in labels, specialty-coated papers, and toners and developers for copiers and printers. Its primary paper and toner production facilities, as well as its research and new product development activities, are located in nearby Merrimack, New Hampshire, close to its Nashua headquarters. Nashua Corporation also has major production facilities in Omaha, Nebraska and Jefferson City, Tennessee.

Francis Bacon wrote in 1625, "Time is the measure of business." Nashua Corporation has stood the test of time for over 150 years. Its roots can be traced back to 1848 when Charles T. Gill, a Nashua proprietor, wanted to profit from the large number of adventurers moving west to California. Charles Gill saw the Gold Rush as an opportunity to sell playing cards to prospectors. Orlando Murray, publisher of *The Oasis*, who was familiar with printing and an inventor of a wallpaper-printing machine, joined him in this venture. Murray enlisted John Gage to perfect printing presses and rotary cutters necessary to manufacture the playing cards. They soon erected a building on Water Street, and John's brother Charles Gage was asked to manage the operations within the new building. Thus, the partnership known as Gill & Co. was formed.

Murray's next challenge was to find a supplier of the cardboard

Finishing operations at Nashua's Specialty Paper Products facility in Merrimack.

rolls needed for production. The only supplier in the United States was a manufacturer in Rhode Island and arrangements were made for delivery. Their business venture seemingly came to a grinding halt when the supplier of cardboard, who proved to be clergyman, refused to sell them his product because of his belief that card playing was sinful. Having already invested a sizeable amount of money to the venture, the partnership decided to solve the problem by producing the cardboard and ultimately glazed paper.

Mr. Murray sold his printing interests on the 10th of September 1849, and Charles Gill died a year later. These events led to the decision to drop the idea of printing playing cards, and the strategy of specializing in manufacturing products from paper was born and is still the backbone of Nashua Corporation today.

In 1861 the company bought the large estate of the Nashua Watch Company on Main Street, because they had outgrown their present quarters. In January 1866, V.C. and H.W. Gilman bought the company, renamed it Gilman Brothers, and continued the business. Nashua Glazed Paper Company consolidated with Gilman Brothers in 1869 to form Nashua Card and Glazed Paper Company.

In 1904, the owners of Carter, Rice & Co., based out of Rockport,

Paper coating machine at Nashua's Specialty Paper Products facility in Merrimack.

Massachusetts, were looking for a new building due to a fire that had recently destroyed theirs. The present owners of Nashua Card and Glazed Paper Company were very willing to sell their plant because of mounting debt, and the company was renamed the Nashua Card, Gummed and Coated Paper Company.

A new invention, waxed paper, was added as a product line in 1907. Bakers used the waxed paper to wrap bread loaves. When an automatic bread-wrapping machine was invented in Nashua in 1915, the company controlled the largest market share of waxed paper bread wrappers in the United States.

After World War I, Nashua's management decided to open a subsidiary in Canada to avoid the high trade tariffs being imposed. The Canadian Nashua Paper Company was opened in 1920. Nashua began manufacturing packing and adhesive tape when it purchased National Binding Company of New York in 1921.

The company's diversity and streamlining efforts of the 1920s prevented the Depression of the 1930s from affecting business too seriously. World War II brought great demand for their products and also pushed them into other areas of manufacturing including the production of power resistors for radar, raincoats, ponchos, protective covers against gas, M-14 primer detonators, M-115 bomb fuse adapters, documents for duplicating, and ordinance wrap. These products were quickly dropped from production at the ceasing of hostilities.

To reflect its broadening product lines, the company name was changed in 1952 to Nashua Corporation. The next 40 years began a series of acquisitions and changes that expanded the com-

Murray: Original advertisement published in Boston, MA newspaper in 1864.

pany into several different areas of manufacturing. A division was created to handle the growing production of office products such as photocopy paper, toners and developers. In 1965, Paramount Paper Products in Omaha, Nebraska was purchased which propelled Nashua into the increasingly important pressure-sensitive label arena. Nashua began producing products for computers in the form of diskettes in the 1970s. The company also acquired mail-order photo finishing companies and claimed the largest market share by the middle of the 1980s. Nashua Corporation was now made up of four main divisions: photo finishing, coated paper, office supplies, and computer products.

If the second half of the 1900s were years of acquisition and expansion of product lines, then the turn of the century will be remembered as the years of transition and the systematic consolidation of product lines. Nashua Corporation divested non-core divisions and is now comprised mainly of three divisions: Specialty Paper Products, Toner Products and Labels. These divisions produce or convert thermal fax paper; carbonless forms; labels with thermosensitive, water activated or pressure sensitive adhesives; labels for data processing, information transfer and product identification applications; and toner and developer products. Flat screen technology is a recent development, as well as PearlFLARE®, a security coating used on printed tickets for theme parks and sporting events to prevent counterfeiting. The acquisition of Rittenhouse Paper Co. in early 2000 further expanded the company's offerings in specialty papers and labels through their product lines specializing in ATM receipt tapes, offset entertainment tickets, point-of-sale thermal register receipt rolls, and fraud-protected security receipts.

Nashua Corporation is committed to supporting their community-at-large. Nashua employees donate to the United Way and have one of the highest per capita contribu-

tions in the state; the company matches their employee United Way pledges dollar for dollar. Their employees participate in charitable activities through volunteer work and company-organized drives to collect food, school supplies and personal care items for the underprivileged. Employees volunteer their time in the classroom by participating in Junior Achievement. Area students are also given a chance to see how what they learn in school is used in business through Nashua Corporation's participation in Job Shadow Days. The company's Corporate Contributions Committee allocates funds to many local groups including the Boys & Girls Club of Greater Nashua, youth sports organizations, New Hampshire Special Olympics, the Humane Society, and Muscular Dystrophy. Nashua is also an active participant in local Chambers of Commerce and the New Hampshire Business and Industry Association.

Cover of the company's 1948 Annual Report

NEW HAMPSHIRE HIGHER EDUCATION ASSISTANCE FOUNDATION

The NHHEAF Network is the largest source for student loans and financial aid within New Hampshire and has a 38-year history of helping families fund and plan for higher education.

New Hampshire Higher Education Assistance Foundation (NHHEAF) owes its existence to the leadership and generosity of the trustees of the Spaulding-Potter Charitable Trusts and the two banking associations in the state. In October 1960, the Executive Secretary of the Trusts, Eugene Struckhoff, convened a group of educators to discuss ways to fulfill one of the missions of the Trusts: to further higher education in New Hampshire. Among the projects they endorsed was a student loan program in Maine and Massachusetts whereby bankers raised a guaranty fund to repay losses on loans made to students. The Trusts offered New Hampshire bankers $25,000 if they would raise $60,000 to establish the guaranty fund.

At the same time, a committee of the New Hampshire Bankers Association (NHBA), under the leadership of James Barker, was exploring the feasibility of a higher education loan plan for New Hampshire. The committee recommended that a nonprofit organization be established to

Governor Jeanne Shaheen and René A. Drouin, president and CEO of the NHHEAF Network, at the second gathering of the first-ever Higher Education Summit in June 2000.

NHHEAF Network office building, Concord, New Hampshire, circa April 1998.

administer the guaranty fund. New Hampshire Higher Education Assistance Foundation (NHHEAF) was incorporated in August 1961 and by June 1962, the Bankers Association had raised the necessary match, provided housing and administrative support. In August of that year, NHHEAF guaranteed its first loan's. Only students who had satisfactorily completed their first year at a post-secondary educational institution could receive a maximum of $500 each year. The interest rate was 5 percent and students had three years to repay the loan, beginning six months after graduation. With the passage of the Higher Education Act of 1965, Governor King designated NHHEAF to become the administering agency in New Hampshire for the Guaranteed Student Loan Program (renamed the Federal Family Education Loan Program in the 1990s).

NHHEAF's loan volume saw modest growth until the late 1970s, spiked and leveled again in the 1980s, but then experienced dramatic growth during the 1990s. It guaranteed $141 million in new federal loans for fiscal year 1999, and a total of $1.5 billion since inception. NHHEAF maintains a low cumulative default rate of 4 percent, which translates into 96 percent of borrowers successfully repaying their loans.

The expansion of loan volume, increasing program complexity and regulation as well as consolidations within the lending community presented new business opportunities for NHHEAF. Responding to the demands for streamlining the student loan process and for quality, local servicing, NHHEAF's leadership created two additional not-for-profit NHHEAF Network organizations. Granite State Management & Resources (GSM&R) was established in 1986 to assume administration and loan servicing of federal and private student loan programs and to provide certain administrative support functions for NHHEAF. GSM&R now services a portfolio of over half a billion dollars for NHHELCO and other New Hampshire lenders.

New Hampshire Higher Education Loan Corporation (NHHELCO) was

Destination College Convention for parents and students, March 1999.

designated by the State of New Hampshire in June 1993 to be a lender and holder exclusively for student loans under the Federal Family Education Loan Program. NHHELCO is now the state's largest student loan lender with fiscal year 1999 loan volume of $131 million. Because all loans are serviced by GSM&R, students receive a continuum of service throughout the life of the loan. Financing for NHHELCO loans is secured from New Hampshire lenders, commercial financing, taxable bonds and tax-exempt bonds.

Initially NHHEAF only guaranteed low-interest loans to students. In the 1980s it added three more federal loan programs: an unsubsidized loan program for students; the PLUS loan program for parents; and the consolidation loan program. In 1983, working with its school and lending partners, NHHEAF introduced a private supplemental loan program (ALPS) which was replaced in 1999, by NHHELCO's competitive loan program, TREE[sm], The Resource for Educational Expenses.

Network staff grew from two employees to five by 1978; to 35 by 1990; and over 115 in 2000! These employees were originally housed in space provided by the NH Association of Savings Banks in downtown Concord, then moved to leased space at the historic Firehouse Building, where it remained until 1998. At that time the Network purchased and built a new facility, where it functions today in the Concord Heights.

During the 1980s and 1990s, the Network expanded services to lenders and post-secondary schools to help automate and streamline the origination and disbursement of loans. Proprietary software allows schools to transmit and exchange loan information electronically and the first phase of web-based reporting was implemented in 2000.

The Resource Center became a focal point for traditional and nontraditional students seeking information about the admissions and financial aid processes and programs of study. It now reaches over 10,000 students and families annually and offers Destination College, an annual statewide convention for college-bound high school students.

The NHHEAF Network organizations have collaborated with their statewide partners on annual financial aid conferences, training seminars, college planning publications, and research on the status of higher education. In 1999, the Network sponsored the first-ever higher education summit. Summit participants recommended the formation of a New Hampshire Forum: a partnership to improve economic and workforce opportunity through higher education. The NHHEAF Network is challenging its business partners to match contributions from the Network and the New Hampshire Charitable Foundation for a three-year start up grant to launch the Forum. And so the circle closes—the organization that began with a challenge grant to help students fund higher education is now offering a challenge grant to create a forum to plan for the future of higher education in the 21st century.

The NHHEAF Network's success would not have been possible without the support of students and their families, New Hampshire lenders and educational institutions and most importantly, the vision and dedication of its leadership. Over the last four decades the Network has benefited from the stability provided by three long-term executives: Eleanor Provencher, executive director from 1963-1978; Mildred L. Dustin, director and then president from 1978-1997; and Rene A. Drouin, president and CEO from 1997 to the present. Also deserving special recognition for their inspiration and support are three board members who also served as chairs. They guided the organizations through change and amazing growth during the last two decades: James R. Reynolds, 1973-1984; Robert C. Condon, Jr., 1978 to present; and Cornelius J. Joyce, 1984 to present.

The Network organizations exemplify the traditional New Hampshire advantage: do more with less, and do it better. They are committed to providing stability and consistency in funding and service to New Hampshire students, lenders, colleges and universities and to delivering them with a higher level of service and quality.

Three generations of NHHEAF leadership, (left to right): Mildred L. Dustin, executive director 1978-1983, president 1984-1997; René A. Drouin, associate director 1978-1983, vice president 1984-1997, president 1997-present; and Eleanor Provencher, administrative secretary 1963-1969, executive director 1970-1978; pose in front of the new facility, April 1998.

PHENIX MUTUAL AND MANUFACTURERS & MERCHANTS MUTUAL INSURANCE COMPANIES

In 1885 a spate of fires, thought to have been set deliberately, destroyed a great many buildings across the state of New Hampshire. The legislature responded swiftly to the needs of property owners by passing what is known as the "valued policy" law, requiring insurance companies to pay damages equal to the sum insured, whether a property had been intentionally overinsured or not.

The passage of the law caused all 58 insurance companies doing business in New Hampshire at the time to pull out, leaving the field wide open for enterprising New Hampshire businessmen.

One of these businessmen was Lyman Jackman, a native of Woodstock, New Hampshire, who has been credited by local lore with the accidental discovery of Lost River, a major tourist attraction in the state. Jackman had served as a captain in the Civil War and

One Sunday morning in November 1935, smoke was seen billowing from the steeple of "Old North," Concord's oldest church. Manufacturers and Merchants Mutual carried the insurance on the church and paid 100 cents on the dollar toward a new building, despite its business slump during the Depression.

when he returned after the war started an insurance agency in Concord. With the passage of the "valued policy" law he suddenly found himself with an insurance agency but no firms to provide policies for his clients. He promptly invested his life savings in four New Hampshire-based insurance companies. The Phenix Mutual and Manufacturers and Merchants Mutual were two of them.

The organization received its charter from the New Hampshire legislature at the end of 1885 and began doing business immediately with Jackman as secretary and Edward Giles Leach, a Franklin lawyer and Meredith native, as president.

Manufacturers and Merchants Mutual's surplus of $2,800 was eaten away only a year later by a huge fire in Lebanon, New Hampshire, which nearly forced the company out of business. Eighty buildings burned in a conflagration that leveled the center section of the town and caused nearly $350,000 in losses.

The Concord-based insurance company had to pay out nearly $6,000 to cover losses from the

Lebanon fire; Capital Fire Insurance, another of Jackman's companies in Concord, insured buildings whose total losses were even greater. As secretary, Jackman convinced the directors of the two firms to allow him to borrow money to cover these losses. By the end of 1887 Jackman had not only repaid this bank loan but had shown a profit.

Lyman Jackman remained secretary and vice-president of the companies until 1914. Leach remained the president until 1928. Upon Leach's death, Charles Lyman Jackman, Lyman Jackman's son, became president of the companies and remained so until 1957, when his son-in-law, Carl G. Gesen, assumed the position. Carl Gesen's son Charles has served as president of the companies since 1975, and his son Rolf H. Gesen, who is currently the vice president of the companies, is the fifth generation of the Jackman/Gesen family to

After nearly 70 years in the Acquilla Block on Concord's Main Street, Manufacturers and Merchants Mutual Insurance Company had its own building constructed in 1970, on Pleasant Street.

Office scene, circa 1904.

more than 14 years. This stability in the work force is vitally important to providing the high level of personal service expected, and it does not go unnoticed by agents and policyholders alike.

The Phenix Mutual and Manufacturers and Merchants Mutual are licensed in five New England states and South Carolina. The primary line of business is homeowner coverage, but commercial coverages are available as well. After its difficult infancy, the companies have managed to grow and prosper and today write premiums in excess of $10 million and have a surplus of $42 million.

Lyman Jackman, founder.

work for Phenix Mutual and Manufacturers and Merchants Mutual.

Outside influences, such as legislation and technology, have brought significant changes to the insurance industry. The Phenix companies have worked throughout their 114-year history to remain true to their roots as small mutual insurance companies, providing a stable and secure insurance market to the more than 175 independent insurance agents which represent them. As many of the agents and policyholders are in small rural towns the company strives to provide them with a high level of personal service and a longterm relationship, both of which are very important to their way of life.

The companies employ just 20 people, all of whom work in the home office in Concord. Because of the "family" environment, employee turnover is very low, with the average length of employment being

PUBLIC SERVICE OF NEW HAMPSHIRE

It may be hard to imagine, but in the early 1900s the small state of New Hampshire had some 54 companies, each competing to supply electricity. Many of these small enterprises integrated into five utility corporations which, in 1926, formed Public Service of New Hampshire (PSNH).

PSNH's first annual report notes the increase in the amount of electricity consumed by residential customers, brought about in large part by the growing use of home appliances. PSNH's Home Service Department helped customers select appliances and taught them how to use them, even going so far as to conduct cooking schools around the state. From 1928 to 1931, in the midst of the Depression, the average residential use of electricity jumped 45 percent.

Originally, PSNH sold appliances on a retail basis and was also in the gas, steam and electric railway business. By the late-1940s, however, the profitability of these ventures paled in comparison to the ever-growing application of electricity. The company's gas business was sold in 1945, and steam sales ended in 1949.

In its early years, the Manchester-based corporation weathered a number of storms, including devastating floods and hurricanes in the 1930s. It also figured critically in the city's comeback after the 1936 shutdown of Amoskeag Manufacturing Company, once the largest cotton textile plant in the world. PSNH bought all of the bankrupt firm's electrical and power installations, allowing a new corporation to leverage enough money to buy the mill property. By the end of 1937, the mills were nearly half-filled with new businesses.

A variety of power generating sources emerged over time. Through 1951, New Hampshire's

Architect's rendering of PSNH's new corporate headquarters, located in the former Manchester Steam Plant at the northern end of the Amoskeag Millyard on the Merrimack River. The steam plant was purchased by PSNH in 1937 and converted to a fossil fuel-fired generating station, supplying energy to PSNH customers until 1981. The company will rehabilitate the former power plant into state-of-the-art office space for up to 200 PSNH employees.

hydroelectric facilities were supplying more than half of the state's electrical needs. However, erratic water flow from year to year made hydropower less reliable than fossil-fuels. Also, new technology made larger fossil-fueled plants more economical. As a result, the organization began retiring some of its hydroelectric facilities. By 1973, 41 small facilities had been taken out of service.

Nuclear energy emerged in the 1960s as a proven technology in some parts of New England. PSNH announced in 1972 that it would build a two-unit nuclear plant on the state's seacoast, in the town of Seabrook. Completion of the $1.3 billion project was expected in 1979. PSNH received its construction permit for Seabrook Station in 1976—and experienced the first public protest at the planned site.

A decade of other protests followed—at the site, inside regulatory chambers, and in New Hampshire and Washington, DC courtrooms. As the construction period expanded, PSNH borrowed money to meet ever-escalating costs. In 1984, the joint owners canceled Seabrook Unit II and formed New Hampshire Yankee, a separate division of PSNH, to manage the construction of Unit I. Seabrook Unit I was completed in 1986 at a cost of $4.5 billion; the plant would not go

into full operation until 1990.

The financial and political difficulties encountered along the way ultimately led PSNH in 1988 to file for reorganization under Chapter 11, becoming the first investor-owned utility since the Great Depression to declare bankruptcy.

In 1989, Connecticut-based Northeast Utilities (NU) reached agreement with the state of New Hampshire, key creditors and other financial groups to acquire PSNH. The NU merger with PSNH was completed in June 1991.

Following the bankruptcy, the company faced major debts, steadily increasing rates and a tarnished public image. PSNH recognized that rebuilding public trust and perception could only be achieved by continuing to provide outstanding customer service and actively involving itself and its employees in important community activities. What it couldn't afford to contribute in dollars in the early 1990s, PSNH made up for in human resources, with employee volunteers responding to community needs in virtually every corner of the state. Inspired by the company's leadership, PSNH's community involvement commitment became a central part of the company's corporate culture and identity.

In 1993, PSNH created a new division devoted to meeting the business and economic needs of its communities. In partnership with the state, PSNH initiated and supported a variety of economic and community development activities, many focused on nurturing small business growth and expanding international markets.

PSNH also devoted substantial resources to protecting the environment. In 1995, the company formalized a landmark alliance with state and federal agencies to develop the Amoskeag Fishways Learning Center. The center features an underwater viewing window built adjacent to the Fishways' fish ladder, allowing visitors to see, and learn more about, anadromous fish in the Merrimack River. In another notable environmental initiative, PSNH became the first utility in the nation to pioneer the use of selective catalytic reduction (SCR) technology to reduce emissions from a coal-fired power plant. PSNH's emission-reduction efforts earned an Environmental Merit Award from the U.S. Environmental Protection Agency.

The company has received numerous other commendations and awards for contributions to education and community involvement. Recognizing the importance of preserving the state's diverse culture and traditions, PSNH assumed a leadership role in supporting New Hampshire's participation in the 1999 Smithsonian Folklife Festival held on The Mall in Washington,

DC. Preserving the past was also the motivating force behind PSNH's funding of the New Hampshire History Curriculum, a valuable guide for teaching Granite State history to students of all ages.

Such contributions to education and environmental protection, along with a proven dedication to economic development and civic involvement, earned PSNH the distinction of being named New Hampshire's Business of the Year in 1997. Moreover, PSNH's president and chief executive officer William T. Frain Jr., was named New Hampshire's Business Leader of the Decade in 2000, illustrating that the company's remarkable culture of community involvement truly did start at the top.

In 1996, the New Hampshire Legislature passed a law that set the framework for electric utility deregulation, giving consumers the ability to competitively purchase energy, much in the same way they shop for long-distance phone service. The delivery of electricity, however, would still continue to be regulated. In addition, the legislature initiated the nation's first statewide "pilot program" on electric competition, allowing about 17,000 New Hampshire customers to choose a retail electric energy provider.

In June 2000, a comprehensive deregulation agreement was approved for PSNH. The deregulation law allows customers to choose a competitive supplier of energy and includes an average 15 percent rate reduction for PSNH customers when choice begins—expected in 2001. The law also requires that the company's power plant assets and energy contracts, including PSNH's interests in Seabrook, be sold off no later than July 2001.

At the beginning of a new century, PSNH remains the Granite State's largest electric utility, pro-

viding service to more than 430,000 homes and businesses. PSNH personnel include over 1,200 employees who live and work in the state and contribute in many ways to their communities. With the anticipated merger of its parent company NU, with Consolidated Edison of New York, PSNH may soon be an integral part of one of the largest electric delivery systems in the country.

For 75 years, through storms, Depression, war, and even bankruptcy, PSNH has never ceased improving its delivery and service to customers. The desire for self-improvement and the motivation to exceed expectations helped the company to overcome extreme adversity and great challenges, and spurred new and innovative ways to operate and provide customer service. The result has often been to break new ground and set the standard for the electric utility industry—a role PSNH is prepared to continue into the future.

In 1998, PSNH became the first utility in the nation to test a program using sheep to control vegetation in its power line rights-of-way. The "Grazing Power Project," an innovative and environmentally friendly alternative to traditional vegetation management methods, earned the company an Environmental Merit Award from the U.S. Environmental Protection Agency.

ST. MARY'S BANK

By the early 1900s, the French-Canadian immigrants who came to work in Manchester's thriving textile mills had begun to sink roots and establish their own neighborhood communities. In fact, the West Side of Manchester was developed primarily to accommodate families arriving from Quebec. The most important local institution for these immigrants was their church, Ste. Marie's. Ste. Marie's Pastor, Monsignor Pierre Hevey, and other prominent neighborhood leaders, found that it was difficult for French-Canadian residents to save money and obtain the credit they needed to build homes and start businesses.

For its first five years St. Mary's operated from the Notre Dame Avenue home of the credit union's volunteer treasurer, Joseph Boivin.

Monsignor Hevey was an innovative, energetic man who had learned of a journalist named Alphonse Desjardins. Desjardins had imported credit unionism from Europe and established credit unions in Canada. Monsignor Hevey invited Desjardins to Manchester, and together they created the very first credit union in the United States—St. Mary's Bank. This not-for-profit, member-owned association was organized in order to help meet the financial needs of the immigrant parishioners.

On November 24, 1908, the credit union was organized and established. From 1908 until 1913, St. Mary's operated from the Notre Dame Avenue home of the credit union's volunteer treasurer, Joseph Boivin. The first safe was a used metal box purchased from *L'Avenir National*, Manchester's French daily newspaper. Savings were accepted from workers, families and children. All the accumulated savings were, in turn, lent out to members to purchase and build homes, establish neighborhood businesses, and meet the personal financial needs of the community. The credit union was charted as "St. Mary's Cooperative Credit Association" and required the purchase of a $5 share of capital stock to become an owner/member. The purchase of one share of stock for $5 is still in place today.

St. Mary's prospered, and in 1913, the office was moved out of the Boivin home and into an office at 330 Notre Dame Avenue. In 1916, the first full-time manager was hired, replacing what had been, up to that point, an all-volunteer staff. In 1917, the state legislature approved a bill, changing the name from "St. Mary's Cooperative Credit Association" to "La Caisse Populaire, Ste. Marie" (The People's Bank). And, by 1923, St. Mary's assets exceeded $1 million. In 1925, an amended charter allowed the institution to be called either "La Caisse Populaire Ste. Marie," or "St. Mary's Bank."

In 1930, St. Mary's moved into the "Marble Building," an impressive landmark in the center of what was then the commercial heart of Manchester's West Side. Additional services and products were introduced, and the credit union began to take its more familiar form—checking accounts, Christmas Clubs, safe deposit boxes, and a wider variety of loan types were introduced. By the mid-1950s, St. Mary's was serving several thousand members and had $6 million in assets. The urban renewal programs of the 1960s resulted in widespread changes in the Notre Dame neighborhood, and in 1970, St. Mary's Bank moved into its present location. St. Mary's has continued to expand its services, locations and member-

In 1930 St. Mary's moved into the "Marble Building," an impressive landmark in the center of what was then the commercial heart of Manchester's West Side.

ship base. At the end of 1999, St. Mary's served over 32,000 New Hampshire families and maintained assets over $350 million.

St. Mary's has survived and grown through some very tough times in New Hampshire. When thousands of banks failed due to the Great Depression, St. Mary's remained open—even during the "Bank Holiday" of 1933, when President Roosevelt closed all banks nationwide. St. Mary's helped its members struggle through the bankruptcy of Amoskeag Mills in 1935, and survived the economic disruptions of the early 1990s, which saw the failure of many familiar Manchester banks.

In 1994, Mr. and Mrs. Armand Lemire donated the Boivin family home, site of the first credit union, to the SMB Charitable Foundation. The Foundation's board of directors accepted the gift and developed plans to preserve the house, create a credit union museum dedicated to commemorating the credit union movement, and build a state-of-the-art training facility. The building has been designated as a National Historical Site.

In 2000, St. Mary's offers membership to anyone who lives or works in New Hampshire and competes in today's marketplace as a full-service financial institution. Throughout their history, St. Mary's has remained dedicated to its original mission—offering access to vital, fairly-priced financial products and delivering those products with a high degree of personal

service. A lot has been written about how much has changed this past century. St. Mary's history of service to its members is usually talked about in terms of change, too. But it's equally important to talk about those things that have not changed. St. Mary's is still owned by its members, not a small group of profit-driven stockholders. St. Mary's remains a community-based organization. Business decisions at St. Mary's are driven by the best interests of the membership. Its origins grew out of unmet needs for credit for a population of underserved individuals. They continue to believe that access to financial services for the underserved is an integral part of their mission.

To this end, St. Mary's has established broad initiatives to serve low-income and minority families in their communities. St. Mary's has pledged $1 million a year for the next 10 years to community outreach programs. St. Mary's Community Outreach Programs are targeted to meet the needs of the underserved in Greater Manchester and are administered through working partnerships with selected area non-profit social service agencies.

St. Mary's has remained true to its heritage and dedicated to its original mission of the founding mill workers—offering access to vital, fairly-priced financial products delivered with a high degree of personal service.

TYCOM LTD

TyCom manufacturing facilities strengthen New Hampshire's industrial fiber.

The men and women who manufacture undersea telecommunications cable at one of TyCom's sprawling industrial facilities are making history. Thousands of kilometers of state-of-the-art fiber-optic cable are loaded aboard the company's ships at the deep-water pier on the Piscataqua River. The cable-laying ships are playing a key role in the creation of a truly global telecommunications network.

In many ways, the scene is reminiscent of the days when the cable manufacturing company, TyCom Integrated Cable Systems, the former Simplex Technologies, used horse and wagon to haul its heavy cable spools to market. Today's differences rest not so much in the company or its employees, but with the technology inside the cable itself. Unlike traditional telephone wire, fiber-optic strands take advantage of physics by relaying digital code as pulses of light, transmitting Internet traffic, voice, data and graphically-intensive video files across oceans and continents at incredible speeds.

TyCom Integrated Cable Systems is one of the core manufacturing facilities of TyCom, Ltd., a leader in the undersea broadband communications industry. TyCom's new goal with the competitive telecommunications industry is three-fold: to sell bandwidth capacity, to supply new undersea fiber-optic cable systems and upgrades, and to provide maintenance and value-added services for such systems.

TyCom Integrated Cable Systems' reputation in the industry as manufacturer of undersea cable is unparalleled. The company traces its roots to a two-man, wire-working firm established in Boston in 1842 by Charles Morss and Oliver

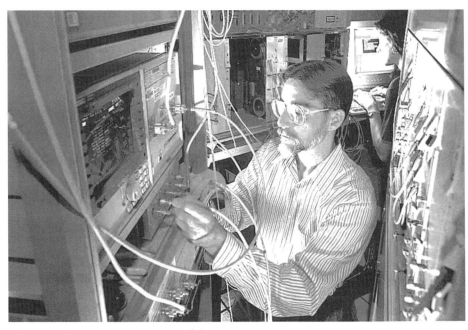

Optical transmission equipment is manufactured at the Exeter facility.

Whyte. The two engineers fabricated wire for such products as coal screens and birdcages. At the close of the Civil War, following a successful trial for street lighting wire, the partnership began to focus on electrical and communications cable as a main line of business. As a result of the street-lighting experiment, which produced enough wire known as TZR to light miles of street lamps in Boston, the company entered the insulated wire business.

In 1898, the company developed the nation's first submarine cable. By the turn of the 20th century, TyCom Integrated Cable Systems had manufactured an unprecedented five-mile length of underwater telephone cable that was laid across the Straits of Mackinac in Lake Michigan.

As the business grew, so did its need for more space. The Newington facility was opened in 1953, the first American plant designed to produce long lengths of undersea cable. The factory, sited on 85 acres of riverfront land, occupies 550,000 square feet, making it one of the world's largest undersea cable factories.

In 1974, the cable manufacturer became a subsidiary of Tyco Laboratories, now Tyco International Ltd., based in nearby Exeter. Work soon began on development of the company's undersea fiber cable program. The world's first transoceanic fiber-optic cable system (TAT-8) was completed in 1988, with TyCom Integrated Cable Systems playing a significant role in the production.

By the dawn of the millennium, the company had produced 190,000 kilometers of optical ocean cable. An estimated 92,595 kilometers of cable were manufactured and deployed for the U.S. Department of Defense. The firm also provided the U.S. Navy with over 12,500 kilometers of its fifth-generation undersea surveillance cable, the first to contain fiber optics.

In July 1997, Tyco International acquired AT&T Submarine Systems, which brought with it world-renowned research and development laboratories, electronic manufacturing facilities, and advanced operations and maintenance organizations. The acquisition also included a fleet of specially designed cable-laying and maintenance ships, and two additional vessels will be constructed and placed into service by 2001. By putting all these pieces together the company became a fully-integrated supplier, focusing on research and development, manufacturing, and installation and maintenance.

The company has deepwater ports in Newington; Baltimore, Maryland; Portland, Oregon; Honolulu, Hawaii; and Valencia and Vigo, Spain. The ships can remain at sea for up to 60 days without refueling, and can carry as much as 8,000 kilometers of cable. After plying the oceans for weeks to install a system, the ships will return to Newington for more cable.

The new strategy of being the foremost supplier of undersea systems and owning and operating the TyCom Global Network, coupled with the company's rapid growth, has had a positive impact in New Hampshire. From 1997 to 2000, the Newington factory increased its annual production of undersea cable from 22,000 kilometers to 60,000 kilometers.

A major manufacturing facility was opened in early 1999 in Exeter. TyCom Optical Transmission Systems is responsible for designing and building the high performance electronics that are used on land to send and receive multiple optical signals along the undersea route.

When the company officially became TyCom in 2000, it simultaneously announced plans to double the size of the Exeter manufacturing facility. In addition to refurbishing the structure, plans call for that facility to increase to nearly 500 employees by 2001—a significant boost to the New Hampshire job market and economy. As of mid-2000, TyCom Ltd. employed over 3,200 employees, and contin-

ues to expand, particularly with the launch of the TyCom Global Network.

The first phase of implementation will span approximately 70,000 kilometers and connect to those telecommunications centers around the world where voice, video, data and Internet demand for bandwidth are greatest. The system is designed to offer multi-terabit bandwidth up to 7.68 terabits per second, which, by industry standards, offers tremendous capacity. Over the next 10 years, TyCom's plans for the Global Network call for it to extend 250,000 undersea kilometers, linking these cable routes to terrestrial networks on all six inhabited continents.

"The concept of building our own global network has intrigued us since the creation of this company in 1997," said L. Dennis Kozlowski, chairman and CEO of Tyco International, and executive chairman of TyCom. "Our undersea fiber-optics business is ideally positioned for this undertaking, based on its knowledge of the market, expertise in designing, building, installing and maintaining successively advanced undersea fiber-optic networks, and its relationships with the world's telecommunications carriers."

Fiber optic cable is loaded onto TyCom cable-laying ships in Newington.

The decision to commit TyCom's undersea fiber-optics business to the creation of a global network was based on projections of growing worldwide communications needs. The integration of the Internet into the daily lives of the world's population, combined with the burgeoning needs of global commerce and industry for data and other broadband applications, continue to drive growth and demand. As broadband terrestrial fiber-optic networks are completed, they require the availability of undersea systems to connect with the rest of the world. It's here that TyCom can fully emerge in the telecommunications marketplace.

By industry standards, the undertaking is massive and positions TyCom among the world's largest providers of advanced broadband communications capacity, systems and services. With two of TyCom's primary facilities in Newington and Exeter, it's clear that New Hampshire's industrial heritage will be part of every piece of data transmitted through the TyCom Global Network across the oceans and continents of the world.

STEENBEKE & SONS, INC.

It was just two years before the federal government's interstate highway program came into being that James and Mary Steenbeke left their New York City restaurant business in search of a better place to raise their three sons.

In 1954 Boscawen, New Hampshire, the town they chose, was a crossroads north of Concord. It was there that state Highways 3 and 4 forked away from each other, 3 going north to the White Mountains and 4 going west toward Vermont.

James Steenbeke purchased a general store and a house on Route 4. At that time Boscawen had three other stores, all of them fairly well restricted to groceries; with Concord a good 30 minutes away, Steenbeke's fulfilled a need for a store that would sell not only groceries but gasoline, kerosene, some simple building supplies such as nuts and bolts, and clothing and shoes.

Steenbeke put his family to work planting corn and potatoes and taking care of 2,000 laying hens. Steenbeke's store sold eggs, homegrown vegetables, meat (even chicken from their own small farm), grain, salt licks, and medicine for cows.

Steenbeke's Grocery Store, as it was then called, did $50,000 in business in its first year, however, when Interstate 93 built past Boscawen in 1960, the days of the general store were numbered. It was sheer accident that three years earlier, Steenbeke had become involved with lumber, the principal concern of the company today.

A local sawmill operator told Steenbeke that he knew of someone in need of a load of finished lumber. Arrangements were made to pick up the load at a wholesaler and deliver it to the builder. Steenbeke saw that the potential for profit was greater in lumber

than it had been in eggs, so he took lumber on as another line. Early in the 1960s Steenbeke even became a contractor for a time, building summer homes that, in those blissful days of low inflation, sold for $6,000.

Steenbeke's three sons all attended the University of New Hampshire, (two of them worked in the corporate world), and returned to the growing family building material business. By 1990 the company had "Home Center" stores in eight New Hampshire communities employing more than 150 people.

The recession of the early '90s took its toll and the company decided to close two of its smaller stores in a consolidation move. At the same time the Steenbekes recognized an unfilled need in the market for a cash-and-carry bargain outlet. Thus, Big Jim's Bargain Outlet was opened in one of the closed stores in Suncook, NH. The store sold seconds and over-inventoried items purchased both from Steenbeke and Sons and other companies. Also during this period the company was expanding its presence in the specialty millwork, hollow metal and architectural hardware market places with a wholly-owned subsidiary, Architectural Specialties, Inc. ASI marketed its products to industrial, commercial and institutional builders.

In 1999 Steenbeke decided to take the kitchen cabinet showrooms out of the lumberyards and open freestanding shops in shopping centers. The thought was, and still is, that upscale buyers would prefer to shop for their kitchens in a less hurried atmosphere than a lumberyard. The first Distinctive Kitchens, Designs by Steenbeke and Sons, was opened in Bedford, followed by stores in Laconia and Concord.

There are plans for other kitchen stores throughout the state. The company now has five lumber yards in Gilford, Franklin, Boscawen, Concord and Manchester. Three kitchen stores are in Laconia, Concord and Bedford.

Also in 1999 James Steenbeke, III became president and COO of the company. In 2000 he purchased the shares of Donald and Raymond in exchange for ASI and Big Jim's shares, and assumed the duties of CEO of Steenbeke & Sons. Donald has full ownership of Big Jim's and Raymond owns ASI. Jim, Jr. and James III retained control of Steenbeke & Sons.

The original general store still stands across the street from the corporate headquarters as a reminder of where the company has been and how far it has come in the last 47 years. In a few years the fourth generation will begin to learn the business and take the company soaring into the 21st century.

James and Mary Steenbeke brought three citified sons to rural Boscawen in 1954 and promptly put them to work gathering eggs and planting vegetables to sell in the general store. At one point, when Steenbeke was building houses, it was possible to buy seemingly everything—from a 1¢ stick of gum to a $6,000 home—from the store.

400 YEARS: HIGH POINTS OF NEW HAMPSHIRE HISTORY

1600 Abenakis live throughout the area later to be known as New Hampshire.

1603 Captain Martin Pring sails along the New Hampshire coast and up the Piscataqua River and sees "groves and woods...also sundry sorts of beasts," but not people.

1605 French explorer Samuel de Champlain enters Piscataqua Bay.

1614 Captain John Smith visits Isles of Shoals: "the remarkablest isles...a heap together...a many of barren rocks."

1622 John Mason and Ferdinando Gorges receive large and imprecisely located grant between the Merrimack and Kennebec rivers from the London Council for New England.

1623 David Thomson, a clerk for the Council for New England, settles with a small group at "Odiorne"s Point (present-day Rye), perhaps to start a fish exporting colony.

1629 John Mason, who probably never visited New Hampshire, names his property New Hampshire, after his native county in England.

The Jackson House at Christian Shore in Portsmouth, is the oldest house in New Hampshire. Built by shipbuilder Richard Jackson about 1664 and occupied by his descendants for over 200 years, it is presently owned by the Society for the Preservation of New England Antiquities. This photo was made in 1920. Courtesy, R. & G. Jager

1630-32 Under Council for New England grants, settlements are established at Dover Point and lower on the Piscataqua at Strawbery Banke (later Portsmouth).

1632 Farming settlements at Dover Point and Strawbery Banke have cattle, sheep, oxen, and they ship corn to Charlestown, Massachusetts, for grinding.

1633 First New Hampshire church (congregational) organized in Dover.

1638 The Rev. John Wheelwright, banished from the Massachusetts Bay Colony, purchases land from Native Americans and settles what becomes the town of Exeter.

—New town (which becomes Hampton) authorized by order of the Massachusetts General Court and settled.

1640 Anglican parish established at Strawbery Banke.

1640s First four New Hampshire settlements (Dover, Portsmouth, Exeter, Hampton), with their makeshift governments, join with the Bay Colony and become Massachusetts towns.

—John Eliot begins missionary work among the Merrimack River Penacook Indians, in their own language.

1642 Massachusetts law requires that parents (eventually including New Hampshire parents) teach their children to read.

—Darby Field and two Native American guides reach summit of Mt. Washington.

1650s Fishing becomes a thriving industry on the Isles of Shoals (up to 1,500 residents), and soon its salted mackerel and dried cod are famed in Europe.

1652 British Admiralty begins regular shipment of white pine masts from Portsmouth.

1660 Passaconaway, in great old age, makes farewell speech to his Abenaki people, urging them to keep the peace with the English.

1662 Quakers are expelled from Dover and Hampton.

1664 The Jackson House, presently New Hampshire's oldest house, is built (vertical plank style) by shipbuilder Richard Jackson in Portsmouth.

1665 The Abenaki Indian Metacomet (known as King Philip), son of Massasoit, begins raids on English settlements.

1672 John Josselyn reports in *New-England's Rarities Discovered* (London) on the White Mountains: "The Country beyond these Hills Northward is daunting terrible, being full of rocky Hills, as thick as Mole-hills in a Meadow, and cloathed with infinite thick Woods."

1676 Wonalancet, son of Passaconaway, signs peace treaty with the English in Dover.

—Major Waldron of Dover betrays Indians in sham fight.

1680 New Hampshire detached from Massachusetts and made a royal province with a town-elected Assembly and a crown-appointed Executive of Governor and Council.

1689 Kancamagus, nephew of Wonalancet, raids Dover and exacts revenge by killing Major Waldron and 22 others, and taking 29 captives to Canada.

1693 New Hampshire Assembly requires towns to provide by taxation for a school and a schoolmaster's salary.

1695 One hundred vessels carry more than 2,000,000 board feet of lumber to Boston.

1697 Hannah Dustin of Haverhill, Massachusetts, reportedly kills her

Native American captors in Penacook, New Hampshire, escapes, and later collects a Massachusetts bounty for scalps.

1700 Census shows there are 50 sawmills in New Hampshire.

1708 New Hampshire legislature requires that a Latin school be kept at Portsmouth, a free school "for readers, writers, and latinists," paid for by Portsmouth and five neighboring towns.

—English Crown lays claim to all trees in New Hampshire over 24 inches in diameter.

1711 Following Massachusetts, New Hampshire puts a bounty on Indian scalps for one year.

1717 John Wentworth appointed lieutenant-governor of New Hampshire—the beginning of the Wentworth dynasty, which ended with the Revolutionary War.

1719 Presbyterian Church opens in Londonderry, the first in New Hampshire.

—Potatoes introduced into New Hampshire by Scots-Irish of Londonderry.

1727 Severe earthquake felt in New England: according to sermons of the time it was one of the precipitating circumstances of the Great Awakening.

1730 Census shows a New Hampshire population of 10,000, including 200 slaves.

About a dozen of these handsome arched dry wall bridges, some smaller, some larger, were designed and built in the Hillsboro area between 1820 and 1840. The claim at the time was that they took no more work and would outlast the covered bridges then being built. The skill required is chiefly splitting granite properly and sliding it into place. A covered bridge is always a design challenge; it may last 100 years, if taken care of, and then will probably require serious repair. This granite bridge on Jones Road in Hillsboro is about 170 years old, it has required little or no upkeep, it won't burn, and it appears to be good for several more centuries. Courtesy, R & G Jager

In this 1858 photo (the oldest photo in this book) the USS Constitution, at age 60, is in dry dock in the Portsmouth Naval Shipyard, for repairs. Today she is over 200 years old and still a commissioned naval vessel, in dignified repose in Charlestown, Massachusetts. Strawbery Banke Museum; Cumings Library and Archives

1732 Anglican parish is reestablished at Queen's Chapel in Portsmouth.

1740 Boundary dispute with Massachusetts settled by the Crown in New Hampshire's favor. Massachusetts loses many towns in present-day southern New Hampshire.

1741 Benning Wentworth becomes governor and starts chartering New Hampshire towns to the west in territory (now Vermont) claimed by New York.

1746 Group of Portsmouth merchants (later "the Masonian Proprietors") purchase Robert Mason's

Half Way House on Mt. Monadnock served as a guest house for hikers. In 1866, Ralph Waldo Emerson and his camping party, driven by the weather to abandon their tents, stayed here. It burned in 1954, and this particular road is no longer maintained. Nevertheless, by other paths an estimated 130,000 people climbed Mt. Monadnock in 1999. Courtesy, R. & G. Jager

uncertain claim in New Hampshire, and start chartering towns.

1752 Record number of masts—554—are sent to England from New Hampshire.

1756 *New-Hampshire Gazette*, the state's first newspaper, founded in Portsmouth by Daniel Fowle: "With the Freshest Advices, Foreign and Domestick."

1759 The famed and feared Rogers Rangers (led by Robert Rogers of Rumford) destroy the Abenaki village at St. Francis in Canada. Their return to New Hampshire is novelized in Kenneth Roberts' *Northwest Passage.*

1761 Stagecoach begins a regular Boston-Portsmouth route.

1763 Peace of Paris marks an end to the French and Indian Wars in New Hampshire.

1767 John Wentworth, friend and Harvard classmate (1755) of John Adams, replaces his uncle Benning Wentworth as governor of New Hampshire.

1769 Eleazar Wheelock's college chartered ("for the instruction of youth of the Indian Tribes...and also of English youth and any others") in Hanover by Governor Wentworth.

Named for the Governor's English friend, Secretary of State for the Colonies, Lord Dartmouth.

1770 Approximately 50 ships per year are being built in and near Portsmouth.

1774 Governor Wentworth dismisses the Assembly but they reconvene as a provincial congress and appoint delegates to the Continental Congress in Philadelphia.

—In the first New Hampshire act of aggression against British authority, John Langdon and John Sullivan lead a successful raid on Fort William and Mary in New Castle and remove the gun powder and light cannon.

1775 Governor Wentworth, with his wife and infant son flee New Hampshire, eliminating British authority in the province.

1776 New Hampshire Provincial Congress adopts a short and temporary state constitution (January 5), which marks the beginning of constitutional self-government in America.

—New Hampshire Provincial Congress instructs (June 15) its Continental Congress delegates to vote "the 13 united colonies a free and independent state."

1777 John Stark, leading a New Hampshire militia to thwart General John Burgoyne's invasion of the Champlain Valley, wins a major victory at Bennington (now Vermont).

1782 Daniel Webster born in Salisbury, New Hampshire.

—George Washington settles Vermont-New Hampshire boundary

dispute, and clears the way for Vermont statehood.

1783 Revolutionary War officially ends with treaty signed in Paris.

—Phillips Academy opens in Exeter.

1784 Jeremy Belknap, Dover minister, publishes first volume of *The History of New Hampshire.* (Three volumes completed in 1792.)

—New state constitution implemented, replacing the war-time constitution of 1776.

1788 New Hampshire becomes the ninth and decisive state to ratify the new federal constitution.

—Sarah J. Hale, future social reformer and *Godey's Ladies Book* editor, born in Newport.

1789 New state law requires towns to have prospective teachers examined by an "able and reputable" person to insure that they are qualified.

—President George Washington visits Portsmouth and Exeter.

1792 Shaker community founded in Canterbury.

1796 First New Hampshire turnpike incorporated, from Portsmouth

The three New Hampshire signers of the Declaration of Independence. (Top two signatures and the bottom one)

to Concord (opened 1803).

1800 United States Navy establishes Portsmouth Naval Shipyard; its location is still subject to a Maine/New Hampshire boundary dispute 200 years later.

—Census records a population of nearly 184,000, including eight slaves.

1805 "Old Man of the Mountain" in Franconia Notch is first recorded.

1808 Concord becomes the chosen meeting place of New Hampshire's General Court. (State House site selected in 1814; construction begins 1816; completed 1819.)

1811 Horace Greeley, future *New York Tribune* editor, is born in Amherst.

1812 New Hampshire criminal code is revised; whipping post and pillory are abolished.

1813 Great Fire (third and worst in a decade) destroys 300 buildings in Portsmouth.

1819 In landmark Dartmouth College Case, argued by alumnus Daniel Webster, the United States Supreme Court shields private colleges from partisan politics.

—New Hampshire Legislature passes the Toleration Act, and Church and State are officially separated. Tax funds no longer to be used to meet expenses of any church.

1820 Census reports "786 persons of color" and no slaves.

1823 New Hampshire Historical Society is founded with historian and former Governor William Plumer as president.

1825 New Hampshire acquires "Granite State" nickname, from Philip Carrigain's lyric commemorating the visit to New Hampshire of General de Lafayette.

1826 Massive landslide wipes out the Willey family in Crawford Notch, an episode memorialized by many graphic artists and also in Nathaniel Hawthorne's *The Ambitious Guest*.

1827 Lewis Downing and J. Stephens Abbot form partnership in Concord which results in the production of the famous Concord

A 1906 postcard view of the Amoskeag and other mills in Manchester. Courtesy, R. & G. Jager

Coach with its pioneering leather thoroughbraces.

—Temperance movement begins in New Hampshire as Rev. Nathaniel Bouton preaches against the use of "ardent spirits."

1828 Thomas Crawford opens the Notch House in the White Mountains, the first of the White Mountain hotels.

1830 Census shows that 83 percent of New Hampshire workers labor on farms.

1832 Residents in northern extremity of the state, weary of boundary disputes, form the Indian Stream Republic, with constitution, legislature, courts, and an army of 40 men—dissolved by the New Hampshire militia three years later, and now the town of Pittsburg.

1833 Peterborough opens the country's first free, tax-supported public library (others were membership or fee-based).

1838 First trains run in New Hampshire between Lowell (MA) and Nashua.

—New Hampshire State Hospital— its name a cautious euphemism—authorized by the legislature (opens 1842).

1842 Webster-Ashburton Treaty establishes New Hampshire-Canadian boundary.

1850 Census shows there are 44 cotton mills and 61 woolen mills in New Hampshire.

—Daniel Chester French, sculptor, born in Exeter.

1852 Franklin Pierce, Hillsborough native, is elected 14th President of the United States (assisted by Nathaniel Hawthorne who writes his campaign biography).

1853 The Republican Party, though born in Wisconsin in 1854, is conceived and named in Exeter, New Hampshire.

1856 St. Paul's School, a boarding school for boys, opens in Concord (girls admitted in 1970).

1857 New Hampshire law grants African American males full citizenship with right to vote.

1860 Forest cover of New Hampshire is at 48 percent, the lowest ever. (In 2000, approximately 87 percent.)

—Abraham Lincoln visits New Hampshire and, after speeches in Manchester, Concord, Dover, and Exeter, emerges as a viable Republican candidate for President.

1861 Carriage Road to summit of Mt. Washington opens.

1862 First Seventh-Day Adventist Church is organized in Washington,

New Hampshire.

1864 Salmon P. Chase of Cornish becomes Chief Justice of the United States Supreme Court.

1866 New Hampshire College of Agriculture and Mechanic Arts incorporated as a "land grant college." Classes open in Hanover two years later with 10 students. (Now the University of New Hampshire in Durham.)

1867 Amy Cheney Beach, pianist and composer, born in Henniker.

—New Hampshire sells the last of its timber lands: 172,000 acres in the White Mountains for less than 15¢ per acre.

1869 Two and one-half-mile Cog Railway opens to the top of Mt. Washington.

1871 Plymouth Normal School opens, New Hampshire's first teacher training institution.

1873 Celia Thaxter publishes *Among the Isles of Shoals.*

—Patrons of Husbandry (Grange) begins in New Hampshire.

1874 Ocean telecommunications cable installed from Ireland, 3,100 nautical miles to Rye Beach, New Hampshire.

1877 New Hampshire constitution amended to permit non-Protestants to hold state office.

—New school law declares that "female citizens of adult age may hold and discharge the duties of prudential or superintending committee."

1878 Female suffrage begins: New Hampshire women allowed to vote in district school meetings.

—First commercial telephone exchange opens in Manchester.

1879 Church of Christ, Scientist is chartered (founded by Mary Baker Eddy of Bow, New Hampshire).

1880 There are 1,000 miles of railroad in New Hampshire.

1881 Horse-powered railway opens in Concord.

1882 Electricity illuminates street lamps in Manchester and in Berlin.

1889 Constitutional amendment sets pay for General Court (Legislature) at $200 per term.

Richard Upton (1915-1996), Concord historian and lawyer, was newly-elected Speaker of the New Hampshire House of Representatives in 1949 when he decided that the presidential primary, held regularly on town meeting day in March, needed more interest. He wrote a bill allowing residents to vote not only for delegates, but directly for a presidential candidate—and he saw it pass. Thus the modern presidential primary was born, and in effect in 1952. Photo by Ken Williams, Concord Monitor

When Strawbery Banke Museum was incorporated in 1958 this area of Portsmouth was slated for urban renewal, and one can see why. Ten acres were to be leveled, including 38, mostly 18th century, houses. This 1962 view cuts across the center of what became the Historical Preservation Project Area. The Museum opened in 1965 and has since become an attractive cluster of 42 historic houses and shops in a tight waterfront neighborhood. Strawbery Banke Museum; Cumings Library and Archives

1891 New Hampshire College of Agriculture and Mechanic Arts authorized to move to Durham. (Classes begin there in 1893.)

1892 First Jewish synagogue in New Hampshire opens in Manchester.

1899 First New Hampshire Old Home Week proclaimed by Governor Rollins.

1900 Twenty-five passenger trains per day enter and leave Concord.

1901 Society for the Protection of New Hampshire Forests is formed, targeting the White Mountains for protection.

1902 Mount Washington Hotel opens in Bretton Woods, capping the Golden Age of White Mountain hotel building.

—Women's suffrage passed by state Constitutional Convention. Later rejected by the voters.

1903 North country forest fires burn more than 200,000 acres.

1905 Treaty of Portsmouth (NH) ends Russo-Japanese War.

—New Hampshire State Highway Department is created.

1907 MacDowell Colony, a retreat inspired by Edward MacDowell, for artists composers, and writers, is founded in Peterborough.

1911 Weeks Act authorizes the creation of the White Mountain National Forest, now over 750,000 acres.

1914 Audubon Society of New Hampshire formed.

1919 State Board Act makes major education changes: acknowledges the state's responsibility for education, creates a Board of Education, a Commissioner, and mandates 36 weeks of school per year.

1920 Women vote in New Hampshire elections, and two are elected to the state Legislature.

—Forty thousand people are employed in New Hampshire textile industries.

1922 First New Hampshire radio station, WLNH, begins broadcasting from Lebanon.

1923 College of Agriculture in Durham is redefined as The Uni-

Jonathan Daniels, born and reared in Keene and a student at Episcopal Theological Seminary in Cambridge, joined many others in Alabama to assist in civil rights work. On August 20, 1965, having just been released from jail for assisting in voter registration, he was murdered on the street in Hayneville, Alabama. A part-time deputy sheriff was charged with manslaughter and acquitted by a jury in 20 minutes. Daniels' death, and the national shock it evoked, helped to bring the turmoil of the 1960s—which had seemed distant and remote—home to many New Hampshire people.

That May, Daniels had written to a friend that one has to be "prepared, in advance, both physically and spiritually, for the gas, arrest, and I suppose, even for death...I decided a long time ago that the Holy Spirit brought me here, that I believe very firmly in the gospel and its faith, that my life is His—which means that before anything else, I am a servant of Christ...that the possibility of death, whether immediate or remote, cannot be a deciding factor...." While in Selma, Daniels stayed with the family of Rachel West, shown with him in this photo.

In historic Canterbury Cathedral, the center of the Anglican faith, there is kept a Book of Heroes and Martyrs. The name of Martin Luther King is inscribed there, and so is that of Jonathan Daniels of Keene, New Hampshire. They are the only Americans. Courtesy, Keene Sentinel

versity of New Hampshire.

—Robert Frost publishes *New Hampshire.*

1929 Currier Gallery of Art opens in Manchester—endowed by former Governor Moody Currier.

1932 League of New Hampshire Craftsmen is organized.

1934 In April the Mt. Washington Observatory records a world-record (still standing) wind speed of 231 miles per hour atop Mt Washington.

1938 Hurricane sweeps through New England and causes $50 million in New Hampshire damages.

1941 Former Governor John Winant becomes United States Ambassador to England.

1942 Constitutional Amendment limits membership in state House of Representatives to 400.

1944 Bretton Woods International Monetary Conference at Mt. Washington Hotel establishes post-war currency regulations.

1946 William Loeb purchases the *Union Leader*, and begins printing ultraconservative editorials on the front page.

1949 New Hampshire law requires votes in the presidential primary to be for candidates, not delegates, inaugurating the modern presidential primary system in the 1952 election.

—Timber Yield Tax, replacing tax on growing timber with tax on harvested timber, is signed into law by Governor Sherman Adams.

1950 Block of New Hampshire granite laid as the cornerstone of the United Nations building in New York City.

—Total number of farms in New Hampshire is 13,391. (In 2000, approximately 3,000.)

1954 First New Hampshire Television station, WMUR-TV, opens in Manchester.

1958 Strawbery Banke Museum formed to preserve Portsmouth's historic waterfront. (Opens 1965)

1961 Commander Alan B. Shepard, born in Derry, is the first American in (suborbital) space. Ten years later he walks on the moon.

1963 New Hampshire Sweepstakes established, the first state-run lottery of the 20th century. By the year 2000 there are such lotteries in 37 states.

1973 "Current Use" Amendment to state constitution allows towns to tax land on its use rather than its development value.

1974 Town of Durham defeats zoning change that would have permitted a major coastal oil refinery.

1986 Christa McAuliffe, Concord school teacher, dies in explosion of space shuttle *Challenger*. Planetarium in Concord erected and named in her honor in 1989.

—"The Great Nuclear Dump Fight": citizen protests defeat plans to put a nuclear waste repository in Northeast region.

1990 New Hampshire population exceeds 1,000,000.

1991 Seabrook Nuclear Power Station goes to full power, the last U.S. nuclear station to be licensed.

1995 New Hampshire Historical Society opens new Museum of New Hampshire History in the former "Stone Warehouse," now the Hamel Center.

1996 Jeanne Shaheen, Democrat, elected New Hampshire Governor, the first woman to achieve this office.

1997 New Hampshire Supreme Court, in "Claremont decision," declares that paying for education through local property taxes is inherently inequitable and unconstitutional, giving legislature a deadline to institute a new statewide school funding system.

1999 Legislature enacts a controversial and temporary statewide property tax to fund schools.

2000 Legislature enacts Land and Community Heritage Investment Program (LCHIP) with 50/50 state funding, to preserve/protect threatened lands and structures.

—New Hampshire House of Representatives conducts high-profile inquiry into conduct of state Supreme Court justices, and impeaches Chief Justice David A. Brock.

NOTES

Page

Part I

16 "within eight . . ." Frederick W. Kilbourne, *Chronicles of the White Mountains* (Boston, 1916), pp. 7-8.

16 "the Country . . ." John Josselyn, *New England's Rarities* (Boston, 1865—facsimile of the 1672 ed.), p. 36.

17 "In great . . ." *Belknap's New Hampshire: An Account of the State in 1792,* ed. G.T. Lord (1973), Intro., p. ix.

17 "Nature . . ." Jeremy Belknap, *The History of New-Hampshire* (Dover, N.H., 1812), vol. III, p. 32.

19 "There is . . . kettle" Jere R. Daniell, *Colonial New Hampshire* (Milwood, N.Y., 1981), p. 25.

20- "all . . . thereof" David E. Van Deventer,
21 *The Emergence of Provincial New Hampshire, 1623-1741* (Baltimore, 1976), p. 72.

21 "live . . ." Daniell, *Colonial New Hampshire,* p. 135.

22 "Course . . ." *New Hampshire Provincial Papers,* vol. XIX, p. 478.

22 "full of . . ." Everett S. Stackpole, *History of New Hampshire* (New York, 1916), vol. I, p. 295.

24 "gives . . ." Jeremy Belknap, *The History of New Hampshire* (New York, 1970—reprint of the 1831 Dover edition), p. 392.

29 "The too . . ." Belknap, *History,* vol. III, p. 197.

29 "husbandry . . ." Belknap, *History,* vol. III, p. 156.

29 "Those who . . ." Thomas Jefferson, *Notes on the State of Virginia* (New York, 1964), p. 157.

30 "We have . . ." Harold Fisher Wilson, *The Hill Country of Northern New England, 1790-1930* (New York, 1936), p. 16.

30 "The almost . . ." Wilson, *Hill Country,* p. 19.

30- "Were I to form . . ." Belknap, *History,*
31 vol. III, p. 251.

Part II

38 "together . . ." *New Hampshire Provincial Papers,* vol. XVII, pp. 501-502.

40 "At great expense . . ." *Historical New Hampshire,* vol. XXVII (Fall 1972), p. 152.

41 "As late . . ." Belknap, *History,* vol. III, p. 192.

42 "They love . . ." Jere R. Daniell, "Lady Wentworth's Last Days in New Hampshire," *Historical New Hampshire,* vol. XXIII (Spring 1968), p. 19.

42 "infectious . . ." Jere R. Daniell, *Experiment in Republicanism: New Hampshire Politics and*

the American Revolution, 1741-1794 (Cambridge, 1970), p. 77.

42 "no jail . . ." Lawrence Shaw Mayo, *John Wentworth: Governor of New Hampshire, 1767-1775* (Cambridge, 1921), p. 145.

42 "All commissions . . ." Belknap, *History* (1970 reprint), p. 361.

43 "explicit . . ." *New Hampshire Provincial Papers,* vol. VII, p. 476.

43 "advice . . ." *Journal of the Continental Congress, 1774-1789,* ed. W.C. Ford (Washington, D.C., 1906), vol. III, p. 298.

43 "that it . . ." *Journal of the Continental Congress,* vol. III, p. 319.

44 "independence . . ." Belknap, *History,* vol. I, p. 367.

45 "We do . . ." Belknap, *History,* vol. I, p. 367.

45 "his hand . . ." Frank B. Sanborn, *New Hampshire: An Epitome of Popular Government* (Boston, 1904), p. 279.

45 "oppose . . ." *New Hampshire Provincial Papers,* vol. VIII, pp. 204-205.

46 "full and free . . ." *New Hampshire Provincial Papers,* vol. VIII, pp. 757-758.

46 "The love . . ." "A perfect . . ." *New Hampshire State Papers,* vol. IX, pp. 846, 845.

47 "When the . . ." *New Hampshire State Papers,* vol. IX, p. 846.

48 "at which . . ." Daniell, *Colonial New Hampshire,* p. 7.

48 "done by . . ." Nathaniel Bouton, *The History of Concord* (Concord, 1856), p. 22.

48 "purposed . . ." Bouton, *History of Concord,* p. 23.

48 "never to . . ." Bouton, *History of Concord,* p. 25.

49 "on a great . . ." *History of Concord,* ed. James O. Lyford (Concord, 1903), p. 74.

49 "and now . . ." Bouton, *History of Concord,* p. 28.

49 "chief sachem . . ." Bouton, *History of Concord,* p. 26.

51- "I have . . ." Lawrence Shaw Mayo, *John*
52 *Langdon of New Hampshire* (Port Washington, N.Y., 1937), p. 149.

53 "We obtained . . ." J. Duane Squires, "A Summary of the Events of 1777 . . .," *Historical New Hampshire,* vol. XXXII (Winter 1977), p. 170.

53 "The most active . . ." David L. Mann, "Bennington: A Clash between Patriot and Loyalist," *Historical New Hampshire,* vol. XXXII (Winter 1977), p. 187.

53 "This success . . ." Squires, "A Summary . . .," p. 170.

54- Quotations from Matthew Patten are from:

55 *The Diary of Matthew Patten of Bedford, N.H., 1754-1788* (Concord, 1903), pp. 342-393 passim.

59 "It is, sir . . ." Irving H. Bartlett, *Daniel Webster* (New York, 1978), p. 79.

60 "extension . . ." Stackpole, *History,* vol. III, pp. 72-73.

60 "at variance . . ." Stackpole, *History,* vol. III, p. 132.

61 "lacks fire . . ." Stackpole, *History,* vol. IV, p. 137.

61 "The true . . ." Frank Putnam, "What's the Matter with New England?" *New England Magazine,* vol. XXXVI (1907), p. 649.

61 "will rule . . ." Leon Burr Richardson, *William E. Chandler: Republican* (New York, 1940), p. 361.

62 "I say . . ." William E. Chandler, *New Hampshire a Slave State* (commonly known as *The Book of Bargains,*) (Concord, 1891), p. 69.

63 "Between 1910 . . ." Elizabeth F. Morison and Elting E. Morison. *New Hampshire* (New York, 1976), p. 181.

63 "always giving . . ." Bernard Bellush, *He Walked Alone: A Biography of John Gilbert Winant* (The Hague, 1968), p. 219.

67 "We spent . . ." *The Journals of Francis Parkman,* ed. Mason Wade (New York, 1947), vol. I, pp. 68-69.

67 "Sitting here . . ." Ronald Jager and Grace Jager, *Portrait of a Hill Town: The History of Washington, N.H., 1876-1976* (Washington, N.H., 1977), p. 487.

67 "Haying . . ." Kate Sanborn, *Abandoning an Adopted Farm* (New York, 1894).

67- "tied . . . farm" Ellen H. Rollins (E.H. Arr),
68 *Old-Time Child-Life* (Philadelphia, 1881), pp. 175-176.

68 "the progress . . ." *Washington & Marlow Times,* November 26, 1903.

68 "I was . . ." Tamara K. Hareven and Randolph Langenbach, *Amoskeag: Life and Work in an American Factory-City* (New York, 1978), pp. 152, 153.

71 "I came . . ." Hareven and Langenbach, *Amoskeag,* pp. 202, 203.

71 "I feel . . ." J. Duane Squires, *The Granite State of the United States: A History of New Hampshire from 1623 to the Present* (New York, 1956), vol. II, p. 674.

72 "given . . . valiant" Daniel Webster, *The Works of Daniel Webster* (Boston, 1881), vol. II, pp. 502, 504.

72- "another scow . . ." Henry David Thoreau,
73 *A Week on the Concord and Merrimack Rivers* (New York, 1966), p. 177.

Page

73 "more pleasing . . . banks" Thoreau, *A Week*, pp. 301-303 passim.

73 "we passed . . . sun" *Journals of Francis Parkman*, vol. I, p. 9.

74 "and asked . . . hospitable" *Journals of Francis Parkman*, vol. I, p. 68.

75 "apparently . . . conscience" Nathaniel Hawthorne, *Passages from the American Note-Books* (Boston, 1900), pp. 538, 542.

75 "Picking . . ." Horace Greeley, *Recollections of a Busy Life* (New York, 1868), p. 39.

75 "Yes . . ." Jager, *Portrait of a Hill Town*, p. 21.

75 "wending . . . again" Charles Carleton Coffin, *History of Bascawen and Webster* (Concord, 1878), p. 206.

76 "Any person . . ." *Laws of the State of New Hampshire*, June Session, 1878, Chap. 38, pp. 170-171.

76 about tramps Haydn Pearson, *That Darned Minister's Son* (Garden City, N.Y., 1950), pp. 194-195, 198.

77 "skimming . . ." Wilson, *Hill Country*, p. 280.

77- "All went . . ." Richardson, *Chandler*,
78 p. 645.

78 "To assemble . . ." Jager, *Portrait of a Hill Town*, p. 162.

79 "To see if . . ." Squires, *The Granite State*, vol. II, p. 755.

Part III

84 "It is . . ." Webster, *Works*, vol. II, pp. 418-419.

84 "I dread . . ." Mayo, *John Wentworth*, p. 93.

89 "endeavor . . ." Wilson, *Hill Country*, p. 35.

101 "If our old . . ." Hareven and Langenbach, *Amoskeag*, p. 11.

103 "a portable . . ." *Report of the Fish and Game Commissioners of New Hampshire*, June 1883 Session.

Part IV

118 "chiefe project . . ." *Annual Report of the Superintendent of Public Instruction*, June Session, 1876 (Concord, 1876), pp. 296-297.

118 "The promoting . . ." Squires, *Granite State*, vol. I, p. 96.

118 "Knowledge and learning . . ." Article 83, New Hampshire Constitution.

119 "physiology and hygiene . . ." *Annual Report of the New Hampshire Commissioner of Education*, 1884.

122 "were unable . . ." Squires, *The Granite State*, vol. II, p. 652.

125 "college where . . ." *History of the University of New Hampshire, 1866-1941*, ed. Fred

Page

Engelhardt (Durham, 1941), p. 8.

126 "agricultural school . . ." Engelhardt, *History*, p. 87.

126 " . . . all the agricultural . . ." Engelhardt, *History*, p. 92.

132 "under pretence . . ." Charles B. Kinney, Jr., *Church and State: The Struggle for Separation in New Hampshire, 1630-1900* (New York, 1955), p. 37.

134 "no person shall . . ." Kinney, *Church and State*, p. 108.

135 "Earthquake in . . ." Elizabeth C. Nordbeck, "Almost Awakened: The Great Revival in New Hampshire and Maine, 1727-1748," *Historical New Hampshire*, vol. XXXV (Spring 1980), p. 28.

135 "Impressions . . ." Nordbeck, "Almost Awakened," p. 43.

135 "one Vain Boaster . . ." Nordbeck, "Almost Awakened," p. 38.

135- "new settlements . . ." George H. Williams,
136 "The Seminary in the Wilderness," *Harvard Library Bulletin*, vol. XIII (Autumn 1959), p. 377.

137 "The wilderness . . ." Williams, *Harvard Library Bulletin*, vol. XIII, p. 400.

139 "A poetic fancy . . ." Belknap, *History*, vol. III, p. 39.

139 "the savage . . ." Thomas Cole, "Essay on American Scenery" (1835), reprinted in *American Art, 1700-1960*, ed. John McCoubrey (Englewood Cliffs, N.J., 1966).

142 "A stern . . ." Hawthorne, *American Note-Books*, p. 561.

142 "She could . . ." John Albee, "Memories of Celia Thaxter," in Celia Thaxter, *The Heavenly Guest with Other Unpublished Writings* (Andover, Mass., 1935), pp. 167-168.

143 "this solemn . . ." Celia Thaxter, *Among the Isles of Shoals* (Boston, 1873), pp. 140-141.

145 "In Cornish . . ." Hugh Mason Wade, *A Brief History of Cornish, 1763-1974* (Hanover, N.H., 1976), p. 45.

145- "called strongly . . ." Homer St. Gaudens,
146 "City Folks in Cornish" in William H. Child, *History of the Town of Cornish, New Hampshire, 1763-1910* (Concord, 1910), vol. I, pp. 220-221.

147 "My dream . . ." Lawrance Thompson and R.H. Winnick, *Robert Frost: A Biography* (New York, 1981), p. 192.

148 "Poetry is . . ." Robert Frost, "The Constant Symbol," in *The Poems of Robert Frost* (New York, 1946—Modern Library Edition), p. xvi.

SUGGESTED READINGS

Adams, John P., *Drowned Valley: The Piscataqua River Valley* (Hanover, N.H., 1976).

Anderson, Leon W., *To This Day: The 300 Years of the New Hampshire Legislature* (Canaan, N.H., 1981).

Armstrong, John Borden, *Factory Under the Elms: A History of Harrisville, New Hampshire 1774-1969* (Cambridge, Mass., 1969).

Bartlett, Irving H., *Daniel Webster* (New York, 1978).

Belknap, Jeremy, *The History of New Hampshire*, 3 vols. (Boston, 1791-92, reprinted in various editions).

Bellush, Bernard, *He Walked Alone: A Biography of John Gilbert Winant* (The Hague, 1968).

Benes, Peter, *The Dublin Seminar for New England Folklife,* Annual Proceedings (1976 —).

Brown, Sanborn C., *Benjamin Thompson, Count Rumford* (Cambridge, Mass., 1979).

Brown, William Robinson, *Our Forest Heritage: A History of Forestry and Re-creation in New Hampshire* (Concord, N.H., 1956).

Calloway, Colin G., *New Worlds for All: Indians, Europeans, and the Remaking of Early America* (Baltimore, 1997).

——*After King Philip's War: Presence and Persistence in Indian New England* (Hanover, N.H., 1997).

Clark, Charles E., *The Eastern Frontier: The Settlement of Northern New England, 1610-1763* (New York, 1970).

——*The Meetinghouse Tragedy* (Hanover, N.H., 1999).

——*Printers, the People, and Politics: The New Hampshire Press and Ratification* (Concord, N.H., 1989).

Cole, Donald B., *Jacksonian Democracy in New Hampshire, 1800-1851* (Cambridge, Mass., 1970).

Daniell, Jere R., *Colonial New Hampshire: A History* (New York, 1982).

——*Experiment in Republicanism: New Hampshire and the American Revolution, 1741-1794* (Cambridge, Mass., 1970)

Dobbs, David, and Richard Ober, *The Northern Forest* (White River Junction, Vt., 1995).

Frost, Robert, *The Poetry of Robert Frost;* Edward Connery Latham, ed. (New York, 1970).

Garvin, Donna Belle and James Garvin, *On the Road North of Boston: New Hampshire Taverns and Turnpikes, 1700-1900* (Concord, N.H., 1988).

Garvin, James L., *Historic Portsmouth: Early Photographs from the Collections of Strawbery Banke, Inc.* (Somersworth, N.H., 1974).

Gilmore, Robert C., editor, *New Hampshire Literature: A Sampler* (Hanover, N.H., 1982).

Guyol, Philip N., *Democracy Fights: A History of New Hampshire in World War II* (Hanover, N.H., 1951).

Hareven, Tamara K., and Randolph Langenbach, *Amoskeag: Life and Work in an American Factory City* (New York, 1978).

Haskell, John D. Jr., and T.D. Seymour Bassett, editors, *New Hampshire: A Bibliography of Its History* (Boston, 1979).

Heffernan, Nancy Coffey and Ann Page Stecker, *New Hampshire: Cross Currents in its Development* (Hanover, N.H., and London, 1986).

Historical New Hampshire, quarterly journal of the New Hampshire Historical Society.

Jager, Ronald, *Last House on the Road: Excursions into a Rural Past* (Boston, 1994).

Jager, Ronald and Sally Krone, *A Sacred Deposit: The Meetinghouse in Washington, New Hampshire* (Portsmouth, N.H., 1990).

Kilbourne, Frederick W., *Chronicles of the White Mountains* (Boston, 1916).

Kinney, Charles B., *Church and State, The Struggle for Separation in New Hampshire* (New York, 1955).

Malone, Joseph J., *Pine Trees and Politics: Re Naval Stores and Forest Policy in Colonial New England, 1691-1775* (Seattle, 1964).

Mayo, Lawrence Shaw, *John Langdon of New Hampshire* (Concord, N.H., 1937; reprinted 1970).

McLoughlin, William G., *New England Dissent*, 2 vols. (Providence, 1971).

Morison, Elizabeth Forbes and Elting E., *New Hampshire: A Bicentennial History* (New York, 1976).

Morse, Steams, editor, *Lucy Crawford's History of the White Mountains* (Hanover, N.H., 1966).

Nichols, Roy Frankhn, *Franklin Pierce: Young Hickory of the Granite Hills* (Philadelphia, 1958; reprinted 1969).

Ober, Richard, editor, *At What Cost? Shaping the Land We Call New Hampshire* (Concord, N.H., 1992).

Page, Elwin L., *Judicial Beginnings in New Hampshire, 1640 to 1700* (Concord, N.H., 1959).

Palmer, Niall A., *The New Hampshire Primary and the American Electoral Process* (Westport, Ct., 1997).

Purchase, Eric, *Out of Nowhere: Disaster and Tourism in the White Mountains* (Baltimore, 1999).

Randall, Peter, *New Hampshire: A Living Landscape* (Portsmouth, N.H., 1997)

Remini, Robert V., *Daniel Webster. The Man and His Time* (New York, 1997).

Richardson, Leon Burr, *William E. Chandler, Republican* (New York, 1940).

Russell, Howard S., *A Long Deep Furrow: Three Centuries of Farming in New England* (Hanover, N.H., 1976).

Sanbom, Frank B., *New Hampshire: An Epitome of Popular Government* (Boston, 1904).

Stackpole, Everett S., *History of New Hampshire*, 4 vols. (New York, 1916).

Squires, James Duane, *The Granite State of the United States*, 4 vols. (New York, 1956).

A Stern and Lovely Scene: A Visual History of the Isles of Shoals (Durham, N.H., 1978).

Swank, Scott T., *Shaker Life, Art, and Architecture* (New York, 1999).

Tolles, Bryant F., *The Grand Resort Hotels of the White Mountains* (Boston, 1998).

Tolles, Bryant F. Jr., *New Hampshire Architecture: An Illustrated Guide* (Hanover, N.H., 1979).

Turner, Lynn W., *William Plumer of New Hampshire, 1759-1850* (Chapel Hill, N.C., 1962).

Turner, Lynn Warren, *The Ninth State: New Hampshire's Formative Years* (Chapel Hill, N.C., and London, 1983).

VanDeventer, David E., *The Emergence of Provincial New Hampshire, 1623-1741* (Baltimore, 1976).

The While Mountains: Place and Perceptions (Durham, N.H., 1980).

Wilderson, Paul W., *Governor John Wentworth and the American Revolution* Hanover, N.H., and London, 1994).

Wilson, Harold Fisher, *The Hill Country of Northern New England: Its Social and Economic History, 1790-1930* (New York, 1936).

Yates, Elizabeth, *Amos Fortune, Free Man* (New York, 1950).

ACKNOWLEDGMENTS

In an earlier version of this book that covered some of the same territory we thanked a number of people who had helped us in many ways. Since this book draws on that material it is appropriate to repeat our thanks to certain of these individuals. They include R. Stuart Wallace, a historian and man of many parts in New Hampshire; he did yeoman service on our earlier book and generously agreed to provide a Foreword for this book. We are especially grateful to him. Also several former and present staff members of the New Hampshire Historical Society: John F. Page, William Copeley, Donna-Belle Garvin, and Joan Desmarais; also James Garvin, Quentin Blaine, and Mary Lyn Ray. Much of the copy work for many of the photos was done by Bill

Finney and Ernest Gould. More recently, Daniel Habib of the *Concord Monitor* was most helpful. Photos came from many sources, and are appropriately credited in the text, but some organizations supplied more than others. Chief among these and deserving of our most sincere gratitude are the New Hampshire Historical Society and the Concord Monitor. Also, the Currier Gallery of Art, the Society for the Protection of New Hampshire Forests, the Department of Media Services at the University of New Hampshire, Dartmouth College, and Strawbery Banke Museum.

R.J.
G.J.

New Hampshire's busiest newspaper publishing company in the 1930s, the Union-Leader Publishing Company is pictured getting out the paper's 75th-anniversary edition in 1938. MVHC

INDEX